Glitter & Grit – The Adventures Of A Ballroom Dancing Journey

Contents

                                                    Page Number

Dedication ……………………………………………………………3

Who Is Ian? …………………………………………………………4

Introduction ………………………………………………………6

Chapter 1 Levelling Up! ……………………………………9

Chapter 2 Snowball Fights & Waltzing In A Winter Wonderland ………………………………………………….24

Chapter 3 The Harmonies Of The Rising Phoenix's ……..47

Chapter 4 "I've Just Taken A Shit In A Bidet" ……………65

Chapter 5 Beach Bods ……………………………………82

Chapter 6 Ducking Lost! ………………………………102

Chapter 7 The Old Damsel In Distress Routine ……..131

Chapter 8 Going Home ………………………………149

Chapter 9 A Front Row Seat …………………………178

Chapter 10 Trade The Day With Dancing Escapades ……203

This part is usually reserved for a dedication,

and so, in keeping with that,

I dedicate this book to the friends and family,

Teachers, partners, and fellow competitors,

who have all been with me in some way or another

and who partake in some of the journeys you are about

to discover...

...And me, I also dedicate it to me too.

Who Is Ian?

With over 30 years of dance experience ranging in a variety of styles taken from a multitude of levels, some of which consisting of an Amateur Competitive Athlete, to Professional Competitor and National representative in International Championship events, all the way up the ladder to being a highly experienced teacher. I feel I am well versed in the world of dance to help provide a structured baseline format to assist any dancer of any level ranging from a beginner level, social dancer level, active competitor (of any level) or a developing teacher, who would wish to develop their own personal understanding of dance further. All of which can be found in the numerous books I've made, and which outline how you yourself can learn how to dance.

Dancing is very much in my blood, having started dancing from the age of 3 and dancing in competitions from the age of 5 (albeit rudimental when compared to the level I've personally achieved in more modern times). I've definitely managed to acquire an extensive number of achievements, some of those consisting of becoming a 2004 Commonwealth Champion, acquiring various Regional & National Titles as well as achieving a Semi-Final Status in National Championship Events and more exclusively attaining European Semi-Finalist status at the European Professional Ballroom Championships. So, it's safe to say, I know my stuff!

My passion in dance has exposed me to a wide and vast array of teachers all with their own merits and elements of understanding which they've graciously imparted to me for my own use in my own dancing career and teaching. It's these soundbite elements of insight, as well as my own veracious appetite for knowledge (I literally have hundreds of books on dancing) which has pushed me higher and further, in both my own personal understanding but also in the direct application of dance. Whether that's been in a training environment, a lesson environment or a competition environment, my personal ambitions and self-motivated drive has pushed me higher than I thought was possible. My personal dancing philosophy (if there ever was such a thing) is that "**Dancing Is Easy**" and therefore anyone can learn at any level to dance because, retrospectively, dancing **IS** easy. "Good dancing" however, high quality dancing, takes practice and patience, I've sought to create an entire body of differentiating works which aims to bridge the gap that people might feel exists, when learning how to dance and to help anyone realise how learning to dance is both fun and easy.

Introduction

The initial idea to write a book about my experiences within the dancing world was, in all honesty, an icky one at first. I viewed the idea as nothing more than pompous postulating and showboating, a desperate grab to satisfy someone's ego from memorable highlights long past by. However, over the recent years of recounting numerous tales and excursions involving the dancing to my friends, to colleagues and to other people interested in hearing me ramble on about my dance career. The idea of sharing my personal experiences has steadily become a more appealing one which has grown on me more and more as the years have progressed. And so, I figured that seeing as though I now find myself acclimating to a different aspect in my dancing career (that being, solely of a dance teacher and adjudicator, instead of an active competitor). And how I have found myself reminiscing and telling stories of the various escapades and experiences which have happened to me whilst travelling and being involved in the world of competitive Ballroom & Latin dancing, that now would be a good time as any to share in some of those experiences. I do hope that you enjoy the little collection of anecdotal stories and snippets taken from an inside view of the world of competitive Ballroom & Latin dancing which follow. However, I feel I should also mention here that although a lot of books might have themselves organised in a very linear manner, their content and chapters usually laid out in some form of chronological order, this one doesn't always follow that particular structure. I tried ensuring that the layout of this book is set out in a way, where if you were to read Chapter 9 then Chapter 5 then Chapter 1, that it shouldn't make too much difference to the overall flow and enjoyment of the reading experience. (Personally, I don't know why anyone WOULD read a book that way, but then again, I'm not everyone). You can still read it in a traditional way of course (Chapter 1, Chapter 2 etc.) I mean I'm not going to tell you what can and can't do (obviously) but it doesn't mean that you HAVE TO read it that way if you really don't want to. The best way I feel I can put across what I mean is if you were to imagine each chapter in this book as an episode on a TV show. You might not fully know the details of each of the characters completely (if you happen to say, tune in on episode 46 of a popular sitcom for example) but you should still be able to have a good time watching the show and seeing what unfolds in the episode.

In all honesty, whilst I was putting together the ideas for each of the chapters which follow here, I did have an increasing sense of imposter syndrome creep up on me though. The thought that 'only famous or well-known people write autobiographies', or an annoying little voice which kept telling me that 'I don't think a book containing just MY experiences would matter or be of any interest to anyone'. As well as a slew of other thoughts, invasively flooded my mind about this books development and all of which were certainly thoughts which made the feeling of writing about it all feel, well, icky. But I figured that seeing as how I personally found these stories enjoyable, both to recount and to retell, and it seemed that other people who have heard some of these stories from me, have also found them enjoyable, I figured why wouldn't anyone else. I should also additionally note here that because I also have a terrible memory when it comes to names, there are occasions throughout some of the stories here, where the use of the real names of people might not be featured. It's not for any other reason purely than the fact that I don't actually know or remember them. However, with that being said, my younger brother Alex does feature quite a lot in these stories and so for full disclosure...

ALEXANDER KILPATRICK WHYATT!

... or Alex for short, will be a name you'll commonly see featured a lot within most of these stories. As funny as it might be though, I won't be mentioning his full name all the time like that, mainly because I can't be bothered to keep typing it out all the time, and certainly not because it lacks any additional comedic impact (plus, I'm pretty sure that reading his full name like that all the time would be annoying as hell for you too). What are big brothers for if not for the occasional embarrassment. I might also sometimes refer to him as Ale (pronounced Al-ay) by the way, not Ale as in the drinking Ale, it's more like Al-ay. I have no idea where this little nickname comes from to be honest, but it's a little nickname that I've had for him since we were kids. So just know that's what I'm meaning when you read his name.

Additionally, because my memory isn't the greatest in terms of accurately pinpointing the exact dates for some of what you're about to read (a lot has happened to be honest, and I can't remember everything). The stories and adventures featured in this book happen to take place between the years 2005 – 2014 and they are what I personally like to think of as, my "*golden years of development*". When I think back to this time, it's with a lot of fondness and appreciation for everything which I had experienced in helping me get to where I am now. It's the time in my life and in my dancing career when I competed and trained as a youth competitor from an Intermediate and Pre-Champ level dancer to gradually branching and dipping my toes into the wider world of the Amateur league. It's where I progressed myself through rigorous practice and torturous training, to the mid stages of an Amateur Competitor. This is the time where I was quite rough around the edges in terms of being a "refined dancer" (whatever that means) and I still had a lot to learn in both life and within the dancing world itself. I personally feel that both mediums, those of both life and dancing, have been a closely interwoven fabric which has resulted in the metaphorical tapestry of stories and adventures you'll read about here. I have every intension of organising another two books which will hopefully depict both my later years of dancing, of which I have already begun outlining in a second book, where the stories and high jinxes help feature my dancing as a more "polished" International competitor, professional and teacher. There are a number of adventurous circumstances which I find myself experiencing during that segment of my dancing career and I feel that the most appropriate way for them to have their own space and illustrate themselves to the fullest with, is within a book of their own. And so, my second book will entail those aspects of my dancing career. I will then add a final, third book, which will hopefully encapsulate my earlier youngster years of dancing. That last book will (hopefully) depict all the variety of dancing experiences, which as a young kid growing up in a dancing world, has come to experience.

Undertaking the task of cataloguing a portion-able wedge of my life has been an interesting one to say the least though, there's a lot of self-reflection that I've found myself experiencing as I dragged myself awake almost every early morning at between 5:00am and 6:00am for the past few months. Putting into words my dancing excursions at that time of the morning has certainly been an opportunistic moment for me to recollect the emotions and experiences of a well lived life which collates my *"**Golden Years Of Development**"*. I do hope you have as much enjoyment in reading the various stories and escapades I've set out here in this little collection, as I did in personally experiencing them.

Chapter 1 Levelling Up!

'STAND UP!!', 'WHY ARE YOU WOBBLING!?' As sweat dripped from my forehead and ran down my face, speckling onto the floor, I could feel my T-shirt sticking to me, the sweat from my body acting as the adhesive which seemed like it kept both my T-shirt clinging to me, like a moist and sticky form of hug and rooting me to the ground. It was hot, hot from the summer weather outside, hot from the room I had been in for what felt like an endless millennium. The smell of an old school hall with its authentic wooden flooring and orange and brown walls were decadent with the scent of perspiration from a nearly 1-hour long lesson I'd been "receiving". These were the only forms of sensory experiences I could take in at that moment; and it was there, whilst my body and muscles continued to ache, whilst my brain was working it's hardest to understand the instructions I'd been given, that I heard once again 'FOOT! TURN YOUR FOOT OUT!' Nicky was a hard task master with her instructions, and although every part of me hurt and I didn't feel I was able to do any more than to try and stand upright, secretly, I was enjoying every moment of it.

The summer of 2005 was something of a baptism of fire as both myself and my younger brother **Alexander Kilpatrick Whyatt** (only time I'll do it, I promise, please keep reading) had started a new journey in our dancing career. I was 16, Alex was 15, when we first entered an old and humble looking school hall where our newly established teachers were teaching down in Wolverhampton. You might initially be wondering how two young lads from Scunthorpe found themselves in a dance studio all the way in Wolverhampton, well, actually, you're probably not wondering that at all seeing as how I've given no prior context which would elaborate to the fact that both me and Alex come from Scunthorpe. A two to tow and a half hour car journey away from Wolverhampton, the humble steel making town, Scunthorpe, known predominantly for its steel works and the lyrical mention "never been to Scunthorpe" from the song Pass Out by Tinie Tempah (full disclosure Tinie, not many other people have been to Scunthorpe either.)

Situated somewhere in North Lincolnshire (by the way my mum prides herself on mentioning she's from North Lincolnshire, rather than the more commonly used South Humberside, all of which are located in the east of England and make very little postal difference). Scunthorpe has been home for our family and it's where me, Alex and our older sister Lynda all grew up. It's also where I, Alex and Lynda started dancing. Our mum and Dad would find themselves dipping their toes in and out of dancing over the years there. But it was me, Alex and Lynda who were encouraged to more actively pursue the dancing and to dance competitively. As such, it was very common to find Sundays for our family, to be taken up with traversing the country in attending all manner of dancing competitions, from Disco (the more modern term now is freestyle I believe) Rock'n'Roll, Classical & Modern Sequence dancing as well as Ballroom and Latin dancing. But it was after me and Alex had experienced and were consequently inspired by the British Open Junior Ballroom & Latin Championships at Blackpool, that we decided to dedicate our time and energies to that particular style of dancing.

Looking back on things I'd have to say that my personal experiences of growing up in a disciplined household, combined with an early form of strict and disciplined instruction in dancing, has probably led me to realise that these discipline aspects have had a big impact on me, and have made me a lot more resilient to various extreme forms of experiences which have come later on in life (whether that's from dancing or from life itself is still something I'm working out, but I'd wager it's probably related to both). What I'm meaning is that I would, personally, be less likely to complain if I found something difficult or tiring, or if the words used to aid a particular element of improvement in my dancing might seem from an outside perspective as belittling or demeaning (stand the fuck up, you look like a sack of shit! Almost has an inspirational message buried within it somewhere). To be honest these are some of the things which I've found myself personally craving, as I've found they've helped me immensely in improving my own abilities and developing my skills in my dancing. Although as I write that now, I realise how unhealthy that may seem, but in reality, the only way I've found to get significantly tougher, stronger or better in anything I do, is by exposing myself to the experiences which have thrown me massively out of my comfort zone and forced me to learn new ways to adapt and thrive. A statement which, ironically, I would hear echoed back to me in my later Amateur/ Professional career from a well-respected sports psychologist. This vague, soup like concoction is what I experienced in the earlier years of my dancing. From lessons with my first dance teacher, whom I have a deep respect for and who helped me start my dancing journey as a youngster, to practice sessions in the living room after school with my mum who sat vigilantly watching from the armchair for any incorrect things I might be doing (in her opinion). All the way up to the competitions I would enter and dance in. All these varying elements have helped serve to act as the reinforced disciplined experiences for me and so, I'd say that my starting point (like a lot of other people, I guess) has been from humble beginnings, routed in a strong resilience to hardships. Plainly said, I'd like to think I'm a tough cookie, unless there's a glass of milk or something like that around, then I might just crumble…badum-tish! I'm sorry, I'll stop there.

Fast forwarding to 2005 and I'd happened to receive an email from a girl from the midlands (I have embarrassingly forgotten her name, so for the sake of continuing the narrative here I shall continue to refer to her as, Susan). Susan had requested me to travel to see her and her dance teacher and so over various back and forth emails to one another, we arranged for a dance trial to be organised in the attempt to establish whether or not we could become dance partners.

By the way, a dance trial is a pretty common thing in the world of Ballroom and Latin dancing, it's where two strangers essentially meet and have a "type of dance lesson" with one another to see if they might make a good match together. I told my parents about little Suzie and the back-and-forth communication we'd had with each other, and it was organised that we should all drive down to Wolverhampton, one Sunday afternoon, to meet her and her dance teacher and to have a dance trial with one another.

The journey down was easy enough, spending nearly every Sunday traversing the English countryside had become something of a normal affair when growing up. So, travelling to Wolverhampton was nothing new to us, it was just different. Different sights, different roads, different scenery, but all the while still having that feeling of familiarity. Whilst sat in the back seat of mum and dads Vauxhall Vectra, mum and dad up in the front comparing maps to see which way we should be heading and with Alex gazing out the window next to me at the passing trees and cars on the motorway. It suddenly dawned on me, that this was the first time in about two or three years, that I'd had another male dance teacher. Growing up as a teenager and taking my early steps into the International Ballroom and Latin world (no pun intended) had meant that I needed to find dancing partners who were the ideal height and committed in the similar way to travelling to the various nationally based competitions, and this pursuit had led me to branch away from finding a "local" dance partner from the dance school I began my dancing journey at. As a teenager, all of a sudden, I'd found myself in the tuitional company of a man named Paul Beaton. Paul was nice, has was extremely flamboyant and he helped guide my earlier years of International Ballroom & Latin dancing as a junior competitor. I frequently remember him saying in my lessons 'you look like William (Pino) so you're going to dance like William (Pino)'. William was an Italian dancing competitor who was a world class professional competitor and who is very well known by a lot of people in "the dancing world". So, when Paul said I was going to "dance like William" what he really meant was, I'm going to give you snippets of his routines for you to use in your own dance choreography, seeing as you look a little bit like him and that should help you dance like him. In fairness though, I think this attribute helped me a lot in many ways and to shape my overall development in dancing, as I'd find myself regularly looking to William as a kind of inspiration, especially when YouTube popped onto the scene. I would find myself glued for hours watching and re-watching older footage from William and his wife Alessandra competing on the computer screen, giving lectures and workshops and dancing showcases at The World Super Stars Dance Festival (WSSDF) all in a hopeful attempt to have a bit of their dancing magic rub off on me.

Arriving at Wolverhampton, we drove to a little village just on the outskirts where an old school hall was situated. This was where the dance trial was being held and where both me and Alex would initially be introduced to our new teachers. Prior to arriving however, mum and dad had managed to navigate us to a different side of the town, where a different teacher was located. After some uncertain back and forth in the car at this "other dance school" we all piled out, the bags with our dancing practice wear in hand, and to which we soon after tentatively made our way to the entrance of the building. After walking through a reception area, we were greeted by a very nice lady who politely and openly asked both who we all were and why we were there. I said I'd been in contact recently with "Susan", a girl who was being taught there and with a perplexed look on her face, this nice lady went into the dance studio ahead "to get someone". The lady that appeared next was not Susan, it wasn't even Susan's teacher, as her teacher was called David and despite the pink coloured tips of spiked hair, this lady was not called David (at least I hoped it wasn't). It had turned out we'd gotten lost (a common trope we'd found ourselves experiencing in the dancing and one which even today still seems to happen regardless of how sophisticated Apple Maps claims to be). The lady's name was Jackie, and she was the dance teacher for the studio we'd found ourselves in. She politely informed us that we were in the wrong place, and she then helped point us in the right direction before we promptly left, feeling rather embarrassed that we'd arrived at the wrong place. Jackie did mention that if were unsuccessful with the dance trial we were heading to, that she had plenty of girls available if we were still looking for a partner. Even after all this time it makes me chuckle to think about that encounter and that comment, it makes me giggle to think there's some form of harem where Jackie claps her hands and assembles a congregation of girls looking for boy partners, "see any you like, hmm?" It was nothing like that of course, it was a genuine and helpful statement from Jackie that informed us, if we were still looking for a dance partner afterwards, that she had plenty of girls who didn't have partners and some of which, would be interested in having a dance trial. After piling into the car, mum and dad conferring the correct way to go via the map and Jackie's instructions, we were back on the road again. Eventually, when we arrived at the old school hall we were supposed to originally be at, we made our way up the steps to the entrance of the hall, the heavily painted, orange door creaked open and we were greeted by a man with silver hair, dressed in a striped shirt with the sleeves rolled up, revealing an array of gold bracelets which fit with the accompaniment of the gold rings adorning his fingers and which contrasted against the black vest top which matched his black trousers. This was David (thankfully), and he pleasantly greeted us as we all entered the hall making our way into the waiting area. There I met Suzanna, she was quiet, but she was nice, and we exchanged the usual little pleasantries of 'hello, hello, how are you? I'm good, how are you?' which were said with embarrassment. I think we both realised, that whilst it was relatively easy for us both to communicate and organise the dance trial with one another, when we actually met in person, it kind of felt weird. Two weeks prior to this we were essentially strangers and now here we were, face to face, about to have a dance trial with one another to see if we can form a partnership. The whole thing felt kind of weird, nowadays this is super common, people meet over the internet all the time, but back then it wasn't as common, you sort of "had to just know someone" who was looking for a dance partner and from there you'd organise something, exchanging phone numbers (usually the parents) which would then lead to organising dance trials with respective teachers. At least that's how it had been for me and Alex. For me and Alex, we had grown up in a dance school in a small (ish) town, occupied by mostly girls, so for us, we'd have a change in dance partner whenever either me or Alex, or our respective partners, grew too tall for the other one (sadly this was more the case for Alex than for me, as although I'm the older one of us both, sadly, he's the taller one of us both). 'The toilets are just through those doors if you need to get changed' David said and with that I made my way down to the bottom of the waiting area to go and get myself changed. Closing the door behind me I saw both Alex and my dad following in toe through the segmented glass windows, clearly the car journey was a long one and they both needed to use the toilet, so like a weird type of lavatory gang we all scurried into the toilets together, where I dropped my bag on the cold tiled floor to begin getting changed.

Nowadays dancers have very sleek looking "practice wear" fitted shirts and pleated trousers for the guys, usually adorned with a belt and if it's "an important lesson" they'll wear a tie and maybe a vest top of sorts, at least that's the typical look they have when they have their Ballroom dance lessons. The girls on the other hand will usually be wearing either an all-in-one practice dress or a practice skirt and leotard bodice combination for the Ballroom. Latin dancers aren't quite as elegant, usually wearing some form of loose t-shirt/ shirt attire for the guys and their pleated Latin trousers and for the girls, usually some sort of two-piece crop top and Latin skirt combo. That's usually the look that dancers have for their lessons nowadays and when I used to compete as a late Amateur/ Professional, the Ballroom look I just mentioned there, with my belt set to one side was certainly a look I also had. But back then, in those early days as a youth dancer, not so much, a T-shirt from the draw and some "older" Latin trousers were the outfit of choice for practices and lessons (I say older Latin trousers because we had some newer, more pristine looking trousers which were for competing in) and Ballroom shoes for lessons in Ballroom, with just a switch of the shoes taking place, to change into some Cubans for the Latin lessons, no frills, no fuss. This was "the look" me and Alex had for our lessons and for practicing and this was my attire for the dance trial which followed that day. The dance trial itself went easy enough from what I can remember, it lasted for an hour, where Susan and myself danced some basic groups of Foxtrot and Waltz steps together for half of the hour and then switching over to dance some Latin in the last half hour segment, consisting of some basic Rumba groups shown to us by David. All in an effort to see how well things felt dancing together, how well we got on and more significantly, whether or not either of us had any talent or potential as a couple. Embarrassingly, I remember being instructed on a lot of things I was doing wrong, starting first with the basics in Foxtrot and Waltz where my movement, posture, frame, and technique was no way near the standard of an open level youth competitor. Both me and Alex had come from a little dance school in Scunthorpe, which was essentially rooted in medallist Ballroom & Latin, Open level Classical & Modern Sequence dancing and Disco and Street Dance (I think they call Disco dancing, Freestyle now because, well, I assume it's because Disco sounds corny in the modern era of dance competitions). So, despite my experiences as a junior competitor in the international field, I was still very, very low on the pecking order in terms of my ability. I suppose if I was critically looking back on my younger self now as a teacher, I'd probably class myself as a mid-Silver/ Gold level dancer at best, competent in knowing what certain basic figures are, but still green on the technique and inexperienced on the advanced figures. I remember having to do Rumba walks down the room for the remaining 10 minuets of the dance trial, by which I think the decision of what was to happen going forward, had already been decided. Afterwards, Suzie and I sat and talked about how well things had gone, about what we thought, and more importantly, what can happen to help move things forward. It was at this time that Alex, wanting to experience something different, asked if he could have a dance lesson with David. So, whilst I talked with Susanna about our dance trial, Alex had a private lesson, working on some basic Rumba and technique. I think that lesson with David was a big deal for Alex, he'd never had a male dance teacher before and he'd not really been present for my lessons with Paul when I was younger either. So, the lesson with David was probably like a type of springboard experience for him, as he'd only ever had female dance teachers up until then and because David "had a gap" before his next series of lessons, he agreed to do some work with Alex. Halfway through Alex's lesson with David, Susan and I finished talking, she was meeting her mum outside and we agreed to follow up with one another in a couple of days as she wanted to talk to her mum about how it had all gone, as well as speak to David later on. After she left, mum homed in, 'so, how was it?', 'it was ok I guess' I answered, I knew I hadn't done very well in the dance trial, I knew there was a lot of things I didn't know which had become apparent as the dance trial continued and I realised I had to get a lot better and ultimately I think this was obvious in the sound of my voice as I replied to mum. 'Well, you could see what needed to happen towards the end of the hour' mum responded, which was a vague statement in and of itself, it kinda means one thing, but it can also mean a thousand other things. At the time, I took from it that mum thought the dance trial went well and that she could see potential in the partnership, dad was stoically quite about it all, he'd accustomed himself over the years to being more of an observer to the dancing, compared with mums more "active" involvement. So, when I asked him what he thought to how it had all gone, he replied saying something to the effect of 'yes, it looked pretty good'. Whether or not he actually thought that or not, I'm not sure as that was his reply to most things which pertained to the dancing. In a way it could have been because it wasn't really his area of expertise, so he might well have felt that to say too much would encroach on our experiences of the dancing, at least that's what I assume it to be at least, especially when I look back on things. I made my way to the open door of the main hall where Alex was now having his lesson, we would regularly watch one another's lessons, picking up little tid-bits of information as we observed each other and watching one another learn what was being instructed to us. If I'm being honest, I think that's what's made us so effective in our later years of dancing, we learnt how to learn (if that makes any sense). I remember seeing David position Alex for his Rumba walks down the room, adjusting his body weight, just as he had done with me and I remember comparing what I was visually seeing in Alex's lesson, with what I had physically experienced in the dance trial with Susan. After watching a bit more of Alex struggling with his balance and David explaining some similar points which he had mentioned to me, I picked my bag up and made my way down to the toilets to get changed into my "normal clothes". There were only 15 minutes left in Alex's lesson so I figured I might as well get changed and besides, I had lot to think about. After Alex finished his lesson and left to go to the toilets to get changed, I got up and went to see him, I wanted to know what he had thought to his experience with David. Alex was midway through getting changed when I found him in the toilets, 'so how did you find it Ale?' I asked eager to know his response. 'It was good' he replied, 'really good actually, there's a lot I need to work on', I could tell he'd really enjoyed the dance lesson and that he was super excited to get working on some of the new things which David had taken him through during his hour-long session.

The drive back home to Scunthorpe went by so fast, as both Alex and I talked about our new experiences to mum and dad from the backseat of the car, talking about this new teacher we'd experienced and all the different things we felt we had learned from this very brief encounter. Looking back, what seemed unique to our experience, was probably the way the lesson and dance trial had gone, I was familiar with having a male dance teacher in Paul when I was younger, like I'd said earlier, but this was Alex's first experience, however most of our dance teachers over the years, as a whole, didn't have the same level of energy and humour. Dance lessons were either, serious affairs which were not to be enjoyed, 'you need to become better and always seek to improve', that was usually the way dance lessons had happened. Or they were more casual affairs because the teacher was of an older generation and didn't have the same energetical input. Our experiences with David contrasted that massively, here was a teacher who not only knew a lot of things and showed us how much more we had to learn, but he was also making the learning fun with cheeky little jokes or quips at our expense, which in all, made us laugh. We'd never had an experience quite like that before and I think that was a big catalyst for us both.

Growing up in our small town, seemingly in the middle of nowhere with humble means to our end, had meant that we were prone to having only our initial dance teacher, a wonderful lady named Jayne, as our primary teacher. In this day and age open level Ballroom & Latin dancers, even most dancers in a medallist setting, all have the experience and fortune of a hand-picked selection of teachers of which they can have their lessons from, growing up, we always only had one teacher. The primary place where we had our dance lessons take place when we were younger was a local community centre and incidentally this place also had a male teacher, teaching across the hallway in the room adjacent, where he would be teaching his own dance pupils and classes. But, despite this proximity to a different teacher and a male one at that, we never intermingled into his dance classes, as that would have seemed somewhat dishonest to our primary teacher. I vaguely remember dancing Disco dancing with a girl from his dance school at one point when I was like 9 years old or something, but aside from that, the two schools never mixed (at least not to my knowledge). And so, growing up, our experiences of a dance teacher and the lessons we'd experience were solely from a feminine perspective. It wasn't until my junior career that I'd meet Paul Beaton, a chance encounter which mum had organised, and which then lead me to have dance lessons in Leeds for my Ballroom and Latin with a new dance partner. Paul was from an older generation of teachers, his age being somewhere in his 60's (as a guess) when I met him. I characteristically remember him drinking glasses of "orange juice" which had a good 1/3 vodka to 2/3 orange juice mixed together (I say that, but it could very well have been the other way around or at the least 50/50). Paul had a very busy schedule and so due to the nature of his busy professional schedule and his travelling commitments, (he would often fly to America quite a lot of the time, as well as other European countries) for various teaching and adjudicating work and because of this, there would often be times when I would have gaps in my lessons with him, making the lessons that I did actually have with him seem almost like "guest lessons". They were the type of lessons which were experienced for a few months and then halted whilst he was away, which were then recommenced when he returned for a few more months again. This meant that the lack of anything consistent resulted in my primary lessons taking place back home with Jayne in Scunthorpe. Suddenly having this seemingly stark contrast of a male teacher for us both in 2005, gave both me and Alex some sort of inspiration, some sort of zest we felt we'd never had as the teaching was more fast paced, the discipline requirements seemed more demanding and the quirky, fun experience meant that the decision was soon after made for us both to part ways with our former teacher Jayne and to start the next part of our dancing journey in Wolverhampton with David.

I don't quite remember how the details of leaving Jaynes dance school happened exactly, but I do know that my mum had been quite direct in her conversation with Jayne over the phone and that, in turn, had seemed to ruffle a few feathers on both sides. My mum has a lot of good merits to herself, but she can be very frank and direct without the consideration of her words or actions sometimes and this sequence of events had all come about from the following lessons after our encounter with David. It was the weekday evening and Alex had experienced a lesson with Jayne two or three days after he had the lesson with David and he was relaying to her, what David had told him to do. Jayne seemed happy to take on board what Alex was saying but I guess there must have been mis-matched ideas about the technique he was relaying or something. I remember Alex leaving the lesson and being sat in the car with me on the way home, saying how he preferred the lesson with David. It was a fair statement, Jayne was a very strict and disciplined teacher and her expertise in the open competition arena was small when compared with David's, so when Alex felt he had learnt more from that Sunday lesson, he wasn't essentially wrong. I think he was just overlooking all the hard work and toil Jayne had put into his development to get him to that point. Later that evening he told mum how he felt and what he wanted to do going forwards and how he wanted to have lessons with David from now on, mum was impressed by the lessons with David as well and she picked up the phone to call Jayne. She asked me what I wanted to do, and I felt that even though I was extremely appreciative of everything Jayne had done for my dancing. I knew I needed to get better, and I needed to push myself more, the dance trial alone had shown me that and it seemed like David was the key to that progression moving forwards. After an intense phone call which mum had with Jayne, that night dad and I got in the car to drive over to Jaynes to organise the prompt return of some school-based trophies we'd received, the saga of my younger years of dancing had finished, encapsulated by the finale of returning those trophies and the new phase of my dancing had just begun.

The following few weeks were a mix of new experiences for me and Alex, having lessons with David and slightly afterwards his wife Helen was so completely new to us both, we'd never been taught by a married couple before and in some ways, it had a familial feeling to it. The dance trial I'd had with Susan didn't amount to anything unfortunately, after not hearing back from her for about a week I'd figured it was a no-go for her. She eventually got in touch not long after that and told me that she was preparing herself for a Duke of Edenborough award, so in a way it was kind of good that things didn't move forwards. The dance lessons which followed for me and Alex, took place on a Sunday and were arranged so that one of us would have a lesson with David and one of us would have a lesson with Helen for an hour. We would then switch and have our second hour of lessons with the other teacher. We really enjoyed it, we felt we were learning so much, we'd spend time working on loads of basic technical elements, dancing basic Foxtrot and Waltz steps around the room with the odd Tango thrown into the mix as well. Then going through Rumba, Cha-Cha and Samba walks down the floor towards the mirrors at the bottom of the hall and back again. Whilst we had our lessons with David and Helen, there would be the appearance of a young dance couple who regularly came into the hall to practice their Latin dancing, it turned out they were National Amateur Latin finalists, and they were in training for their next big event on the calendar. They would sometimes be in the hall at the same time as me and Alex and more often they would have a lesson after we had just finished ours. The girl was short and petite, with jet black hair and blue eyes, she would usually be wearing some form of crop top and hotpants with her 3-inch Latin shoes to match, the guy was tall with dark and curly "wet looking" hair, usually wearing some type of loose shirt with a low open V neck, he wore Latin pleated trousers and his black Cuban dance shoes just added to the enormity of his height. Not only were this dance couple National Latin finalists in the Amateur division but they had also been quarter finalists in the world championship events. Me and Alex were both in awe of them as soon as we saw them, they had a way about themselves which just oozed that type of quality you see from top performing athletes. As they warmed up and ran through drills and practices, me and Alex were completely blown away by them. They were powerful and dynamic, fast, and awe-inspiring, without a doubt they were a definite true inspiration to us both and they were worlds apart from what we had ever seen before. We just had to get better! We had to look like that! After seeing this couple for herself and chatting to them when they would arrive, during the lessons which me and Alex would be having with David and Helen. Mum tentatively approached David and asked if it would be ok for Alex and myself to receive some additional lessons from this couple. I think all parents have their innate flaws, but credit where credit is due, when my mum sees something opportunistically, she reaches out to grab it. After talking with David and requesting lessons from this impressive Amateur couple, David agreed for it to be ok and so for the following months, myself and Alex would interchangeably receive lessons from Will and Nicky as well as David and Helen. Altogether we must have had between 3 to 4 hours of lessons every Sunday, each, it sometimes happened that some weeks that was dropped to 2 hours, primarily if David happened to be away adjudicating and Helen was busy at home with either their young daughter or dealing with administrative office work. Will and Nicky became a pivotal role in the development which both me and Alex experienced, so much so, that we still talk about our experiences from back then, now and to which we fondly look back and laugh at some of the things which happened.

And so, during a hot Sunday afternoon in summer, the room scant with the scent of perspiration, the smell of the wooden floor enhanced by the heat of the day and the sun beating down on it from outside through the windows, clear blue skies apparent from the windows and the emergency fire doors at the bottom of the hall, which were wide open in a vain attempt to receive some type of cooling breeze. Nicky, in her assertive tone shouted once more "STAND UP!! I SAID STAND UP!". This was the state of things for me and Alex for the first few months or so of lessons with Nicky and Will, with all our merits we were still greatly unskilled, and we needed a hell of a lot of work to even be in a position where we could strongly stand on the competition floor, let alone actually compete alongside some of the country's best and up and coming talents. Nicky was far more stricter and the more authoritative one out of the partnership and Will, although he was tough as a teacher, was a lot more accommodating and sympathetic. For all the learning difficulty involved for me and Alex, we never ever complained, for us this was everything we ever wanted. It felt to us like this couple, who were so talented and accomplished, along with David and Helen, genuinely gave a shit about us and our dancing, that they actually wanted to make us better and that it was up to us to make sure we didn't let any of them down. The instruction was generally the same from Nicky, she'd be repositioning me, kicking my front foot which should be turned out, pulling my hip back to stretch and twist me into the correct position and by using her dagger like nails, she would jam them into my diaphragm and proceed to forcefully push it up, 'LIFT YOUR CENTRE!' she'd shout and I would try my absolute hardest to do what she wanted. Inevitably though, something would give, my muscles would tire, I'd stumble with my balance and fall, or one of the technical details she was instructing to me would be lost. I'd realised quickly after my first ever lesson with Nicky, that this was the first stage of it all and it was hammered home to me when she would say 'we haven't even started moving yet and you're wobbling all over the place'. Nicky would then adopt the position she was asking of me herself, effortlessly (as you'd hope from someone of a national and world status) and I'd be then told 'Like this, see, now do it again! POSITION!'. Out the corner of my eye I'd see Alex's lesson with Will though, 'What the hell?!' I thought, 'He's doing it! He's dancing the Rumba walks with Will down the room!'. I couldn't believe it, how was he able to get everything correct and now be ready to not only start dancing Rumba walks down the floor, but make it all the way to the bottom of the hall by the mirrors? HOW?! I think Nicky must have seen me catching a glimpse of Alex's lesson though as she sternly jibed at me, 'Focus on what you're doing! You're not even stood up correctly!' and once again those talon-like nails came back in again, stabbing and moving what felt like my entire insides upward. After the lesson with Nicky had finished it was "half-time", a quick drink and towel down to dry the hard-earned perspiration away, evaluate some life choices and we were back into it with the other person. Now I was with Will, Alex with Nicky, Will had a very calming presence about himself and it seemed as if he was a type of yang to Nicky's Ying. I'm not sure if this had anything to do with him being French or not, but it was a definite

European vibe he had about himself, which contrasted the more brash and laser like attitude of Nicky who was born and raised in the midlands. 'Rumba walks?' Will asked, 'uh huh' I nodded to him to confirm, the sweat from the previous lesson now splattering to the floor as I nodded. 'Ok, let's go' Will instructed and I once again adopted the position for setting up to dance my Rumba walks down the floor. As Will assessed my positioning he mumbled to me 'Ok, good, ok, yes, just move this, lift this, good!' all the while making minor alterations in my positioning. 'Good?!' I thought 'how can this be good?!' I was barely able to keep on balance when I was with Nicky, but now, now I feel almost perfectly poised. 'Now start to move' Will said as he moved backward away from me, I looked at him with astonishment, fighting hard to retain this position I'd worked so desperately to achieve in Nicky's lesson, I took two steps and then lost balance. Will just looked at me, 'it's ok, go again!', I couldn't believe I'd managed to take two steps, I set myself up again, Will corrected a few minor things and I began to walk down the floor again, five steps this time! I stepped a sixth time dropping my centre and my foot pointed straight forwards 'No' Will said, 'go again!' and he pointed to the top of the room, I was frustrated but I was also excited, I was making progress. As I turned to walk back to the top of the room again, I saw Alex being barraged by Nicky's onslaught, her dagger like nails repositioning his centre just as she had done with me and it was with a newfound self-confidence that I assumed the position again and began to dance my walks down the floor, the echoes of "NO, WHY ARE YOU WOBBLING ALEX?! STAND UP! LIFT THIS!' acting as a musical compliment to my walks down the floor.

As I'd mentioned earlier, this was how things went for the next few months, metaphorically speaking, Will and Nicky took some very cold, unmoulded clay with twigs and bits of dirt and stones buried within it, and tried to create some form of clean, identifiable Vase like shape to us. After many weeks of tough, enduring lessons and countless nights practicing through the week in the hopeful attempt that the next Sunday training day down in Wolverhampton would be a better one, and that we'd finally be able to not only do what's been asked of us, but that we might ACTUALLY be able to dance some choreography and figures soon. It was then, seemingly overnight, as if by magic, when it happened! In that old school hall one Sunday afternoon (after months of being barraged by Nikki and the odd reprimand from Will) in both Will AND Nicky's lessons, that we both found ourselves dancing our Rumba walks down the floor, to end of the hall, no mistakes, no issues and with the music to boot no less! There was the odd correction or two, of course, but nothing like what we'd been experiencing in the months prior. It was a really big moment for us both, it felt like we'd spent an eternity trying to acquire this seemingly impossible, seemingly intangible skill and technique and now, all of sudden, here we were, moving down the floor towards the mirrors with no stopping, no wobbles, no sudden halts in our progression which required us to drudge ourselves back to the top of the hall in an attempt to get the next attempt right. We had finally gotten to a place where we were able to dance our Rumba walks down towards the bottom of the hall and then switch ourselves to moving backwards. It wasn't always perfect and both Will and Nicky would regularly interject with their necessary corrections, stopping us to restart the whole sequence only if it was a terrible shamble, but we were doing it, we were finally making identifiable progress and we were clearly getting much better. 'Good work Ian' Nicky said, her face showing a slight smirk which seemed to share in my accomplishment, I was lost for words, both Will and Nicky were so inspirational to us and now here Nicky was giving me praise, I didn't know what to do. But fortunately, Nicky did, 'Now we move onto the Cha-Cha walks!'. I was caught off guard and completely unaware. I'd been spending so much time fixated on improving my Rumba walks, so desperate to receive the sought-after praise from Nicky and Will. This imaginary little badge of honour which would be bestowed to only the best and most accomplished of students, that I'd completely forgotten that there were walks to be danced in both the Cha-Cha and in the Samba as well. Needless to say, all the constant struggle and challenging toil I'd experienced with trying to master the Rumba walk movement was re-experienced again with the Cha-Cha walks and later on with the Samba walks. Two steps forwards and a 4 & 1 backward was the state of progression it seemed. Climbing the ladder of success was difficult and I imagine that if a lot of other people were thrown into that situation (provided they even got that far) they'd have thrown in the towel. But not us, not me and not Alex, we're tough and resilient, especially when we believe in what we're doing. I knew that if I'd managed to make so much improvement in the Rumba (in what I see now, as a short period of time) that it was definitely achievable in the Cha-Cha and in the Samba as well. And so, with sweat once again pouring down my face, my muscles aching, my head, and body hurting from the stresses thrown upon it both physically and mentally, that I heard it, once more, the inspirational melody which seemed to endlessly ring around that old school hall in the summer of 2006, 'STAND UP!!', 'WHY ARE YOU WOBBLING!?'

Chapter 2 Snowball Fights & Waltzing In A Winter Wonderland

On the run up to March of 2010 the country had been experiencing a turbulent winter period, everyone's always hoping that they'll see a bit of snow on Christmas Day and when it doesn't show, or worse, when it rains, it can seemingly put a little bit of a downer over the festive period for people. They want that winter wonderland scene that you see in all those holiday movies, where the houses are covered in snow and kids are building snowmen. That's rarely, if ever, been the case when I've been growing up, a light dusting is the best I've ever experienced at Christmas and even if the country would be so euphorically enamoured with the frosted scenery, when it would be pasted over the news stations, it would unfortunately be mentioned as a cause for concern. After a bleak Christmas in 2009 (in terms of the weather) the commencement of 2010 saw weather warnings being put out over January and February which predicting horrendous snowfall due to dowse the entire country in a blanket of winter wonderland scenery in 2010. Putting in mind the kind of scenery that you'd expect to see on the front of old Christmas cards, which show kids sledging down hillsides white over with snow. As is always the case with things happening in the UK regarding its weather, even something as minor as a spot of rain or a light dusting of snowfall can easily be spun into a wild declaration of danger and extremity from the news and weather reporters, and for us, with traversing the country over the years doing the dancing and partaking in competitions here, there and everywhere, we'd seen and experienced pretty much anything and everything the wonderful British weather had to throw at us. It almost seemed fitting that the news stations were proclaiming nationwide mayhem all over the country with colourful charts and forecasts showing the coming conditions. The talk on the tv was the kind that you'd expect to see in apocalypse movies, where people abandon their vehicles on the motorway (or highway, if you're an American reading this) and where townspeople are fighting tooth and nail just for a tin of beans and a packet of bandages. But in March 2010, the weather which had been falsely predicted for January still hadn't arrived, and that was then projected into February with no avail. But eventually it did arrive, and it hit the little British island with a wallop in March, resulting in transport, businesses, and most of the general public being severely affected. Something as simple as a local school run for parents, had turned into something you might expect to see from a disaster movie like *The Day After Tomorrow* or something. Supermarkets were being heavily shopped as people decided to stock up on essentials, in case the weather happened to get a lot worse, and the news was filled with the usual bleak and gloomy reports of accidents, public transport services being stopped, which in turn resulted in national delays for anyone brave enough to travel. All of which was advisably broadcasted from the news stations and weather channels on the TV which were telling people to stay home unless you absolutely had to travel or if it was an emergency, the extreme weather had brought the UK to a bit of a grinding standstill.

After turning off the TV with its bleak news channel story, in the early hours of a Wednesday morning, both myself and Alex were getting ourselves organised for a full day of dance lessons, practice and training all the way down in the midlands dance studio in Wolverhampton. A dynamic, which by this point, was a regular and well organised affair. We'd been experiencing the regular routine of travelling down south to the midlands for dance lessons, practicing and training for several years now and so everything from organising our practice gear and bags, to filling up the car, to travelling, was almost second nature to us both and well-orchestrated into a routine of efficiency. At this time both myself and Alex were still living in Scunthorpe, Alex was living with our parents, and I was house sharing with a friend, in an attempt to gain some independence and personal freedom. What would of usually happened on a Wednesday was this, I would travel to my mum and dads from the house I was living in, me and Alex would organise our dancing gear and fill up the car, and one of us would jump in the driver's seat and drive the two of us to Wolverhampton, depending on who's turn it was to drive that week (we used to alternate each week, who would be driving, so that the driving didn't fall on just one person and that we'd be able to give each other a bit of a break). In March 2010 the snowfall that had come down seemingly overnight at mum and dads house was at least 12 inches deep (wink, wink…nothing? No? Never mind then) and by the time I'd arrived at mum and dads house, dad had already been outside to clear the pathways leading to the house, piling the additional snow onto the grass, and creating this chasm like walkway which led you nicely, straight to the house, without your footwear being covered in snow. The snow was still gently coming down as I made my way to the front door, banging my trainers against the side of the house to knock off any additional snow that I might unintentionally be trapesed into the house. As I opened the front door, knocking as I did so, I shouted through the hallway, 'It's just me!' the warm heating of the house almost felt like a loving embrace compared with the contrastingly cold air outside. I'd always entered mum and dads house openly like that, there was never any need for formerly waiting to be invited in like a devious vampire on the prowl for his next drink. So, I'd always make my way into mum and dads house with a little knock, to hopefully reassure them that I wasn't a crazy person who was breaking into their house in an attempt to rob them or something. It hopefully meant that mum and dad wouldn't be worried as to why the front door was opening of its own accord, especially so if they were in different parts of the house. Alex was still eating his Weetabix when I made my way into the living room, and he looked at me with the type of look that said, 'are we really doing this today?' the news station providing its gloomy reports acting as the background noise to his unspoken question. That was the funny thing with me and Alex back then, we could almost "telepathically" have this strange type of communication with one another which was based solely on and communicated via facial expressions and that allowed us to know exactly what the other person was thinking. This was used to full effect when we were out in public places and was especially the case when we were at competitions. I remember on one occasion being at a dance competition in Stockport, after arriving and putting our dance gear in the changing rooms, located off to the side of the main hall. Alex, I, or dad would make their way to the little table beside the stage where entries would be received for the events taking place on the day. You'd be issued with a little form to fill out that required your name, address, your competitor's number (a little code given to you by the governing body of dancing) and a listing of all the desired events you wanted to take part in that day. You'd then be soon given a number for your competition events and the form was kept by the person giving the numbers. When it came time to go get changed before Alex and I's competition events started, we had to walk from the seats where mum and dad were sitting down by the stage, walk out and around the perimeter of dance floor, to the opposite side of the room to go and get yourself changed. Seating was never assigned at these types of "Sunday Comps"; you just grabbed some seats where they were available. Now, the usual etiquette in competition dancing is that if you ever need to leave where you are and you have to go to the other side of the room for whatever reason, you should ideally wait until the people dancing their event on the floor have finished their dance, that's the unmentioned etiquette which would allow you to then go to wherever you wanted to go to. Not everyone follows this etiquette mind you, but it is a known thing to do. It also would feel strange walking and moving around the outside of the floor whilst people are dancing, as the audience are watching the competitors dancing and that would also mean that they're watching you as well, so I guess that's another reason why people wait before they then go to wherever they need to get to. It was during a particular competition at Stockport town hall that Alex found himself on the opposite side of the floor where the changing rooms were situated and I was adjacent to him on the opposite side of the floor, we were waiting for the current round of dancing to finish so that Alex could get his number from mum and dad, and I could go organise my competition gear. The round being danced was for people dancing in the Intermediate or Pre-Champ level (I don't really remember to be honest), watching that level of dancing, at the point where both of us were personally at, at the time (By this point we were branching into dancing just the Amateur division of competitions and had subsequently moved past the requirement of dancing lower graded events) was interesting to say the least. You'd see all the familiar mistakes you'd done yourself, but you'd also see how the competitors handled themselves, it was very raw, very pure in a way. Sometimes competitors of that level would be bold and slightly arrogant, despite where they were on the pecking order and others were more timid and milder mannered when they danced. As me and Alex watched the dancers in this particular round, we caught the glimpse of someone dancing past, we both clocked him. The way he moved the way he was trying to present himself was all, well, it was all wrong let's just put it that way, but it was carried with a sense of bravado that if you were only looking at his face, you'd think he was the best on the floor, especially with how he arrogantly blazed past another couple nearly knocking them off balance. As soon as he danced past the eyeline of Alex and myself, I looked back to Alex, he instantly looked back at me and with a smirk on his face and a glint in his eye, he "telepathically" said 'what the fuck was that?'. All I could do was look away and laugh, Alex is a very blunt character at the best of times and especially so if he's involved with something he cares deeply about, what you'll hear from him is a very direct, very frank way of talking. Personally, I'd like to think I've managed to establish a good balance of honesty (what I genuinely think, even if it's not great) with a decent amount of diplomacy. Even to this day Alex will still communicate something to me in this way with a look, or me to him and we'll just smirk and laugh to ourselves as we continue to watch the thing, we're both clearly noticing.

Back in the living room in March and Alex's "telepathic" look was saying to me, 'are we really doing this today?' The news station on the TV was blurting out its usual topics of doom and gloom, people were getting into accidents, more severe weather was on the way, public transport was almost at a standstill and motorways were slowing to a crawling pace as motorists were being forced into one lane of traffic from the typical three lanes, due to accidents. I looked at him and said, 'don't worry we'll be fine, we've handled worse' (full disclosure we hadn't, we'd experienced "different" situations and we'd experienced numerous situations, but not worse). With a sigh, Alex finished his breakfast and made his way upstairs to get changed, his dance gear for the practicing and lessons was somewhat already organised (mainly because it was the same stuff, he was wearing from the week before, only this time he'd be wearing a different coloured T-shirt. At this point in time Alex was still dancing 10-dance events, he'd soon make the decision to specialise and to only compete in Latin American dancing though, he was never fond of wearing the suits in the Ballroom and couldn't hold himself to the required element of discipline used in the Ballroom dancing. He'd always had a deep passion for his Latin dancing, and it showed whenever he competed, that passion and enthusiasm coming out to the fullest when he danced his Jive, his favourite. Jumps, kicks, flicks, quirky rhythm changes, he loved to show it all and in credit to him, the audiences that would watch him, loved seeing it all too. I, on the other hand, deeply enjoyed being a ten dancer, I loved being able to dance all of them and I enjoyed the personal challenge of trying to master ten dances instead of the specialised five from either the Ballroom or the Latin. There was a common trope I'd regularly hear through the years of competing in both Ballroom and Latin and it was that ten dancers try to get good at both Ballroom and Latin, but ultimately, they're always better at one of them. I didn't like that idea; I didn't like the thought that I'd have to make a choice to specialise, I wanted and greatly enjoyed dancing all ten of the dances in Ballroom and Latin. So, when Alex made the decision to specialise in just his Latin dancing, his packing for competitions was made easier because he literally only needed his Latin top and trousers and his shoes, all of which could fit in one bag. Whilst Alex sorted himself out upstairs (maybe even questioning what we were doing at that point) I went to see mum and dad, mum was in the kitchen, folding laundry before she went to bed. I gave her a hug and asked how she was, we talked for a bit, and I asked where dad was. 'He's out the back, clearing the paths' she said, and so I popped my head out the back door to find dad in the garden. The cold chill of the air greeted my face, a pleasant reminder that no matter how cosy and warm the inside of the house was, outside was still a cold winter tundra. The light snowfall dropped onto the top of my head as I scanned the back garden looking for dad, I couldn't see him out there, but I could hear the scrapes of his snow shovel (a wooden, custom-made construction he had created himself using an old bit of plywood and a broom stick) he was in the midst of clearing out the build-up of snowfall and you could hear the scrapes of the "shovel" the groans and occasional clatter as the "shovel hit the bins or wall in his efforts coming from the side passageway of the house. 'Ready!' Alex shouted to me from the hallway, the cold air outside was making me shiver and I quickly made my way back inside again, leaving dad to continue his battle against the elements outside. Alex's nose was red from being outside himself, not only had he gotten himself changed and organised his dancing gear, but he'd also cleared his car of snow. 'Have you got everything?' mum asked, 'Yes', we both replied, somewhat in unison. 'Right. Drive. Carefully' mum purposely spacing out her wording to emphasise the way she sternly told it to us both. 'We will' Alex replied and after giving mum a big hug, we packed the boot of the car with the remaining dance gear, and we soon jumped into the car seats. It was Alex's turn to drive this week, as I'd driven last week, and when I think back to that time, that's probably why he was "telepathically" looking at me with the expression of 'Do we really have to go today?'. Alex fired up the engine to his red Fiat Punto, I popped in a CD from Feeder (that's right kids, we used to listen to CD's years ago! Which we would slide into a stereo system of the car. Not like today with the likes of using Bluetooth and Spotify), and he gingerly reversed the car onto the small road of the cul-de-sac to the tune of Buck Rogers, mum waving to us as Alex carefully made his way down to the end of the street. Because the interconnected streets where mum and dad's house was situated, wasn't on any form of main road or bus route, the gritter trucks which would help clear and grit the main roads in the town, wouldn't venture down them. This would mean that the roads were particularly precarious at the best of times where mum and dad lived. Whenever there was snow and ice predicted for the weather forecast, the generalised sentiment meant that if you were brave enough to start venturing out, you should definitely proceed with caution. Alex braked at the end of the street, his car sliding to an eventual halt against the smooth trye marked snow on the road, with the juddery feel of the car breaks being used to their fullest extent, the car did eventually stop though, sliding its way onto the next street. The roads were completely white over with tyre tracks imprinted from other cars creating some makeshift guides in the snow, which had been made by people who had also braved the roads in an effort to get themselves to work. Alex indicated to turn out onto the next street, and he carefully made his way around some of the back streets, heading towards the local garage where we would fill up the car with petrol and "pick up supplies". Fortunately for us the garage we were heading to was situated on a main bus route which meant the gritters had managed to at least clear something of the road for local traffic to get around with. Alex pulled up to the pump and got out to fill the car, we had a pretty good system by this point, the person who was driving us there and back on the Wednesday would fill the car, the other person would buy the petrol (seeing as the other one of us was driving) and pick up snacks and drinks from the garage shop. 'Do you want anything else?' I asked Alex, our usual array of supplies would consist of between six and ten Red Bull cans, mainly for me, with a couple left in the car for Alex on the way home. We would also pick up bags of Haribo sweets both the fizzy kind and the normal kind, a big bag of skittles and anything else that might take Alex's fancy, today it was a tin of spaghetti hoops which he'd heat in the microwave down at the studio for his lunch. 'Can you also pick me up some of those Pro Plus tablets as well?' Alex asked, 'sure thing' I said, the Pro Plus and the odd little "shot like" energy drinks were something of a god send for us when driving late at night as we'd have a couple of Pro Plus tablets washed down with one of these concentrated energy drink "shots". That way, we were wired for the trip and all its precarious hazards (usually other motorists not paying attention). With the supplies in the footwell of the back seat behind Alex's chair, we made our way out from the petrol station and back onto the road. Heading out of town the roads were relatively clear, it was something like 10:30 in the morning and so a large amount of traffic had already passed over the gritted roads that morning, which meant that for us, we had the joy of driving through the slush like concoction usually amassed from melting snow and ice. The snow was still gently falling as we neared the M181 Motorway leading out of town, the gravitas of the situation of the weather and how it was affecting everything in the country, suddenly setting in. Even as we drove along the dual carriageway leading to the M180 motorway we could see the impact of the snow storm, two or three cars were pulled over to the hard shoulder with their hazard lights flashing and the odd accident or two where someone had tried to overtake someone else which had resulted in a collision, had meant that the traffic leaving Scunthorpe was in one lane and not two, with cars scattered on either side of the lane we driving in, the victims of fate to the gods of weather.

When Alex and I would drive ourselves to lessons or competitions the stereo (one of these detachable ones where the front of the system came off, to deter would be car thieves) would be loud enough to drown out the strangled cats noise of our singing, but quiet enough to not deafen us, it was only if we were lost or we didn't know where we were going, or if there was a serious problem, that the volume on the stereo would be dropped to a subtle background noise. I think it goes without saying that on this day, that's exactly what was the case in the car. No Karaoke session on the road today, it was clearly going to be a serious affair and Alex needed all his concentration faculties if we were to make it to the studio in one piece. As we made our way down towards the M1 junction of the M180 the snow started to come down more heavily, Alex had the window wipers working their hardest to keep the windscreen clear. I tried to make sure I didn't say or do anything too distracting for Ale as he really needed to concentrate but with only the dull sound of Seven Days In The Sun, by Feeder playing ironically in the background. Our usual chat in the car was all dance related (naturally) we would talk about stuff we were working on, what we were hoping to go through in the lessons and what we might practice that day, the conversation would be paused when a car or lorry drove past Alex, who was now driving at a steady Fifty to Sixty miles per hour in the "slow lane". The middle lane was too wet and precarious with its slush like mix of snow and ice and the "fast lane" (the lane on the far right) was a no go, no matter how desperately you needed to get somewhere. And so, it was somewhat inevitable that we would be overtaken by vans, lorries, BMWs, and Audis (it's always those types of cars which are desperately nudging you out the way by driving too close to you) who were all clearly in more of a rush to get where they were going. As we drove past the Woodall service station on the M1, me and Alex deeply engrossed in a discussion on Paso Doble technique, talking about all the nitty gritty stuff which we enjoyed comparing and talking about, especially when we talked and compared what we were saying with the top-level Amateur and Professional dancers at the time. Suddenly, seemingly out of nowhere, a huge lorry bellowed past Alex, creating a wave of slush and snow which dowsed the windscreen and darkening the inside of the car, the dull blue and red light from the stereo system was the only light we had, and Alex immediately flicked his wipers which desperately and through a massive amount of strain flexed as they tried to shift the bestowed road slushy from the car. When you have a moment like that, it's incredibly scary, you're doing between fifty and sixty miles per hour and you're essentially blind, you know you're still in the same lane as before because you haven't felt the bumps of the cat's eyes on the road, so all you can really do is pray that the blanket now covering your windscreen, clears so you can see again. Alex was good though, we'd experienced all sorts of things whilst driving around and this was no exception, he gently eased off the accelerator to give the window time to clear and to ensure he didn't collide with whatever vehicle might have been in front of us at the time. Eventually after what had felt like an eternity, the bright white glow of the blanketed snow-covered English countryside appeared again (it must have only been five to ten seconds where we couldn't see anything, but it certainly felt a lot longer when it happened). Like I said, we'd both experienced a number of different things when driving at that point, so we knew to stay calm when the slush from the road hit us.

When both me and Alex had reached the age where we'd finished school and were going to college (English college and not the American version of college) It was mum who gave us the 4-1-1. 'When you finish college, both of you can either get full time jobs to help pay towards your dancing, or you can give up the dancing and go to university, you can't do both!'. Growing up, mum was quite the disciplinarian, and it wasn't uncommon to be given forms of ultimatums when they arose, I remember quite distinctly receiving a letter to take home to mum and dad when I was 14 which said the school was organising a trip to the north of Italy to go skiing. I took the letter home so enthusiastically; I'd never been to Italy, but I'd constantly experienced all the Italian dancers who would try to speak to me and to which I would give a gesturing nod to them in an effort to communicate with them (all the while being completely oblivious to what they were actually saying to me). Here was my chance to see the culture, to go and visit Italy, surely mum and dad would agree. Lynda had gone to France for a week on a class trip when she was in school and mum had said yes to that (a big deal really, because anything which interrupted the dancing, was viewed as detrimental), 'how was this any different?' I thought. I remember handing over the paper for her to read, saying 'I think they're organising some sort of trip to Italy which sounds pretty cool', the tone of my voice probably conveying the optimistic reply I hoped I might get back from her. Instead, mum looked at me from the paper and then handed it to dad, who was beside her, for him to read. 'You can't go Skiing' mum firmly stated, 'because if you go, and you fall over, you'll break your leg, then you'll be in a cast for six weeks! And that'll be it!', I sighed, this wasn't the first time I'd heard mums' espousal of "that'll be it", it was a turn of phrase that had surfaced and re-surfaced over the years with anything that could be seen as a hinderance to the dancing. So, when me and Alex were finishing college, mum gave us the stern dilemma of choice, Lynda had given up her dancing in order to pursue an academic path, she was a good, strong and successful dancer in her days as a juvenile, she'd become a Juvenile British Champion in her earlier years. But she also worked super hard in school and college with a vision of going on to university, and in all honesty, I don't think that sat right with mum. So, when me and Alex neared the stage of going to university, we were told bluntly that we would have to make a choice of one or the other, we were not allowed to pursue both. We obviously made the choice to work full time to help pay for our dancing, but it was around this time that we'd both passed our driving tests, Lynda had passed her practical test with only four minors, pretty good going when you think about it. So naturally, when I did MY practical test, I had to pass with less minors (which I did, only three minors!) Alex was the last one to pass (being the youngest and all) and the cheeky sod passed with only two minors! I was pleased when he told me he had passed his test first time, but I was slightly pissed that he'd gotten only two minors on it. Because we'd passed our driving tests, we were itching to become a little more independent, so over the following years mum and dad gradually transitioned to attending the odd lesson with us and to coming to the odd competition with us. We'd found ourselves in our very early twenties driving all over the country by ourselves for lessons, for practices and for competitions, which I guess allowed mum and dad to spend some good quality time together.

Back on the motorway and the junction for heading towards Derby was nearing, as we banked around the curve of the motorway, passing the Tibshelf service stations on the way, we saw the gradual unfoldment of the road leading off the motorway. The slip road was at a standstill, Alex gradually slowed the car to gently stopping and we joined the extending traffic. I remember thinking 'this will be fun', the slip roads were covered with a lot more snow and ice than what the motorway was and Alex's car, although being somewhat scrappy, was at that point fighting it's hardest to even drive us back and forth to lessons on a regular basis, its overheating engine being the primary area of concern all the time. Now it had to battle its way up hill, try not to stall and to not slide back down the inclined slip road. Eventually, through some over compensated revving and the combinations of breaking, accelerating and using the clutch, almost to the effect of being like a 10-hit combo from the Tekken games (it's that really long combo, which each character has, that few if any people aside from hardcore gaming enthusiasts ever learn). The problem was that the roundabout which the slip road was taking us towards was structured in a way where there were traffic lights at nearly every junction leading both towards and away from it. So, as we rolled up to the traffic lights, becoming the "pack leader" of the slip road, the worry of the cars arduous climb uphill was now put to rest as the road was now level again. This meant we were now able to see the contrast of the blizzard like conditions we'd been experiencing from the weather all along the journey of the motorway, now gently easing up into a gentle fluttering snowfall. We rolled our way through two sets of lights and waited at the third and final set which would put us onto the A38, the dual carriageway which would send us on the outskirts of the Derby ring road and ultimately towards the Litchfield direction. 'Hey look there's a couple of lorries waiting over the other side there' Alex light-heartedly said, I think the car journey was stressful for him in many ways which could have easily been gleaned from the lack of singing and the brief amounts of conversation we were having, it was only when we talked about dancing and technique and the competitors and competitions that he seemed to be a bit more himself. 'It's almost like they're preparing themselves for a race or something', he continued, I looked across to where he was pointing, 'oh yeah' I replied, the cabin areas of two lorries were side by side on the dual carriageway which was looking to join the roundabout we were currently on. The lights turned green on our side and Alex gently rolled onto the A38, the odd impatient driver zooming passed us, it was as we started down the incline of the A38 that we saw it, the extensive tail back of traffic back logging itself way off into the distance, 'holly crap!' I exclaimed, 'look at all that traffic!'. A stupid statement really because Alex was so pre-occupied with driving the car and not crashing, that for him to look away even for a second, just to see stationary vehicles on the other side of the road, would have been a dumb thing to do. After passing a few cars, lorries, and vans there was a break in the traffic, 'that's weird' I said to Alex, 'why hasn't the rest of the traffic moved up?'. As Alex drove us steadily down the incline of the A38 it became all too clear why, two lorries (one trying to overtake the other) had gotten stuck in the snow, the lorry in the left lane had also punctured one of its main tyres and the other lorry, trying to overtake, had gotten itself stuck. The A38 was still blanketed in snow, both lanes were white over on both sides of the dual carriageway and so everyone was driving a lot more carefully than they were on the main motorway prior. As we drove our way past the two static lorries and the backlogged traffic behind them, we saw a flurry of snowballs whizzing back and forth over parked and stationary cars, it was clear that no one was going anywhere for a while and so a bunch of drivers had gotten out of their cars, vans and lorries and were now engaged in a winner takes all, royal rumble, snowball fight!

Alex and I thought it was hilarious, seeing these grown men (because let's face it, having a snowball fight on the motorway is something only they would do) pummel one another, ducking and diving like soldiers in a battlefield all the while the "sensible drivers" looked on, was so funny to us. We laughed about it for ages whilst driving down the A38, passing all the other stationary motorists as we did so. Glancing over to the other side of the dual carriageway we could see other small pockets of people who had decided to do the same thing, it wasn't just one little battle at the entranceway to the M1 roundabout, it was a full-on war! With pocket sized skirmishes taking place all along the A38 which banked and sloped its way down to Derby. It was such a stark contrast when you compared what was happening on that dual carriageway to all the doom and gloom that surrounded the weather from the news stations, it was like there was a weight which was lifted from the veil of severity that had eclipsed the country and that people were actually able to enjoy the weather, despite everything which was surrounding it all, well, it at least came across that way from the grown men playing outside on the road. As we made our way around Derby's ring road to continue on to Litchfield me and Alex joked with one another about how these burly, tattooed blokes were playing like five-year-olds in the snow, unfortunately, despite all that joking, everything seemed to almost dissipate when we left Derby and started on our way towards Litchfield and Wolverhampton. As the severity of the weather situation once again loomed its ominous head over us. The traffic navigation was taking a toll on Alex now, he was become a bit stressed, he wanted to drive steady and to properly accommodate for the weatherly circumstances, but other drivers were impatiently driving super close to him, cars, delivery vans and the occasional lorry would all occasionally fly past him in that second lane, the "fast lane" if you will, and this would result in the those vehicles kicking up slushy mixtures of snow, ice and other bits of crap from the road, which would fly onto the car windscreen of that little red Fiat Punto. Alex would then frantically try and get the window cleared so as to not have a "blinded" repeat from earlier. Cars and vans were strewn along the hard shoulder of the dual carriageway, their hazard lights blinking like little beacons of hope for those who had either gotten stranded or worse, had some form of accident. Warning signs urged motorists to drive at a steady 50mph but with no security measures to keep things in check and with police services prioritising other emergencies. Drivers were at the mercy of each other's "good manners", which unfortunately consisted mainly of people who were late or wanting to get off the roads as quick as they could. The snow had begun to come down heavily again by this point and the stereo was still at its low mumble as Alex needed every aspect of distraction removed so that he could properly concentrate. After reaching from the back seat for a can of Red Bull, two sets of eyes being as vigilant as possible were better than one and I'd probably been a bit lax in helping Alex with traffic beforehand. But something was up, something didn't feel right, maybe it was because of the amount of traffic trudging its way along the A38 combined with the extremity of the weather which had now worsened again combined with the sights of cars and vans and the odd lorry halted in the hard shoulder. That the stretch of road leading towards Litchfield and Wolverhampton now seemed so ominous and this is when things came full circle as we neared the exit for Litchfield.

After logistically managing some skilful manoeuvring, Alex was now clearly just trying to get us to the studio as soon as he could, the stresses of driving the A38, battling against the elements and other motorists, were now seemingly taking a bit of a toll on him and he was now driving a little too close to a BMW situated in front of us (possibly for some form of retribution-al payback from the way other BMW drivers had been with him up to this point I'm guessing). Apparently, when it's raining motorists are required to drive about five car spaces apart to allow for appropriate breaking distance, when it's snowing, that number jumps to 10 car spaces, Alex, regrettably, was driving a steady 3 or 4 car spaces, so unless his little red Fiat had the breaking capacity of a Formula 1 car (it didn't) he could technically be classed as driving too close. In front of the BMW was another little car, which through the snowstorm had to hit its breaks, this led to the BMW in front of us needing to break suddenly, and like a chain reaction, Alex slammed on the car breaks hard in an effort to not slam into the back of the BMW. The juddering feeling of his well-worn brake pads meeting the stresses of the road and the snow, in an effort to not collide with the car in front of us. Alex sharply swerved to the "fast lane" but he lost control of his little Italian punto in the snow and ice concoction, heavily smeared across the road and we slammed into the central reservation with a wallop (the central reservation was a metal barrier which by the looks of it would crumble under the gentlest of breezes, let alone stand as a pillar of protection to the other side of the road, if an eighteen-wheel lorry collided with it at 60mph) Alex, in a desperate panic, over corrected trying desperately to keep 4 wheels on the ground and to not have us ending the adventure, upturned in a ditch on the side of the road. His over correction resulted in us spinning 360 degrees, both of us screaming as we did so, we were shitting ourselves (to say the least) and the half can of Red Bull I had in my hand was crushed whilst I slammed my right hand on the dashboard of the car. I looked to Alex for reassurance (and with panic in my eyes) who was also looking back at me with the same worried look. The situation in the car reminded me of that scene from Planes, Trains & Automobiles where John Candy and Steve Martin are travelling in a car on the highway and at one point during the trip at night, they end up driving the wrong way down the road, as the chaos unfolds, they happen to graze between two lorries, with sparks flying everywhere. Steve Martin then turns to John Candy in a panic, who suddenly goes from wearing the normal clothes he's had on, to wearing a devil's costume, and then switching back again all whilst maniacally laughing. That's the scene that flashed through my head as the car continued to spin, we ended up colliding into the side barrier in the left lane, now facing the opposing direction with the oncoming traffic heading our way. 'Not good!' I shouted, as a navy-coloured Audi rolled to a sudden stop in front of us, its hazard lights blipping on and off as it did so, the remaining traffic gradually all began to stack up as the snowfall started to ease up. We were both shaking and were lucky to be alive, let alone lucky enough to still be in relatively one piece on the dual carriageway as opposed to the more severe scenario, upturned in a ditch at the side of the road. Alex's knuckles were as white as could be from the severe grip he'd managed to maintain on the wheel during our little spin. Slowly, his fingers began to unwrap from the wheel, and I slowly released my own grasp from the dashboard, my left hand unclenching the Red Bull can which was now a crinkled mess in my hand. The fizzy contents had spilled all over my hand revealing to me a cut which I'd received from the ripped can which was now stinging me badly, the resulting damage from a desperate clench of safety, from our Waltz across the A38.

As both me and Alex left the car, my face was hit by the freezing cold chill of the wind and its wintery gusts. The snow which had barraged us up until that point had now softened to a gentle snowfall again, with the accompanying wind blowing its sporadic gusts against us. We were shook-up, but alive, approaching us was the lady who was driving the Audi car, which was now securely parked in front of us. The traffic which had back logged itself was now re-routing itself around and past us, it turned out that the lady (we'll call her Tracey for the sake of the narrative here) was an off-duty police lady and after asking us if we were injured or not, she signalled for us to move behind the barrier at the side of the road which by now, we'd recently become cosily acquainted with and to where Alex's little Red Fiat Punto was now "resting", for us to wait for the arrival of assistance. The biggest issue we had now, was that the little portion of road where we'd now taken up residency, didn't have a hard shoulder, so our car and Tracey's car were now essentially blocking half of the A38. After waiting there for about thirty or forty minutes we were eventually greeted by a police car who parked behind our stranded little fiat which was now gradually accumulating a little blanket of snow to gradually cover it completely. It wasn't soon after the police officer had arrived, that there was an arrival of a tow truck as well, Tracey was super nice and friendly throughout everything. She must have known that this was all new to us. We were still shaken from the whole experience and Alex's face must have said it all as she talked with us, making general conversation to help ease and relax us both, and asking about where we were heading to. After conferring with the police officer, Tracey told us that the police officer was going to handle things with us now and she got back into her car and gently drove away. When I think back to the whole experience, we were lucky that Tracey was there, sure we could have dealt with informing the police and break down services ourselves, but there were other things which helped us immensely. The little orange triangle and cones, Tracey happened to have in her car boot were super useful at redirecting the backed-up traffic, the way she helped us both (especially Alex) feel so much calmer about everything and the way she organised the arrival of the police and tow truck for us as well. It all made the experience go a lot smoother and we were certainly appreciative that she was there.

The police officer who had arrived to help us gave us the usual Q&A's that the police do, where are you going, where have you come from, what brings you all the way down here etcetera, etcetera. We were both given a breathalyser test and then promptly asked to wait in the back of the police car out of the snow and cold, of which by now we'd been stood outside in, for about an hour to an hour and a half, the both of us jigging around to help keep warm. Sitting in the back seat of the police car I turned to Alex, 'you ok man?' I asked, my nose red and my arms pulled into my jacket sleeves, my shoulders lifted and squeezed tight to help keep my warm. Alex looked back to me and nodded 'yeah, I'm good' practically mirroring me with his hands pulled into his jacket, his Rudolf red nose sniffing at the dribble of excretion from it and his shoulders tensely lifted trying to keep himself warm. I found the experience super weird, I'd never been in the back seat of a police car, I didn't and still don't have any desire to experience it either, but it reminded me of all the movies you see where the "bad guys" are put in the back seat of a police car at the end of the movie. Now here me and Ale were, albeit without the handcuffs, sat in the backseat of a police car, the grown-up equivalent of the naughty step. Not too soon afterwards, the police officer who had arrived to help us, got into the front seat of the car, 'we're going to drive you up to the boat yard ahead of us here and drop you off there, so that you can sort your car out, with your breakdown provider' the police officer explained, and he soon after started up the engine to his police car getting us out of the way of the remaining traffic.

Rolling into the boat yard ahead, with the sound of crinkling snow crushing beneath the police car tyres, we could see the tow truck ahead leading the way, our pathetic looking little red fighter mounted onto the back of it, like a prized kill made by a lion on the Serengeti plains of Africa. The police car rolled to a gradual stop, and I instinctively went to get out of the back seat, realising straight away as I did so, that the police cars are designed to not allow their "passengers" that luxury and something which Alex, mockingly, reminded of. We waited there for a few minutes whilst the police officer who had brought us here, spoke to the tow truck guy and soon afterwards he came sauntering over to open the back doors to let us out. 'We're going to go inside here and see if it's ok for you both to wait here for your RAC van' he said as he gestured to the open door of little shack covered in snow, which had the appearance of a garden shed more than anything of significance, and off he walked gesturing for us to follow him. The back seats of the police car were certainly a welcome break from the cold winter weather outside. First and foremost because there was heating inside it, but secondly because it was a nice secure barrier which acted as a nice defence against the windy and downpouring snow conditions outside. As we walked across the open area of the shipping yard, the wind had died away and the snow had changed to a lighting fluttering, a very different type of scenery compared with over an hour ago by the roadside. I took one look at the tow truck, the snow crinkling underneath every step I made across that yard, to catch a glimpse of it now halfway through dismounting Alex's little Fiat from its rear end and I followed the police officer and Alex inside the little shack.

It was such a surreal experience at that boat yard, after walking through the doorway of the little shack, you were immediately greeted with a sharp incline of very low, very narrow stairs, which in an effort to get down, you had to walk slightly sideways on. Downstairs in what was essentially a basement, dimly lit with those yellow kinds of lights, bouncing everyone's shadowed reflections off all the wooden walls, the long "Viking" like table and benches being the primary focal point of the room, aside from the small family which were clearly living there. Below that little shack was a husband and wife who were staring at these new arrivals in perplexing glances. A couple of young lads similar in age to me and Alex, were sat near the top end of the table busying themselves in their own activities. The husband of the family, now talking with the police officer about what had happened, was a tall and broad man with dark features and he towered over Alex and me, whilst he talked with the officer about us staying with them for a little while. His wife, a very mild-mannered lady, gestured to the table and benches in front of us and Alex, and I were asked to take a seat. She then asked us if we wanted a cup of coffee to warm us up and we politely confirmed, our bodies were still freezing cold from the long exposure we'd had outside. 'You boys are going to wait here with these folks,' said the officer 'I suggest one of you gets in contact with the RAC whilst you wait'. No sooner had the officer finished explaining the situation and thanking the family, did he promptly leave me and Alex in the basement of this little shack with a group of strangers. They were super kind to us, and we greatly appreciated them allowing us stay with them for a little while, unfortunately, the whole room smelt of damp wood and piss and regrettably, the coffee I enthusiastically tasted to begin with (acquiring a huge mouthful in a quick attempt to warm myself up) tasted no different. I swallowed the "coffee" hesitantly so a s to not offend our new hosts and then turned to Alex, in an attempt to use our "telepathy" which fortunately came into its own once again. The look and feel of the place was warm enough for us to get ourselves back to a temperature a living body actually have, and the family were super nice. But the whole scene looked something similar to one of those murder TV shows where you're told the gruesome way someone unfortunately met their end, usually at the hands of their former lover or something. The "telepathy" we had was something to the effect of 'are we going to die here?' and 'I hope not' Alex then stood up and looked at me with a glint in his eye that said 'I'm leaving you in here' and proclaimed to the room, 'well I better give the RAC a call, like that officer told me to do' and he swiftly left up the stairs and back out into the yard. I felt super awkward, the family didn't really speak very good English, they spoke enough to get by, but it was difficult trying to make out what they were saying. Don't get me wrong, they weren't foreigners (at least I don't think so at least) they had that midland twang to their speech that people from Wolverhampton and Birmingham normally have, but I still couldn't understand a bloody word they were saying. After some minor exchanges where I nodded more than actually spoke, I slowly stood up, saying how I should probably let a few people know what's happened and with my phone in hand, I made my way out and up that narrow staircase into the winter wilderness outside.

Outside in the yard Alex was by the car on the phone with the RAC, the passenger car door open with him sat on the seat sideways, his feet softly kicking the snow on the ground beneath him. As I walked over to him, I saw him holding his RAC card and calling out the number on the back of it for verification. I waited until he'd finished calling it all out and then quietly said 'everything ok Ale?' gesturing two thumbs up whilst he looked back at me. He waited for the person on the end of the phone to finish what they were saying and gave me a quick nod, before then carrying on the conversation with the operator on the other side of the phone, promptly swivelling his feet inside the car, to gesture for some privacy. I walked around the car to see what damage had been done, with everything which happened before, neither of us were able to see what had actually happened to the car, a few scrapes along the sides and corners of the car. A new additional dint in the drivers rear door to add to the collection of other "memories" already acquired from our little adventures over and around the country and two flat tyres one on the passenger side where I'd been sat and one the drivers rear side. I walked next to Alex by the open door of the passenger side of the car and mouthed that I was going to call everyone, and I walked away, my phone at the ready to call the first person on my list, David. A few rings and eventually he picked up, 'Hi David' I said, 'Hi Ian, what's up?' I think he was probably expecting a call to say we weren't coming or something; he'd already received a bunch of calls from other people who had said they weren't going to go to their lessons today because of the weather and I guess he thought that we were going to give him the same type of phone call. After explaining what had happened and what we were doing now, he asked, 'so will you be going back home?', I paused, to be honest I wasn't completely sure, In theory we probably should have (well in full retrospect we probably shouldn't have gone in the first place) but I wasn't fully sure if Alex was still going to still drive us there or whether he was going to decide to turn us around at the next junction and just head back home. 'As far as I know, we're still coming' I said, 'but if it changes, I can let you know, Alex is on the phone to the RAC at the moment so they'll be able to tell us what we can do next'. 'Not a problem, keep me posted' he said, and we hung up the phone to each other. Alex was now walking towards me, the car was locked, and he'd finished his call, 'they're going to be about an hour before they get to us' he said, the snow gently coming down onto his head and shoulders. 'That's fine' I replied, 'I just spoke to David, and he was asking if we're still going to the lessons. I tried to say it in a way where I was both telling Alex what I'd told David, but also saying it in a slightly questioning way as well, like, 'Are we still going?' Alex nodded to me a confirmational verification which was accompanied by a 'yeah we are', 'we haven't come this far not to have our lessons', he was so fed up that I guess in his own mind, turning back now would have meant that everything we'd experienced up until that point was a waste. 'That's ok then' I replied, 'I'll call Nat as well as mum and dad and let them all know what's happened' then, somewhat signalling to Alex that I was taking the lead on it all and that he should go back inside to the warmth of the basement shack (and its accompanying smell of a gent's urinal).

I promptly called David back again, 'yep, we're still coming' I proclaimed, 'jolly good' David replied, a slight chuckle accompanying it, 'how long will you be?' he asked. 'I'm not sure to be honest, the RAC will take about an hour to get to us and then there's the case of changing the tyres and stuff, as well as actually getting over to you as well still, so I'd like to say it'll be two hours, but it could honestly be two and a half to three hours before we get to you'. There was a brief pause, 'that's ok, just get here when you can and we'll sort the lessons out later, have you informed your partner?' David asked, 'not yet, I'm going to call her straight afterwards' I answered, and after confirming some rough times for our lessons to be changed to, we once again hung up the phone to one another. Next on the call list was Nat, my dance partner, I knew she might not have set off just yet and I was hoping that if was able to catch her, that she could at least have a couple of hours extra for herself before driving down. Nat lived in Bolton and so for her, travelling to Wolverhampton was relatively easy, she'd hop on the M6 and drive all the way down to the Wolverhampton junction and from there, she would just follow the usual back roads we did, to get to the studio space. Unfortunately for Nat, she was constantly met with delays and road works on the M6, they were expanding the motorway and that meant that large sections of the M6 were set to regulated speed zones and traffic reduced from three lanes into two. 'Hello' Nat answered in her usual upbeat tone, she was very bubbly, very girly and "super fabulous" as she liked to say, 'hey Nat, me and Alex have gotten into a little accident...', 'Oh, no?! are you both ok?', she worryingly asked 'yeah, yeah, we're both fine thanks,' I calmly replied 'we're just going to be a little late getting to the studio, so if you haven't set off just yet, you don't need to rush yourself, we're stuck here in this boat yard by Litchfield for a couple of hours anyway'. During the little back and forth with Nat about planning the rest of the day, I found myself gradually sauntered around the boat yard, the gentle snowfall covering me, of which I would promptly shake and dust myself free from, only to be covered once again which would repeat the whole thing again. The freshly untrodden snow crunched beneath each step I made around the yard where stacked river barges were arranged for storage. Before we hung up, we'd decided that after the lessons and after a little bit of practice which we used to do. That Nat was going to shoot off back home at around 8:00pm, it meant that it would still give us a solid five- or six-hours of both practice and lesson time together and it would also mean that she could get back home safely. The final call was mum and dad, they were used to hearing from one of us about the odd accident or flat tyre or something and so when I called dad and he picked up, hearing me explain what had happened wasn't a big surprise to him. 'Are you both okay?' he asked, 'yeah, we're fine, Alex was a little shook up' I boldly proclaimed, masking the fact that I'd also gotten shaken by the spin across the A38. 'Ok' dad calmly said, 'just let us know when you get to David's', 'we will' I replied and with a press of the red icon n my phone, the call ended. This all seems a little blah-zay when I read it back to myself, but the truth was that we'd always experienced something, in one form or another, whilst travelling for the dancing. Some sort of escapade or scenario where the usual aspect of the experience was juxtaposed by an unplanned event, circumstance, or situation and this just seemed to be another one of those escapades. I jokingly remember saying to Alex as he pulled up to the roundabout which leaves Scunthorpe on our first ever excursion to the studio together. Just me and him, In the summertime of 2007, without mum and dad in the car with us for the first time, 'let's go on adventure!' I was genuinely serious about it, but the irony I guess, is that you should always be careful what you wish for, because that's exactly what we got in the years that followed.

Back in the boat yard and I slowly made my way back to little shack and its pungent smelling basement where Alex was waiting, I'd been on the phone for just over an hour which conveniently meant that I didn't have to sit and wait inside for too long. I made my way back down the narrow staircase and into the basement area where Alex and the rest of the kind family who had taken us in were situated. 'I've called everyone and let them all know what's happened I said to Alex, who was slowly and unwillingly sipping his coffee, I guess he'd also tasted the same taste I had and wanted to keep up the appreciative appearances of hospitality and gratefulness. No sooner had I sat down, and Alex's phone began to ring, 'It's the RAC' Alex said with a relief 'they must be outside' we gave a subtle nod to each other and thanked this lovely little family for the coffee they'd made for us and for letting us wait in their erm... shack, basement place, and we headed upstairs and out into the yard to greet the new arrival to the scene. Alex had already gotten to the RAC man before me and had explained the situation, 'Not a problem lads, I'll have this sorted in about twenty minutes and you'll be back on the road in no time!' This guy was super enthusiastic, either this was his first call of the day, or he'd been out and about all day and was already familiar with people having accidents in the snow. Either way, he was reassuringly calm and upbeat and like a whirlwind he got the car sorted with two new tyres. 'That'll be two hundred and fifty quid please boys', Alex looked at me, his "telepathic" powers coming into fruition once again "Shit! I'd forgotten we need to pay for the tyres!" was the vibe he was giving me, I knew full well Alex didn't have £250 to spare and quite frankly, neither did I, but I did have a wonderful little invention called the credit card at my disposal, the miraculous piece of plastic which allowed you to get what you wanted even if you didn't have the money for it at the time. I'd already used my credit card numerous times before, purchasing new Ballroom & Latin music and dance DVD's and racked up an impressive £1500 by that point, all with the good-willed intent of repaying the money back, but without the actual means to do so. Nevertheless, it was something of a god send in little pinches like that and I whipped out my wallet, 'don't worry I'll pay for it' I told the RAC man and with a few taps and a signature it was all done. He handed me the receipt and as he made his way back to his van, he told us to drive carefully. Alex looked at me, I think it was in the odd little moments that happened like that, where he was truly thankful for me being with him on the road, at least that's how it aways came across to me in those moments. If I hadn't had been with him, then he would have had to have the car taken to either a nearby garage or towed back home, instead not only were the car tyres sorted and paid for, but we were able to jump back on the road again. 'I'll pay you back' he said to me as he put one hand on my shoulder (an empty promise if there ever was one) he never did, but to be honest, I never chased him for it either, we were in the dancing together, a duo, a team, we helped and supported one another no matter what happened and this was just another occasion when that was the case. 'Let's get going' I said, and we hopped back into the car, Alex back in the driving seat and this time, he was going to drive a lot more carefully, he indicated from the hard shoulder which led both into and out of the boat yard, which we'd been previously residing at and he gently made his way out onto the A38, the snow gently falling down still, and I picked out my phone again. 'Hi dad, just letting you know we're all sorted now and we're back on the road again, I'll let you know when we arrive at the studio', 'very good' dad replied, 'drive safely', 'we will' I reassuringly replied, and I hung up the phone. It was no sooner had I put my phone in my jacket pocket, that a little car came speeding past Alex in the right-hand lane, clipping his back end slightly and essentially doing the same Waltz-like spin manoeuvre that Alex had done. We were both in shock and Alex reacted quickly, breaking, and hitting the hazard lights as soon as the car hit him, slowly driving past the opposing car which was now nestled by the side barrier of the road, and we checked if the people were ok. All good, nobody was hurt, they were shaken up, just as we were, judging by their faces, but they were fine and without so much as a second thought Alex looked at me and said, 'We're not stopping, we're already late' and pressed his foot down hard on the accelerator to speed off.

He should really have stopped and dealt with the whole insurance exchange business, but I think he genuinely had had enough at that point. He'd had it with all the doom and gloom of the weather reports, the cold bite of the air and standing in the freezing snow. He'd had it with impatient drivers urging him to go faster in the dangerous roads and the slushy messes which could dowse the vision of the windscreen in an instant but in turn, take way too long to clear again. He was tired, both mentally and physically and he just wanted to get to the warmth of the studio and to dance and forget the day, and in all honesty, so did I, the day was certainly turning into a long one and we hadn't even gotten to the studio yet. Our dance lessons and practicing would allow us an opportunistic escape from all the crap we'd experienced up until now and it was what we loved to do more than anything. So, with his foot pressing into the accelerator, the newly stranded car disappearing in the distance from the view of the wing mirrors, we continued on, ready to escape this turbulent day and to dance our problems away.

Chapter 3 The Harmonies Of The Rising Phoenix's

Every calendar year, in the first or second week of January, dad would come find both Alex and me, to hand each of us a four to five page print off he'd organised from the computer. It was always carefully arranged in chronological order and was neatly stapled together in the corner with a single staple. This masterful print off would consist of a collated list of any and all competition events taking place in the given year and it's what both Alex and I would use, when planning what we were going to be doing for the year ahead. Like a strategized military campaign, me, Alex and occasionally dad, would all stand around the dining table in the living room and strategically plan out using various highlighters and pens, the print off that dad had provided along with the stolen calendar from the kitchen wall, which if we were quick about it, mum wouldn't realise had gone missing. All in an effort to collaborate on which of the available events we would most likely be attending, which events we SHOULD probably be going to, and which ones would be a no-go for us, in the year ahead. Occasionally, dad would provide a map of the UK, which he would roll out to cover the entire table helping us to pinpoint where and how far away some of these events were taking place. All of these locations would be given a rough explanation outlining how we would (or should) be getting there by our dear papa. The inclusion of the map adding to the militaristic element that it felt like, the scene should really have been viewed in black and white with wooden dance icons representing other dancing couples and "the competition" (those couples we were hoping to beat that season) in red and we should really have been using those shuffle stick things that old military films had their generals use, you know what I mean, those wooden sticks that would be used to shuffle troops and tanks around a large scale map and that all the official military personnel would be wielding? Anyway, that militaristic element would come to its completion when mum would enter the room. I guess if I was overstating it (which I am) we'd stand to attention and salute our "superior officer" and report "the plan of attack" (whilst also handing back to her, the recently acquired P.O.W, the kitchen calendar). I'm joking of course, but when it came to the dancing, every element was covered as best as it could. Planning and organising the calendar year was the first thing we did, and we tried to do it with the upmost extreme efficiency in the early weeks of the new year, with me and Alex confirming to one another which events we thought we should be attending. There were often events taking place on the same day though, and when a decision needed to be made on which particular event we should go to, ultimately, it came down to two factors, the first being proximity, 'which one's closer?' One of us would ask, and we would use our judgement to weigh up the pros and cons for the travelling involved. Honestly speaking though, practically every competition we attended was at least two hours away from us, so it was more like a flip of a coin was used to help make the decision sometimes. Driving all the way from Scunthorpe meant that the closest event we ever had "locally" was in Sheffield, just over an hour away, everything else was a minimum of two hours away, in the car. The second factor and the most crucial one at that was; was it a ranking event? You see the open Ballroom and Latin scene in England and the UK was a very different landscape when me and Alex used to compete as juniors and youths and eventually into our early amateur careers. Especially when you compare it with how everything is now. Back then, dancers in the UK would traverse the country attending all manner of EADA (Eee-aah-daah) events. EADA were the respective, competitive dancing body of which all competitive dancers would be required to register themselves to (the organisations acronym standing for English Amateur Dance Association), and they were closely linked to the British dancing body for Ballroom and Latin dancing who governed the whole dance scene in England, Wales, Scotland, and Northern Ireland with rules and regulations. At that time, dancing the World Championships and the European Championships was an exclusive privilege, a "club", that you couldn't just walk into, you had to be invited to it, and that "club" only catered to the top contenders of their respective nations, if you weren't in the top two spots by the time that period for assessment came, you wouldn't be going, it was that simple. It was a brutal affair, but it was effective, and we all loved it! Competitors of all ages, classes and divisions would traverse the length and breadth of the country, in an attempt to acquire one of those top two positions. From Juvenile dancers right the way up to senior level dancers, we would all compete for the glorious accolade of being one of England's "top-two". This "set-up for selection" needed a regulated format, and so "dance promoters" (as they now prefer to be named) used to host EADA competitions, ranking events which would allow competitors to acquire points and essentially climb the national leader board for a chance to have a shot at glory in the World and European Championships. If you wanted the points, you had to dance the competitions and if you wanted to stand in the running for climbing the leader board, you not only had to be making finals, but you also had to be winning as well. This is what fuelled me and Alex, we were hungry, desperate to make something of ourselves, we'd thrown our heart and soul into doing the dancing, literal blood sweat and tears from the years of lessons, practices, and competitions. (Not to mention every penny we had). Climbing that leader board, even if it was only for the mere CHANCE to go to the World and European Championships, was something we would try to make happen any way we could, to make it a reality.

The living room at mum and dads house was filled with the buzz coming from the back and forth of me and Alex deep in the planning stages of the competition calendar; 'Let's go to that one', 'what about this one this time?', 'we haven't danced there yet', 'hey look there's a new one, that wasn't on the calendar last year'. I remember feeling like we might have had some sort of slight edge over some of our competitors. I'm sure they were all organising and planning their own competition calendars (at least the serious and top-level dancers were) but we both felt like we had something they didn't, we felt that we had a winning secret formula that would help propel us further than those other "idiots". 'What an arrogant thing to say!' you might well think to yourself, I know, I hear you, but we were so confident because in retrospect, we had each other, we were a unit, a team, a deadly duo, "The Whyatt Brothers!", other competitors only had themselves and their respective partners. When attending the various competitions right across the country, people would recognise Alex and me as "The Whyatt Brothers", to which Alex would give a very crude (but funny) chuckle brother, to me, to you, referenced joke about anal sex (don't ask me to repeat it because I thankfully don't remember it). All this planning and excitement would happen every year, initially dad would have organised what events we would be going to do and when, he'd done this all through our junior careers and into our early youth careers too (the junior division was from the ages of 12-15, the youth division was from the ages of 16-20). In a way I think this helped him feel more connected to what we were doing, he was always there at the competitions with a camcorder or something, filming the earlier years of our dancing as juniors and youths (which I recently saw some footage of, and as I watched some older competitions, in a swirl of emotion and memories which I'd associated from it originally, I realised it had regrettably blinded me from the fact that the overall dancing wasn't that great, especially when viewed from the cockpit of knowledge I personally have now as a professionally qualified teacher). When I think back to moments like this and to the times dad helped organise our competition calendar, I'm sure it was all because he was proud of us and of what we were trying to do for ourselves. It was only when we started to take the reins of our "dancing destiny" more, that he took more of a back seat to it all and allowed us to get on with it ourselves. Because Alex and I wanted to travel to all the different competitions together and to go to our lessons on our own, I guess to feel like we were taking more ownership of our dancing or something. We soon realised that when we would train all day and have lessons and practicing sessions as well, that mum and dad were essentially just "tagging along". It was always a long day for them both to come with us, to just sit and essentially have nothing to do, so one evening me and Alex approached them both, asking to talk to them. We knew it wasn't a bad conversation we wanted to have with them, that there wasn't going to be a big deal made about it or that anything serious was going to happen from what we were about to say, so we simply explained that whilst we were extremely appreciative of them coming along with us to our lessons, etcetera. We felt that we wanted to do this more on our own accord and that we knew they would always be feeling tired from the long days in the studio doing nothing, driving here, there, and everywhere for us. They were really thankful with what we'd explained to them, but I'm sure, despite all the tiredness they seemed to endure, they probably enjoyed every moment, seeing us hard at it in the dance studio and competitions.

Back at "HQ" and Alex and I had decided what competitions and events we were doing, we'd mapped it all out, all the competitions we were planning on doing, 2010 was going to be a big year for us both. During 2009 we had both begun new partnerships, Alex had started dancing with a lovely and sweet girl named Katherine who's Mediterranean like features contrasted nicely against Alex's more universally bland and "British" appearance. Katherine wore lovely bold and striking colours for her dresses which complimented her dark hair and olive features and which I think worked contrastingly well, when compared against Alex's slenderer and very "English looking" appearance. Alex and Katherine had started dancing together not long after I had started a new partnership myself with Natalie (or Nat as I would refer to her as). Natalie was brilliant, she wasn't afraid to tell you what she thought despite the fluffy pink accompaniments she would contrastingly have with (her pink notebook for writing down notes and her pink and fluffy pen which would be her choice of writing utensil being only a minor element of that) she worked hard, harder than anyone I've ever danced with, and she experienced every hardship that I did in her personal development. Every time I've recounted back to the years when we danced together, I'd always and still continue now, to hold her in the highest regard and with the deepest respect. So, 2009 for both me and Alex not only saw us establish new partnerships, but we also began the transition of bidding farewell to our Pre-champ status, we felt so accomplished. During late 2007 and most of the course of 2008 we'd both been alternatively winning near enough every Pre-champ competition we'd chosen to enter (Pre-Champ was the level below Amateur and is where competitors not skilled to hold their own in the Amateur league would be able to compete and develop). All with the preparatory view of dancing and winning the 2010 Champs Of Tomorrow event at Blackpool and encapsulating that time as Pre-champs by winning the biggest event in the category. This, we felt, would allow us to boldly move forward into the amateur division feeling unhindered, regrettably however, things didn't quite go to plan though. The Champs Of Tomorrow event would always take place on the first weekend of January, which meant firstly that the competition planning we would do, back in the living room, always took place directly after that competition and this meant we would need to accommodate Champs Of Tomorrow in the previous year's planning of events with the full understanding that the first comp in the new calendar year was going to inclusively be Champs Of Tomorrow. Alex and I prepared ourselves in the upper balconies of the extremely familiar Blackpool Winter Gardens Ballroom. A place which was almost a second home to us from the near two decades we'd spent dancing there. When stepping out onto the floor things felt a little off though, something wasn't quite right I thought, there were a hell of a lot more competitors on the floor than I normally would remember. With Alex looking on from the side of the floor, where he'd been drawn into the second heat, which incidentally worked out better for us, as it allowed both of us to watch one another in the earlier rounds, before then meeting in the semi-final to duke it out against each other where the two heats would be merged. I looked at him in an attempt to "telepathically" ask him what was up. He just looked back to me and shrugged, to which he then encouragingly bellowed my number, as a gesture of support. The music began for our first dance in the Ballroom section, the Waltz, Nat and I took up our hold and we began our first swing into a Natural Turn, as we danced and turned and shaped all around the floor, we would occasionally be met by numerous nudges and bumps, a common element in competitive dancing and the unfortunate result of poor floor craft ability from other competitors. But we seemed to get knocked around more than usual this time, with elbows colliding into my face and the back of Nat's head. The dance eventually finished, and we presented ourselves to the audience, trying to compose ourselves so as to not let on that we'd been bombarded by a series of rough and tumble situations. I remember walking past Alex and giving him a quick pat on the back, as he walked past me onto the floor, my token of supportive good luck to him, all the while trying to maintain the same element of professional looking composure, expected from all competitors and that I'd vigilantly seen from the top-level Amateurs in World Championships. I grabbed my towel and drink of water, which I'd sneakily stored behind a pillar situated at the back of the lower seating and then promptly took up position at the side of the floor. Not only to prepare myself to go on to the floor for my second dance, but to also support Alex and Katherine strongly and boldly with my own voice-truss bellows, shouting their number as they turned and swung past us in their Waltz. That's when I realised it, some of the familiar faces of competitors on the floor in that second round, of which Alex was now valiantly battling against. Both he and Katherine were also fighting against the argy-bargy nudges and occasional facial adjustments of competitors elbows. The face on the floor were faces I'd seen before, but I couldn't initially pinpoint who they were, and it was whilst I watched them all dance past, that I recalled it. I'd recalled where I'd seen some of these faces before, they were some of the low-level amateurs, the type of competitors who were not good enough to make decent recalls in the Amateur division. They'd purposely dropped themselves down a level and were now trying to win the entire competition at Champs Of Tomorrow. This was highly unfair, me and Alex (with our respective partners of course) had battled and worked our way up the rankings in the Pre-Champ division all season, driving all over the country and winning various Pre-Champ events. And now all of that was going to be zeroed out because these "Amateurs" who weren't good enough to contend with the upper echelons of the division, wanted to win something for themselves. Unfortunately, there was no real way to police such a thing back then, I scanned the side of the floor, looking at all the competitors waiting to come onto the floor with me for the next dance, 'yep, they're in my heat too' I thought, and with the applause of the crowd, Alex's heat finished and I was back on the floor with Nat for our next dance, the Tango. Like I'd said, it had turned out that a bunch of the Amateur level competitors who were good enough to beat me and Alex in the regular Amateur events, but not good enough to make it through the significant rounds of the big Amateur Championships against Britain's best, had chosen to dance the Pre-champ event here at Champs Of Tomorrow. Needless to say, despite how fiercely and valiantly both Alex and I battled in the following rounds of the Ballroom and during the entirety of the Latin section as well, we just weren't able to make it to the finals, our hopes of winning the biggest Pre-champ event of the competitive season, encapsulating an entire year's worth of hard work was somewhat stolen away from us and we ended the event as semi-finalists in both the Ballroom and the Latin.

And so, after returning back home and licking our wounds from the farce which had happened at Champs Of Tomorrow, me and Alex planned our path for 2010 with a vengeance. We'd been advised by our teachers to once again, dance the Pre-champ event the following year and to win what was deservedly ours, but we weren't interested with it. Yes, we COULD spend another year, winning the Pre-Champ division all through the calendar year again, but what if it happened again? What If the low-level amateurs decided to drop down again and take the winning positions at Champs Of Tomorrow for themselves, which deservedly should be awarded to Alex or me? We'd both built up in our minds that Champs Of Tomorrow 20010 was our last Champs Of Tomorrow event (because Amateurs are deemed as too skilled to partake in the event and so it's an event, which quite rightly, only caters to the lower level competitors and youth dancers, of which this would be Alex's final year of dancing the Youth division with him soon moving up age categories into the Amateur division). The rest of the competition season in 2010 for us both was going to be totally different, we decided whole heartedly to only compete in the Amateur division, with Alex dancing the remaining season of his youth/ Under 21's events as well. We were on a mission in 2010, to climb the ladder of the EADA charts in the Amateur and Youth divisions, just like we'd climbed the ladder in the Pre-Champ division. To do this successfully though, we needed a plan, we needed to be cleverer than the rest of the competitors and so, we got to work.

The plan we made was simple, (cue heist music) most amateurs are either too busy or too lazy to attend all manner of competitions hosted by event organisers, even if they are EADA registered events, not all Amateur competitors will traverse the entirety of the country to attend them all. At best amateur competitors only attended one event a month, this was in part because the top-level Amateurs would acquire double points at the big national championship events and because of this, it meant that they would only ever need to attend EADA events in order to retain their top positions or to "top up" their points if you will. The remaining Amateurs were lazy and would compete only once a month, there were a select few who danced more often, but politics and specifically choosing to go to local events would prohibit them from dancing everything available. This was what Alex and I worked hard to exploit, we'd exploit the fact that the amateurs wouldn't go everywhere across the country to dance ALL the available EADA events, English dancers are inherently lazy that way (or at least they used to be) but WE would, other competitors would normally dance "locally" to themselves, or a large majority would feel "too important" (despite being ranked 32nd or something in the country) to dance particular events. There was no way we would ever beat the top-level couples at the big national events either, we wouldn't even scratch the mid-table competitors either, we just weren't good enough (or politically favoured enough) to do so. But we did have an unmatched work ethic and a hell of a lot of persistence, no-one would beat our deterministic mindset. I'd regularly be found close to every night, practicing from the hours of 10:00pm at night to 2:00am in the morning in the living room, weights around my arms and legs dancing through finals (five dances either in Ballroom or Latin, with full energy and performance in the mix, as if I were in a competition at the World finals). With the sweat pouring off me, honing technique and doing exercises, ready for whatever might come my way in the next lesson I'd be getting that week or in preparatory build up for the next big competition. Competitors from the north seldomly travelled to London for EADA events, it was only the national, international or BDF competitions which would draw them down that way, and the competitors from the south would rarely travel too far north to places like Manchester and Sheffield, the furthest both northern and southern competitors would usually traverse, would be to the midlands (that being Birmingham/ Wolverhampton area, which was now becoming an additional home to Alex and me).

The plan we made was simple, we'd aim to compete in every single event we could during the season, if the game was to acquire points and to climb the EADA table, then all we metaphorically had to do was "play more games". We looked at all the logistics (and costs) and decided that a minimum of two competitions a month was what we needed to enter, to allow us to have a shot of climbing the ranks. Sometimes we'd do a third if we could manage it (and if our partners would agree to it as well) and using mums' calendar from the kitchen, we marked up which events we'd be going to, where they were happening and when they were taking place. We'd beat the rest of the field on the numbers alone, we didn't always have to win, but we did need to rack up points and make regular finals.

It goes without saying then, that Alex and I managed to spend a lot of "quality time" together as we traversed the country completing our goal, we'd travel across to Liverpool and Manchester for EADA events, to the formerly mentioned and locally run Sheffield event. We'd traverse regularly to the midlands and Birmingham, of which we already did twice a week anyway, attending any and all comps we could there, alongside our usual lessons. We travelled down south, to London, Heathrow, Essex and Oxford and we even branched into attending and dancing the Welsh Open Championships too, where EADA points were doubled (for some reason), despite technically being in a different country. Additionally, this wasn't including the nationally based and internationally classed events taking place across the UK either, where again, the points were double. Travelling around to all these different events meant that the car was constantly filled with talk about dancing, things Alex and I had seen from top amateurs or professionals, things we were currently working on, ideas about the "bigger picture" of dancing along with chat from what we thought about the competition we'd just attended that day/weekend. The travelling to Wales was probably the most arduous journey we'd do, frankly because the event was four and a half to five hours away from us, even longer on the way home in the dead of night with the manoeuvring of roadwork detours. The music selection was exceptionally varied in Alex's little red Fiat Punto, we'd listen to Feeder, Greenday, the Keiser Chiefs, the extensive and complete collection of Enrique Iglesias, with a Now That's What I Call Music collection CD thrown into the mix for a little bit of spicy variety and to quell any disagreement on music selection that Alex and I might have had. We would howl away to all the well-known and "rehearsed" songs, Alex even managed to sing a little bit in Spanish with the odd Enrique song too. Now, when I use the term sing, what I'm really meaning is that the musical and vocal ranges coming from the stereo system, were horrifyingly drowned out by the almost glass shattering and ear bleeding vocal experiences, created by both Alex and me. We were in no way, shape, or form singers and if you were unfortunate enough to have been sat in the car with either of us on those long,

long journeys. You'd have probably jumped out of the window, deciding to take your chances with the impactful collision of the road or the likely impalement of local scenery, than to suffer any more of our banshee cries of musical ignorance.

Heading towards Wales for the Welsh Open Championships and the consequently related FADA supported Ballroom and Latin events, myself and Alex prepared the car for a very long journey. We'd done the journey over to the Welsh Open a couple of times already, but we still needed the trusty guidance of the satnav, powered by the lighter section of Alex's car, to guide us to the sports hall venue where the competition was taking place. It was a nice and hot summers day as we navigated the various Motorways which led us over to the M50 and our karaoke session went through some of the usual CD's we'd howl away to. I remember distinctly driving around the various twists and turns of that M50 to a Stereophonics CD Alex had put into the player, it was the greatest hits compilation with all the main songs you'd recognise from the band, and with the windows rolled down on both my side and Alex's side, the heat of the summer sunshine blasting through the windshield and the cars heating turned up to full blast, in a vain attempt to keep it from overheating, our arms resting on the rolled down window frames. We'd be "singing" away, the occasional moments where we'd both be genuinely trying to sing properly (and failing miserably mind you) would be interrupted with Alex switching the lyrics to something crude or funny which rhymed with the previous verse of the song and we'd both end up bursting out with laughter together.

The musical arrangements which me and Alex would organise were a little varied to say the least, Alex liked to listen to indie bands, groups like the Keiser Chiefs, Kings Of Leon, Oasis and The Automatic. I wasn't a big fan of these bands really, the odd song maybe, but I wasn't much of an indie music listener. The only real reason why I could tolerate listening to it all was because I knew the trade-off would be that Alex would have to listen to my music choices too. My music selection was contrastingly different, the bands I used to listen to consisted of Feeder, Greenday, Blink 182, I used to listen to Enrique Iglesias and like I'd mentioned before, I'd throw on a Now That's What I Call Music CD if Alex and I couldn't agree on anything to be played, a type of "punishment" to us both for the lack of decisiveness and agreement. Whenever we travelled together though, we always tried to keep the music choices even, if Alex had popped in one of his CD's first, then the next CD we would listen to would be mine and we would flip flop the music choices back and forth as even as we could, on the various excursions we'd do to the EADA events. Because our lessons were in Wolverhampton (a good two hours to two and a half hours drive away) it meant that we would manage to be proficiently bad at all the music we would listen to. Despite the weekly "practice" we'd have at "singing" we never managed to get any good, we were terrible! Once, we were listening to the music loudly, the windows wound down on a sunny Wednesday afternoon in July, as we headed to the dance studio, that the attempted "singing" which ensued, sounded more like 1000 strangled cats being choked at once, it was seriously that bad! After pulling up to a set of traffic lights, one of the familiar Kings Of Leon songs came on stereo system, I didn't really like the band but it was Alex's turn to have a CD playing in the car. With a stationary car pulled up beside him, he let rip with the vocalisations he felt passionately resonate with himself, I honestly couldn't tell you what song it was because I was too busy trying not to burst out laughing at his embarrassment, as the girls who were in the car next to us were laughing hysterically at Alex who was hitting every single note, except the right one, completely oblivious to his new found audience. The lights turned green and both cars drove onward, the girls turning right and heading away (possibly to escape Alex's poor rendition from the Kings Of Leon repertoire). As I began to laugh out loud, Alex ending the last verse of the song he'd wonderfully and in his own way, had artfully butchered, he turned and defensively asked 'What?! What's so funny?!' I composed myself, Alex was so engaged with the music that he hadn't noticed the girl's car next to him and the scene of the situation. 'You mean you didn't notice the girls in the car next to us?' I replied, wiping a tear from my eye. Scenes like that were hilarious to me, especially when it was at Alex's expense, the hilarity of his innocence and of his obliviousness, compounding on the comedic effect which would add to the entire situation we'd usually find ourselves in.

Back in the car with our journey to the Welsh Open Championships and we were driving our way through the Welsh countryside, the winding twisting roads and hilly scenery adding to the exploratory aspect of adventure which it felt like. With the last song of the Stereophonics CD playing, I opened the glove compartment of Alex's red Fiat Punto, ready to randomly catch one of the eight CDs which would undoubtedly fly out. It was my time to choose some music and aside from the variety available in the glove box we also had a pariah of selections in both Alex's door pocket and mine, it was like a type of Jukebox on Wheels, with the most horrendous "singers" you'd ever NOT want to hear. I popped in Enrique Iglesias's Escape CD and as the first track began to play, Alex and I psyched ourselves up to give the performance of a lifetime. It was horrendous! We were so shit, so horrendously bad that in fact, I think the lovely scenic Welsh countryside would have begun to melt, if it were able to actually hear us. Our car journeys would often entail this, aside from navigating the various terrains and roads to get to our competitive destinations, we'd have the soothing melodies and harmonies of our out of tune noise to help make the car journeys seem less intensive and to seemingly reduce the duration it took us to travel to the events. Our karaoke sessions in the car were certainly a good way to help with all that. Passing the time on long journeys like that, we'd have our psyche up situations when we were at the venue, the two Ipod's I used to use for training purposes would act as psyche up harmonies to "get in the zone" with and prepare one or both of us for the competition ahead. But in the car that was all enjoyment, no need to psyche yourself up when you're merely travelling to the destination right?

The Welsh Open Championships was always a good event for Alex and me to attend, firstly because loads of other Amateurs wouldn't attend it despite it having EADA Ballroom, EADA Latin AND EADA 10-Dance events (possibly in a bid on the organisers part to increase ticket sales). We'd enter everything on the day that we could, Alex had enduringly driven us both to the competition, but he wasn't dancing it this time, his partner either couldn't make it or didn't want to do it, I honestly can't remember. But Nat did, we'd agreed to all the events together that we'd be doing for the year beforehand, and she trusted and believed in the plan that had been made from the living room planning session, earlier in the year by Alex and me. This meant that Alex was a spectator and was additionally assigned to camcorder duties, recording the events I would be dancing in so as to allow me to watch it all back later that night or the next morning, where I'd watch and see for any mistakes or corrections and ultimately learn from what I saw. The EADA events went well enough, I made finals in everything, the 10-dance event was essentially a straight final and consisted of a "warm-up" round and then a final because there weren't enough Amateurs which would dance that section. With the EADA Ballroom and the EADA Latin events requiring me to dance through semi-finals and then finals. After making the EADA Ballroom final (I think I was placed 5th or 6th in the event) and completing the EADA 10-dance event (where you dance both Ballroom AND Latin sections as one big event) it was the EADA Latin section to go. It was late, the competition was long and there were Welsh

Closed National Championship events taking place on the same day as well, which increasingly padded out the run time. I had quickly nipped to the toilets to make sure my tan, hair and make-up was unhindered from all the perspiration of the previous events. With my make-up and assortments in hand I quickly nipped off out the sports hall and into the nearby toilets (I guess you could say I'd gone to the toilets to powder my nose?... Nothing?... Fine!). Anyway, after making some minor additions, adding a little extra bronzer to my face, and sorting my hair a little, adding yet another layer of hairspray to an already "crash helmet" strengthened hair, I made my way back to the double doors of the sports hall. Through the glass windows I noticed the room was silent, couples were on the floor, but they weren't dancing, 'typical' I thought 'we're already behind and now the organisers have to wait for some idiot who's in the toilet'. I pulled the door handle leading into the main hall, casually swinging my bag of effects with me. Scanning the floor judgmentally I remember thinking to myself 'what inferior event is holding the organisers up?' and I looked across the floor at the grouped couples standing together. 'Hey, that girl looks like Nat' I thought, seeing the side profile of a girl in a pink Latin dress, her hand raised (a common signifier to the organisers that she was without her partner), and I looked up to the seating area where me, Alex and Nat had been sitting in, to point her out. That's when I saw Alex stood and frantically pointing to the floor, his face said it all, that girl didn't just LOOK like Nat, I damn well was, which meant that I was the idiot in the toilets! As the realisation dawned on me and I turned to see Nat looking to me, gesturing me to come to the floor, David (who was adjudicating the event and conveniently was stood by the side of the floor nearby) turned with a smirk and said, 'this is you'. 'SHIT!' I thought as I threw my bag to the side, its contents of make-up, hair gel and hairspray rolling out everywhere on the carpet, as I bolted onto the floor to join Nat for our Semi-final round of the EADA Latin event. I gestured an apologetic wave to the organiser on the stage, his mic held to his chin and took Nat by the hand to find a position for the first dance, quickly telling her I was sorry. She quickly replied 'it's ok' as the organiser did a quick count to ensure he had all couples present and the first dance, the Cha-Cha began. The worse thing about that experience for me was the fact that the event was packed, tiered seating was filled on the right-hand side of the floor, surrounding the entrance to the hall. The stage, and organisers at one end of the hall and large circular dinner tables scattered on the remaining two sides of the floor. All filled with the onlooking eyes of parents, competitors, and kids. I was embarrassed of course, I was NEVER late onto the floor, but I quickly shrugged it off and didn't allow for it to affect my performance, points were up for grabs, I had to get to the final and to secure the next position in the EADA leader board.

Regarding competitions let me tell you about one of the other biggest EADA events that was recognised as a "must go" on the calendar. It was an event run at the Kings Hall in Stok-On-Trent, this event was always packed, EADA Ballroom, EADA Latin and EADA 10-Dance events ran all through the days schedule and ranged extensively from the juvenile level (kids up to the age of 11) right the way up to the senior level (derogatively anyone over the age of 35 who wasn't a professional) and everything in between, If you wanted EADA points, this was THE event to go to. As with most things though, it would seem almost too good to be true, an entire competition day filled to the brim with ranking events for everyone dancing Juvenile, Junior, Youth, Amateur and Senior events! Everyone and anyone should be going to it, and in most cases, a lot of people did. The problem was that the event was always, always running late. Now when I say the event was running late, I don't mean ten or fifteen minutes late, I mean like four hours late, if you were "scheduled" (a loose term to encapsulate the proceedings) to dance at say 1:00pm you wouldn't get onto the floor until 5:00pm (at best). Normally, (as you might expect) a lot of people wouldn't stick around, some competitors would leave exceedingly early, having paid to enter, waited for three or four hours, only to be told that their event wasn't happening for ANOTHER two hours, which would consequently result in them picking up their gear and then leaving. When it came to all the Amateur events however, the EADA points were double, that meant, despite the long, long waiting period, it was really in your best interest to stay and dance, regardless of the fact that the EADA Latin and the Latin section of the EADA 10-Dance would have their first rounds (out of three or sometimes four) start at 9:00pm. You'd probably assume it was due to numbers, a high and unexpected influx of competitors which would require more rounds to accommodate them and therefore would resultingly pad the run time out even further. But that just wasn't the case, this happened every, single, year, so much so that if anyone mentioned "Alan's Comp" it was advised that you should take a tent with you as you'd likely be spending the night. When Alex danced as a youth competitor, days like these were exceedingly tough, it wasn't too bad for me personally as I'd missed out on the last two years of my youth career (my partner at the time being 21 meant that I couldn't dance as youth competitor, as it would be deemed unfair and thus, go against the rules). This meant that while Alex continued his Youth career, I would predominantly be dancing the Amateur events and Pre-Champ events as well. Alex's last year as a Youth dancer saw him dance the Ballroom sections (all of which consisting of five dances to be danced consecutively after each other) in the Youth category, the Amateur category, and the Ballroom part of the 10-dance category. With the later fortune of dancing the same in the following Latin sections (also consisting of five dances to be danced consecutively in their respective categories) in the Youth category, the Amateur category, and the Latin segment of the 10-Dance category. Not to mention the Open Foxtrot and basic rumba categories in the respective Ballroom and Latin sections which would be used to "help keep your legs warm". The event was brutally long, when the Amateur competitors for the Ballroom event, for the Latin event and for the 10-Dance event were about to dance their first rounds respectively, they would all be ushered into the corridor adjacent to the hall to take part in a "parade of Britain's best" with a march theme played as the competitors for the specified event took to the floor; uniformly organised in order by their competition number, of which you would then be required to parade around the entirety of the floor, lining up in front of the stage for one huge photo, which would be published on the front page of a future edition of the Dance News newspaper (a big deal at the time, or at least it was for me and Alex). Because Alex and I would enter all three Amateur events (Ballroom, Latin and 10-Dance) it meant that we would take part in this parade three times on one day if they were all EADA events. The music of which we would march to, still ringing strongly in my ear as I type this all out. The spirit, atmosphere and overall encompassment of the event was brilliant, the difficulty which always transpired with it all, was its run time, the organiser (Alan) was an elder gent who despite his exposure to the dancing scene had no real clue on running an event. He'd sporadically divert away from his programme to run a different category, which would then mean that the category he'd missed, needed adding in somewhere else, it was always a shambles and things like that and the fact he hadn't accounted for the time of his parades, resulted in the competitions running massively behind schedule. Competitors leaving early and not dancing their events didn't help matters and meant that the numbers on the floor didn't match what was on the entry form list, and so Alan or the Chairman of adjudicators would be required to do a head count of everyone on the floor, wait and work out tallies, and then eventually run the event with an altered marking system based on the new number of competitors (reduced of course) now on the floor.

During the closing part of the Ballroom rounds of one particular event (now scheduled to take place around 5:30pm) Alan must have suddenly realised that he needed to run the remaining finals of the EADA Amateur Ballroom event, the EADA Youth Ballroom event and the final of the Open Foxtrot event (a one dance event which anyone could partake in). The problem for Alex was that not only had he made the final of the Youth Ballroom and the Open Foxtrot (guaranteed on both accounts, as his Ballroom skills as a youth dancer were pretty good and we'd both made the Foxtrot final together in any competition we would enter) but it turned out he'd beaten me into the final of the Amateur Ballroom as well. As Alan went through the numbers recalled back to the final of the Amateur event, literally about to take part straight after the Open Foxtrot event (which was run literally straight after Alex's Youth Ballroom event) announcing some of the numbers associated with the expected top-level Amateurs who had attended the event that day and managed to stick around. My number was just ahead of Alex's, no sooner had we both left the floor for the Open Foxtrot, and I heard that my number was skipped, a sign that I hadn't made it through into the final and a little disheartening to hear but I didn't let it show, however Alex's number WAS immediately called out. Katherine was understandably ecstatic despite being slightly out of breath from the previous events she'd just finished, Alex, not so much, he'd just given everything he had in the Youth event. The tough competition from all the other Youth dancers on the floor required him to pull out all the stops and now after dancing the Open Foxtrot final, he had to go out and do it all again for the Amateur section. There was chance for catching a break, for allowing him to catch his breath, without having the chance to get a break or even a drink or to towel down the perspiration from his face. He shot me a quick "telepathic" look which read 'for fucks sake' and he soon composed himself with Katherine and took to the floor for the Amateur final. You'd think that I would be disheartened, not making the final of such a big and important event, but I never felt bad, not once, when Alex made the round ahead of me or if he won the category and I didn't, I never once got upset or complained about anything. For one very simple reason, it helped push me harder in my training for the next big event, if Alex had done better than me, if he'd won and I'd come second or something along those lines, then I would just work harder and become stronger so that the next time we'd find ourselves in contention on the floor, I would be the one to come out on top. The other reason was because we both felt the same for one another, we both wanted and enjoyed duking it out together on the floor with one another, that's what made the semi-finals of big and important events so much fun for us both. As the heats would be merged into one big collection of competitors at the semi-final stage and if Alex and I were in separate heats (as we often tried to make happen) then we'd have to battle through the rounds independently, earning our way into the semi-final before then enjoying the resulting clash in the semi-finals. But only one of us could ever win the event, so whenever one of us lost to the other and was subsequently knocked out of the round before the final, the other one of us would always cheer from the side lines with tremendous support and pride in what the other had achieved. And that's exactly what I did that day, Nat and I stood at the side of the floor, the sweat still glistening from our faces of the Open Foxtrot event that we'd just danced the final of, and we cheered and shouted during the whole five dances for Alex and Katherine.

As the day drew longer, the competition slowly progressed, with the 1st round of the Latin section of the competition commencing at around 7:00pm, following the conclusion of the final parade of the day. After my personal defeat in the Amateur Ballroom section of the competition, I had to try and claw a victory back over Alex in the Latin segment. Due to the prolonged wait times, a number of Amateur competitors had decided to leave and go home, which in theory should have reduced the amount of rounds we all should have danced, regrettably though, this wasn't the case. Rather than having three rounds including the final, Alan had decided to keep the fourth round and made the competitors dance a "warm up round". I think he must have been doubling down on the running of the event his own way, no doubt the chairman of adjudicators (the person responsible for any split decisions or rulings which require an oversight) had ruffled the feathers of him after approaching the stage a number of times to not only talk during the rounds taking place about re-structuring the time table to get things moving quicker, but he would also be marking the dancers on the floor as well. Fortunately, the chairman knew what he was doing, it was David, our teacher, he was the chairman of adjudicators, and not only did he have the capacity to handle the lack of structure, but he was up against it all, trying to get things back on time again. To no avail, the competition ended at around 1:00am in the morning, with everyone then needing to drive themselves back home straight afterwards and it was on that long journey back home to Scunthorpe, where

Alex and I then began to dissected what we felt we'd experienced in the competition, what we felt had worked really well, the brilliant string of results we'd gotten (because loads of people had abandoned the event all together) and where we might find ourselves on the Leader board after the results were updated in the EADA charts. Because Alex had driven us to the event and danced nearly double the number of events that I had done, I figured I'd drive us both home. That way Alex could relax after the competition and re-charge himself a little and we could also have chance to talk extensively about the competition as a whole and how we both felt it had all gone. I navigated the night-time streets using the Satnav, eventually getting us to the A38 which would eventually lead us to the M1 and back home. As soon as the car reached a point where it was essentially a straight run, I turned to Alex to ask him how he felt he'd done in the events he'd danced that day. Not needing to worry about narrow streets, one-way systems and traffic lights in Stoke-On-Trent and focussing on staying awake on the A-roads and motorways. Nestled into the seat belt, his arms folded, and body slumped into the seat, Alex was fast asleep, he'd given it his all at the comp in the Kings Hall, another valiant effort collating in his personal accumulation to add to his collection of points for the EADA leader board. Alex had made finals in everything, which meant that he'd scored double points and large amounts of points at that, in every EADA event he'd entered. I knew I had to work on some stuff myself after getting back and watching the competition footage the next morning, I knew I couldn't end the season behind Alex, I also couldn't allow the results of that one event, to affect the goal of climbing the leader board. Each competition would be a kind of skirmish or battle we would "fight" and, in order to "win the war" we had to keep ourselves focussed on working hard and making finals. I had a lot to work on and I was excited to get stuck into it all, with the stereo playing one of my Feeder albums, I drove us both home, the track, comfort in sound, playing quietly from the stereo, acting as my companion whilst Alex slept in the passenger seat alongside me.

Chapter 4 'I've Just Taken A Shit In A Bidet'

During my Junior, Youth and Amateur career in Open Ballroom & Latin competitions, it's not been an uncommon fact to find dancers break-up and form new partnerships, there's always a number of reasons for this, some of the most common being related to the couple having height issues (one person suddenly becomes taller than the other) if the dance couple have involved themselves with one another and formed a romantic relationship and then they suddenly break up, then that can also end a dance partnership. Another reason would be if the parents of the dancers can't agree with one another, then that can also end a partnership, regrettably, I'd have to say that I've had my own fair share of dancing partners. Each with their own personal and differing merits and each one unfortunately ending for one reason or another. As a junior it was mainly because of a height issue, standing at a towering five foot four (and a half) would mean that the array of available partners suitable for me, weren't always easy to find. My first Youth partner (when I was 16) was a lovely girl named Faye, she was a year or two older than me and we danced open level competitions from the intermediate level through to Pre-Champ level, as well as dancing the occasional amateur event (the order I've stated them, being the order which they are categorised with intermediate being the lowest and Amateur being associated as the "top-level"). I don't remember all that much from dancing with Faye to be honest, I remember dancing the National Championships in 2005 with her as well as travelling to York for dance lessons with her teacher, although as I type that I realise that I recently came across a photo taken by either Alex or my dad, of Faye and me dancing in the Winter Gardens at Blackpool. Late 2005 was my first year of dancing the adult division and like I just mentioned, I'd enter everything and anything available at the competitions. The National Championships was always a big one though, the only events I could dance there were the Youth (in both the Ballroom and the Latin) the North Of England Championships (Ballroom only for some reason) and the Amateur events (both Ballroom and Latin). Over the ensuing season, I'd become familiar with some of the main faces in the Amateur league, seeing the top couples winning or being placed in the top three of all competitions I'd personally attended. They all needed the EADA (Eee-aah-daah) points and so at that period of time, it wasn't uncommon to see a lot of the top-level amateurs attending most of the Sunday competitions, of which I would be attending myself. When it came to the Nationals though, everyone was at their peak, and everyone was in attendance. All the events I'd chosen to participate in, were separated over the three days which the entirety of the National Championships festival would take place over (the British National Championships runs Thursday through to Saturday). This was where I remember having my first taste of the rough and tumble of the adult division, I was terrible in terms of my technique, and I'd have been lucky if I'd made any form of recall in any of my events, a first-round knockout was what I'd commonly experience at that time. However, due to everyone's surprise, Thursday (the day where both the North Of England Championships and the Youth Latin Championships would take place) was a busy one for me. With Alex watching from the seats in the Winter Gardens Ballroom, I danced my first round of the North Of England Amateur Championships, I was very rough around the edges and my technique was a shambles, but I was able to cobble together with Faye, something which seemed acceptable. The first round was busy, four heats and a very fast and busy floor meant that my inexperienced self along with Faye, were getting bashed and knocked around all over the place. After dancing the first round of the North Of England, Faye and I raced to the back of the ballroom, we had between fifteen and twenty minutes to get ourselves changed to go and dance our Youth Latin event, the senior category which followed the North Of England Championships, acting as a type of buffer to allow for Faye and I to do a "quick-change" into our Latin outfit. Fortunately, dad was there, having laid out my outfit for the Latin event he helped undo my collar and remove the studs, his fingernails jabbing into my throat as he wrestled with the slightly moist and intricate collar stud. Tail suits are an artful construction in and of themselves, the shirt is a collar-less attire which required separate studs to close up (no buttons unfortunately) with longer studs which would be placed on the back of the neck under the fabric and a longer stud at the front, both of which would have a foldable clasp which would help secure the plastic collar which you separately had to attach before completing the shirt ensemble with a pristine white bow tie. Next were the trousers, black and high waisted, secured with a cummerbund and braces with a thickly padded black tail suit jacket and its additional white pocket hanky. It was an art to just to get the whole thing on, and after that first round of the North Of England Championships, I had to race to get it all off as soon as I could. Taking everything off was easy enough, dad was fortunately there to help clear the mess of me dumping my stuff to the ground as soon as it was removed from my perspiring self, I then speedily got into the Latin outfit, hoping not to rip and tear the more delicate fabric against the sweaty mess of my body which still clung to me from the previous event. With the first round of the senior ballroom section dancing their last dance, the Quickstep, I tied my laces, completing the mad scramble to get changed. Faye had just returned from getting changed herself, her mum carrying the bag with her ballroom dress inside it. No need to warm up for the Latin, we were already warm from the mad scramble of changing and with the crowd applauding the valiant efforts of the senior category. Faye and I took our position at the side of the stage, joining a majority of the other Youth dancers, opposite to where our families were sitting, ready to be announced onto the floor to dance our Youth Latin event. After dancing the four test dances in the Latin segment (those comprising of the Cha-Cha, Samba, Rumba and Paso Doble) with my teacher Jayne, encouragingly giving advice in between the numerous heats before the next dance commenced. Youth dancers have bundles of energy (as you'd expect) but they're also quite unreserved and fierce when battling on the floor for open spaces which allow them to showcase their hard grafted dancing skills and technique. With the end of the last heat in the Paso Doble, we raced back to our parents on the other side of the Ballroom, there was another fifteen-to-twenty-minute segment where we needed to get changed, I wasn't optimistic for a recall in the Ballroom, I mean I always hoped to make the next round, but I wasn't an idiot either, I knew the other competitors were better than me. The suit was back on, and Faye once again returned wearing her lovely Ballroom dress with a black coloured bodice covered with rhinestone which faded down into a white skirt with white feathers, the live band on stage (now returning from their designated break period) played the fanfare commonly used to signify to the whole Ballroom, the re-commencement of the competition with the distinguished panel of adjudicators being announced back on to the floor. These judges were the best of the best, all of them former World, European and British finalists or champions and they all knew what they were looking for in terms of quality and skill. I waited by the bar at the back of the seating, expecting the usual scenario of my number to be skipped, thus signifying the fact that I'd not made it through to the next round. I was lost in my head for a moment and that's when I startingly heard an almighty 'YEEEES!' I looked across to where the cheers had erupted to see Faye's family and my family all cheering for us, we'd done it! We'd made a recall; I couldn't believe it. I walked so proudly to the floor wearing a smirk of personal self-satisfaction which beamed across my face as the remaining numbers for the first heat were announced to the floor and I prepared myself for the first dance in this next round, the Waltz. I was ecstatic that we'd made a recall, this was my first "proper" competition as an adult, and I'd managed to make a recall! But I knew I had to compose myself, there were still four test dances to get through and with the band starting the introductory bars to the Waltz, we took up our hold. There were a number of things probably going through my head and an even larger number of experiences taking place as well, the primary one I remember, was when I was dancing the Foxtrot (the second test dance at Blackpool, normally it's the third dance in the sequence at a regular competition, but in Blackpool the order is slightly changed, and Foxtrot is danced second). As I danced into a Feather Finish facing one of the corners of the Ballroom and preparing to dance a Three Step (a common combination) I had to suddenly stop, the top couple, Marco, and Joanne, scheduled to win the entire event, were dancing my heat. I'd seen them both many times, becoming somewhat inspired by Marco's dancing and his mannerisms from the various competitions I'd attended and had seen him dance at, as well as the occasional brief conversation I'd managed to have with him. I looked up to him as a type of guide and inspiration for how amateurs are supposed to look, how they're supposed to dance and how they should conduct themselves overall. Being the current British Champion, you'd expect nothing less than the highest of decorum, conductivity, and skill, this was all encapsulated in that moment as I attempted to continue into my Three Step. It wouldn't have been hard for Marco to see my inexperience, to see my poor quality as I tried to completely stop a progressive movement which is designed to continue moving. After he completed what I would later learn to be as a Curved Feather and Outside Spin movement, he paused about a metre away, clearly seeing the potential collision about to unfold. I was able to see him execute this sequence of steps because I was somewhat motionless, unable to decide which way I should go next and unable to interpret where he was going. The last thing I needed was to collide with Marco on the floor, I knew that if we accidently collided that he would knock me flat on my ass. With a look in his eye and a subtle nod, he signalled for me to continue forward and dance past him, which I immediately did with a relieved sense of confidence dancing my way into my Three Step and the remainder of my choreography. That was such a big and inspirational turning point for me, dancing was always brutal, competitors were always fierce, but I knew I didn't have the skill or quality to hold my own or house any of that ability, not with the low-level ability I personally had at the time at least. It would be many years later, after seeing a dancing interview with Simone Segatorri (Italian) and Anette Sudol (German) (the Amateur World Champions at the time) that it hit home to me, why that experience resonated so much with me. In the interview, Simone and Anette were asked why they look like they're holding back sometimes in the earlier rounds they dance in, why they don't dance to their fullest especially when we comparingly see them in a semi-final or a final. A good question when you think about it, they're the best (at the time) and they can be clearly seen not dancing their fullest, they can noticeably be seen dancing more reserved and restricted. Simone stated that despite them being world champions (at the time) they were fully aware that a lot of the other competitors dancing in those first and second rounds are only ever going to dance the first or second round, they're not going to make it any further in the competition. Simone and Anette know they're going to make the final, maybe even win the entire event if they can, but for a lot of those other competitors, that first round or second round is all they'll do and so they should be allowed to enjoy the time they have on the floor. That really hit me, it was something I'd subconsciously also done, especially when partnering students as a professional later on down the dancing road. Marco had given me chance to experience that second round, the first ever significant recall I ever made as a young adult competitor and the degree of professionalism and masterful use of floor craft with which he used, was something I personally aimed to attain for myself. I remember getting back home after the festival had ended brandishing some new Blackpool dance CDs to add to my collection now amassing on an Ipod I had recently bought, feeling inspired and excited, a fire was burning strongly, and I was ready to do more.

As Alex and I became more known within the National Sunday circuit, making regular finals in the Youth division and winning the Pre-Champ competitions alternatively, the exposure to our other competitors and some of the top-level dancers in the country was inevitable. We'd made friends with quite a lot of the other dancers, and it was always fun seeing our friend Jack or Kyle (who had a personal rivalry between them both at the time) John and Katherine Giannini (the brother and sister combo) as well as numerous others. It felt like, even though we were all separated by distance and dates of competitions which would be the circumstance of when we would next see each other, it still felt like we had a little type of community, a little amalgamation of friendships, it was nice. It was during late 2007 into 2008 where Alex and I began venturing into the territory of going to lessons and competitions by ourselves, with our dad occasionally joining us in Alex's little red Fiat Punto and with the occasional accompaniment (on a Wednesday) of both mum and dad, who would drive us to our lessons sometimes. Despite all the upward trajectories made in competitions, in training and in results, we always tried to remain ourselves, dancing was always fun, and it was never a chore. We wanted to climb the ranking table so much, that every yearly comparison was just a form of measurement towards that goal. We were competitive, especially against one another and I feel that it was this primary element that helped push us higher in our results and in our overall progression and quality. The lessons would serve as the feedback on what needed to change, what was working well and what still wasn't right, with Will and Nicky now actually able to assess and actively teach us, rather than disciplining us on our walks down the room. With all this variable seriousness surrounding the dancing you'd expect it all to be stressful, but that just wasn't the case, we always had an outlet, some form of joke, or silliness that would help to diffuse any tense circumstance or situation.

Alex and I had amassed a large collection of Stand-up comedy DVD's and would frequently watch them, telling jokes from what we'd heard of whichever particular comedian we'd just seen. I guess if I had to classify my humour and Alex's humour it would be that Alex is a lot darker with his jokes, he'll tell you jokes on race, religion, and a number of other taboo subjects, and because they sort of come from left field, you never really expect them. Combine that with the dead pan way he usually tells them, and you'll find yourself laughing for hours with him. My humour is a little sillier, I might say a silly thing, use some type of particular wordplay to alter something so it sounds funny or sometimes do a silly action in one form or another. Alex can also be silly, and I'll sometimes have the odd taboo joke, but I'd say the ratio is about an 80-20 split (Zipf's Law) on the two types of subject matter. On Wednesdays after a long day of lessons and practicing and training down in Wolverhampton, mum, dad, me, Alex, David, and a guy named the Stagman; would all venture to a nearby pub close to the studio, the conversation mainly flowed about dancing, but as soon as Alex started telling jokes, that was the end of it. Alex just had a way of telling them, so much so, that locals in the pub on Wednesday would saunter over and listen in on his jokes, to which Alex would embarrassingly but eventually start reiterating. I was always amazed at how many jokes Alex had remembered from those DVD's, I'd only have a handful of jokes, but Alex, he was on a whole other level. Every Wednesday saw the little corner we used to all sit at, boisterously ooze with comedic gold spewing from Alex, with David wiping away tears from his eyes with whichever off the cuff joke Alex just said, and mums belly laugh which had less and less restrain the more drinks she acquired. Because we would find ourselves regularly in the company of David and the Stagman in the more intimate evenings, it meant that Wednesdays was a day where we'd also be able to talk about some of the antics that had transpired within the dancing scene as well. Maybe there was a new couple on the scene, maybe something had happened politically, it was almost like a little hub of dancing embroilment with David maybe talking about one of his international excursions adjudicating. I remember asking David occasionally about dance related things pertaining to my own dancing, what he thought I should maybe be working on at home before he saw me again on Saturday, the answer was usually the same, something relating to technique or movement of some description, but because we weren't in the studio, I guess, looking back, he would be a little reserved in saying too much. 'So' David said looking at Alex and me, 'Are you both going to Coventry on Sunday?' we'd already planned our competitions in January and the Coventry event was a new one which wasn't included in the list from January, it had emerged on the calendar a few months afterwards as a new event for dancers to attend. Alex and I looked at each other, the new event had been listed as an EADA Youth (both Ballroom and Latin) an EADA Amateur Ballroom event and an EADA Amateur Latin event. It was a triple whammy of points and David was judging the event as well, so it would have been a silly idea not to go and do it. The difficulty was in its distance, Scunthorpe to Coventry was around two and half to three hours away, and then you had to add on the fact that we'd spend another half an hour finding the venue. 'I'm not sure' I said, 'where's it being held?' 'It's being held at the Coventry football stadium' David replied, 'which means it'll be easy to get to' 'You're going!' mum said assertively, 'David's going to be there as well, so you're going' and with a glance back to David, his face saying something to the effect of "you've been told" the plan was made to go to the competition that weekend.

Me and Ale had never been to Coventry before, we'd ventured to Nottingham the odd time for competitions, but never to Coventry, fortunately for us though dad had. Dad was in his mid to late sixties at this point and we knew it wouldn't be fair to make him drive us all the way to the competition and all the way back again, so Alex and I decided to share the driving. With Alex driving us all there (I'd be assigned supportive navigational duties alongside dad), and I drove us all back home again after the competition had ended. Dad was assigned to the primary role of navigator, if we were lost, he was to use the maps in the back (if the Satnav failed us as well) to get us to the football stadium. The drive went well enough, music in the car playing away to help make the three-hour journey seem shorter, chat in the car about various topics and dance related things, which would be interjected with dad reassuring us of the Satnavs guidance as he cross referenced our route with the big map book of the UK, which he'd picked up from WHS Smith, in the back seat. Eventually we arrived at the stadium, all three of us pouring out the car to stretch our legs and begin unloading the boot of the car. Alex and I looked up at the stadium in slight disbelief, we'd never danced in a stadium before, but we'd aspirational and inspirationally seen countless international competitions, with top-level dancers dancing in grand sporting arenas all across Europe and the world. Now, here we both were, about to experience the exact same thing, my mind flooded with scenes from world championship events from across the globe where spotlights and cheering crowds with thousands of people are all supporting their favourite competitors. That was going to be us in a few hours' time, and I grew ever more excited as we joined the que of people lined to go inside. As we stood in the que at the bottom of a staircase, just on the inside of the building, leading up to the ballroom, Alex and I began to talk strategy, 'Ok, so we need to get numbers and entry forms' with Alex confirming as I told him the plan, 'you're on first Ale, so you'll probably need to go put your stuff in the changing rooms as soon as we get up stairs'. I then turned to dad who stood one step below us, 'that'll mean I'll need our EADA cards for registration dad, do you still have them?' dad looked back at me with a blank expression 'no', 'What?' I responded in a nervous panic 'he's joking Ian, of course he has them' Alex retorted and gestured to dad to hand the cards over. As dad reached into his inside jacket pocket, revealing the EADA cards he'd been retaining for safekeeping, he handed them to Alex, the que gradually making its way up the stairs and into the venue. After walking through the double doors at the top of the stairs and paying the entrance fee, Alex and I looked around, all the excitement and visualised pre-conceptions about what the competition venue might look like, were all instantly dissipated. It turned out that the competition was to be held in the V.I.P suit of the football stadium, which overlooked the Coventry Football Club's playing field. This was a far cry contrast to what Alex, and I had previously imagined the venue to look like. it was essentially a regular Sunday competition with large circular dining tables and white tablecloths spread across the entirety of the carpeted area of the venue. It was certainly a positive contrast when you compared it to the regular competitions that would take place in old town halls with their "authentic aroma" of damp or leisure centre sports hall venues with their tiered seating. But it was far, far away from the glamourous ideas that me and Alex and had seen on YouTube videos from the big IDSF competitions. After finding an empty dining table, somewhere near to the back of the room, Alex and I made a plan of what we were going to do. The events we were dancing that day were quite extensive, I would be entering into the Pre-Champ Ballroom and Pre-Champ Latin categories, the EADA Amateur Ballroom and the Amateur Latin Events as well as the Open Foxtrot category and Basic Rumba category. Alex would be entering the exact same with the addition of both the EADA Youth Ballroom and the EADA Youth Latin categories. After looking over the running order in the programme which contained the entire listing of events for the day and that had been widely distributed amongst all the tables for people to refer to, I told Alex that whilst he went to go put his dancing gear into the changing rooms, I'd look at organising our entries, filling out the entry forms and collect our respective numbers. Alex's EADA Youth Latin event was scheduled to be first in the running order so it was best he take his gear into the changing rooms so that he could then spend the rest of the time before having to get himself changed, "getting in the zone". Alex picked up his bags with his suit and Latin outfit and the bag with the rest of his effects and made his way out the side door of the main hall and into the corridor, leading off down towards the changing rooms. I, on the other hand, made my way to the entry table to collect the entry forms for myself and Alex. Whenever Alex and I used to compete there used to always be a gentleman named Michael who would be responsible for organising entries of each and every competitor on the day. Michael was a short, heavy-set man with thinning dark hair, somewhere in his late fifties (as a guess). He had an almost Mediterranean look with his features and my dad used always find ways of conversating with him, whenever he attended the numerous and varied competitions. Michael smiled at me as I made my way to the entry table, Michael was always at the various competitions and because me and Alex traversed nearly everywhere, we'd gotten to be regular, familiar faces to him. As Michael handed me two forms, he smiled as he asked, 'are you both dancing today?' 'yes', I happily replied, reaching out my hand to collect the two forms Michael had presented. One would be for me, and one would be for Alex 'looking forward to seeing you both out there'? Michael responded as I smiled and thanked him, who then greeted the next person in the small que which had begun to form behind me. Making my way back to the table area we'd confidently acquired, I couldn't help but notice, there were an exceedingly large amount of dining tables (there must have easily been at least 50 to 60 tables, all seating a potential 10 people) placed all around the dance floor and extending right the way back to the end of the room. A large chandelier poignantly hung in the centre of the room over the dance floor area, of which didn't seem to look so big, I was concerned about how the other couples would operate on such a small floor (when I say small floor, I mean in comparison to the usual size of a sports hall venue or some of the more familiar locations we'd competed in). Amateurs, Youths and Pre-Champs would battle every inch of a larger floor, with no restrain for knocking into or barging past other couples and now we were all going to have to contend against one another on something smaller, that meant only one thing. Floor craft was going to be the priority of the day for me, not only would I have to look at adjusting my choreography to match the floor sizing, but I'd also have to consider what type of expected situations might occur due to the size of the floor and the voraciousness of some of the other dancers (as well as their own poor floor craft ability) especially within the Amateur division where EADA points were available. Because we were further down south, that meant that a lot of the London couples, the "top level" dancers, would be likely attending the event as well, that meant that the competition was going to be a tough one for both me and Alex. Considering as well, the fact that Alex also had EADA points to collect in the Youth sections, which were rife with unapologetic and boisterous competitors. As I sat down with the forms for Alex and me, I contemplated what way I should approach my dancing today containing any form of trepidation I might have about the upcoming proceedings. Dad leaned over wielding a pen, 'here you are' he said with a smile, and I took the pen from him ready to cross compare what events we should be entering for the day. When it came down to the entry forms at various competitions, each organiser had their own way of organising the categories, some organisers would have Y01, Y02, A01, A02 to signify that specified categories would be Amateur event number one, Amateur event number two, Youth event number one, Youth event number two, which would also trickle down and extend into the other categories of intermediate, beginner etcetera. Other organisers just numbered the events, and others had an almost cryptological approach where you'd need a master's degree and twelve years' experience with Indiana Jones to work out. Fortunately, every event was also named alongside whatever letter, number, or batman symbol the organiser had associated to the event you would be looking to enter. This is more for the organisers than for the competitors and in reality, it's a very efficient system, it's just that near enough every event has a different formula for short handing their listing of categories. So, providing the events are named as well, you'll find that it's very rare for you to have any real issue when filling your entry form out. I was part the way through completing Alex's EADA number from his EADA card when I heard the pattering of running feet, no sooner had I looked up, had Alex thrust himself into the chair beside me, barging his shoulder into mine as he knocked into me which almost made me mess up his entry form.

'What the fuck's wrong with you?' a joking tone coming from what seemed to be a very direct and curt response to his arrival. Alex had a look of concern on his face, he didn't have his dance gear with him and as I asked him if he was ok, I scanned the area around him, looking for his dancing gear in an attempt to convey the question, 'have you lost it all or something'. 'Where's all your stuff?' I eventually asked, now a little concerned myself, at this point dad had the camcorder bag on the table and was rifling through the contents to find and organise a blank tape to record the days dancing on. 'Don't worry, it's all in the changing room' Alex replied, clearly reassuring my initial concern that he might have lost all his dance gear or that maybe it had been stolen. I breathed a sigh of relief and turned back to the entry form for Alex, scanning the reference paper from the table to find the relevant categories for him to enter that day, Alex then leaned into me and as he did so, my eyes raised, looking straight forwards, I had a feeling that something was up. Being brothers and considering the fact that we were very close, there was always a sixth sense that you would have if the other one of you had some sort of issue. One example of this was during a regular competition in Worcester, for us, that drive was also somewhere in the region of three hours as the venue was somewhat on the border of Wales, and It meant that Alex's little Fiat Punto had to traverse the width of England to get there. The competition was run by a very nice man named Tony Hunniset, he was a regular face on the judging panels, and he would host twice a year, his Worcester competition which would feature alternative EADA Amateur events running on each of the different occasions that the competition was on. One competition would have an EADA Amateur Latin event along with an EADA Youth Ballroom event, and the other competition, later in the year, would play host to the EADA Ballroom and EADA Youth Latin events. It meant that anytime you danced Tony's comp, you'd always see a couple of the top-level dancers attending the event. In one particular competition, Alex was dancing the EADA Youth Latin event (I was only dancing the EADA Amateur Ballroom event that day, so I was on camcorder duties for his Youth section). Tony used to run either EADA Youth Latin or the EADA Amateur Latin event early and alongside the semi-finals of the Junior and juvenile events, that way all the youngsters would have a chance to see some inspirational dancing and the competitors for the Latin event would have a decent crowd to perform to. This was because after all the adult Ballroom events had finished, a lot of people would leave and go home, not a lot of the adults would dance the Latin sections which meant that the crowd, which was also them, would disappear (it wasn't uncommon to find yourself dancing a regular Amateur final to an entirely vacant side of the room, as I often and unfortunately found myself doing quite a lot of the time). As Alex finished his Paso Doble, his fifth and final dance in the EADA Youth final was about to begin, he prepared himself for the last dance, he'd battled a first round (where three couples were knocked out) and then faced fierce opposition in the semi-final managing to come out ahead of some rivalling couples and securing his position into the final where he was now giving it his all, in the hopeful attempt of securing a decent number of points that day. The music played and Alex began his choreography with his partner, they jumped and turned and flicked and kicked, Alex's energy rising with the crowd's enjoyment and support. When It comes to performing Alex and I have a very different selection of styles, I'm a little more charismatic (as told to me from numerous people) and I like to be slightly cheeky when I dance, showing some form of complex movement or my interaction with the audience. Alex is a little more reserved, Alex will show his performance aspect through an element of reserved and interconnected movements which culminate into a form of impacting stop movements with his face saying something to the effect of 'did you see that? It looked pretty good'. That means that when he lets rip with the energy, anything can happen, and that unpredictability is intoxicating to watch. As Alex danced his choreography hitting the highlight points of his routine, he danced a movement leading away from his partner, usually this would signify a series of flicks and kicks in what is known as an Open Extended Position, a position of the couple in Latin dancing where the Leader and Lady are a couple of feet away from one another. It was during this moment of unbridled separation that Alex decided to perform an improvised spin, jump and splits movement down to the ground, which he'd seen from one of the top Russian dancers he liked to gain inspiration from. To his credit, he landed the move perfectly and the crowd went ballistic, he got a huge cheer and the audience screamed for his number. He then proceeded to dance a form of bounce action on the floor maintaining his splits position, 'that's weird' I thought 'why is he doing that?' he was bopping to the Jive rhythm, so it was all on time and from the outset, it looked like it was part of the entire series of movements he'd just executed. But I knew Alex's choreography like the back of my hand (I'd purposely learnt it all to understand things he did better than me as well as learn what he was learning) that bounce action was all new, he'd never done that before, eventually after some nervous walks on time forward by his partner, signifying an unspoken 'get the fuck up from the floor' he sprung back up, held position for a couple of bars and then more loosely and casually continued for the remaining ten seconds of the music with a more tamed Jive. When the music ended, he presented to his newfound fans, all of whom erupted with an almighty cheer and support, as I'd mentioned earlier, the EADA Latin events, whether that was for the Amateurs or for the Youths, were run whilst the venue was still packed with people, so you always felt a personal enjoyment from the buzz of crowds and with the kids watching you. After finishing with his presentation, he made his way off the floor and past where I was standing, shooting me a nervous and worrying look, something was wrong, he grabbed his towel and his water and made his way into the corridor where the cold Sports hall became a god send which contrasted the heat of the main hall. I followed him out into the corridor, 'well done mate, that was brilliant, did you hear the crowd they all bloody loved that!' Alex still had a nervous look in his eyes, despite my positive praise. After catching his breath and nursing the two stitches he had in his sides, he made his way down the corridor to the changing rooms, not saying a word as he passed me, 'oh man' I thought, 'this is bad, what's happened?' I quickly followed him, walking and probing him for answers, scanning him to see if he was injured or something and that he didn't want to tell me for some reason, all the while, Alex remained stoically silent, his eyes firmly fixed on getting into the changing rooms further down the corridor. As Alex burst through the door of the male changing rooms, with me quickly following camcorder in hand, I'd not had chance to put the camera away and so was still wielding it like I was about to shoot a student film or something. Alex grabbed his bag with his Latin gear inside it and began rummaging frantically inside it, 'will you tell me what's wrong Ale, did you hurt yourself or something?' It was just me and him in the changing rooms and without any hesitation, he whipped his trousers off, still wearing his Latin shoes, and held them to me sprawling each trouser leg apart. I suddenly understood what had happened, why he'd not said a word to me and why all of a sudden, he'd made a B-line to the changing rooms. Staring back through the ripped inside seam of his trousers was Alex, 'You, see?' he barked at me in frustration, he'd not only ripped his trousers, but the seam had been pried apart from the knee area up to the crotch, an irreparable job, especially from either of us at the competition. I burst out laughing so hard, thankfully he'd finished his Latin section for the Youth, but much later in the evening he had the Amateur Latin and Pre-Champ Latin categories to dance. 'What are you going to do?' I asked holding back the remaining laughter I desperately wanted to release, fortunately Alex had come prepared (for a change) well, I say prepared, the dance bag he used for housing his competitive Latin gear was the exact same bag he would take to the studio for lessons and practicing and because of his possible laziness, he'd not taken his practice gear out of the bag. He whipped out the slightly stained (from dried sweat) and slightly pungent pair of practice trousers he had stowed away in his bag from the day before with a facial expression that didn't hide his personal satisfaction of relief and contentment to the resolve-meant of the situation.

As I stared forwards, mentally preparing myself for whatever form of caper Alex had now found himself in, he whispered, 'can I just ask you something?' I looked back at him, our faces only a couple of inches apart 'yeeeees?' I nervously said in judgmental response to what he was about to say. 'Y'know when you go to the toilet...' I pulled myself backward away from him, 'Ale I don't want to hear about that!' I retorted, turning back to the half-completed entry form I was filling out for Alex 'no, no, no, no, no' Alex said trying to reel me back so he could elaborate further, our faces once again inches apart, this time my eyes staring at his entry form, severely concerned as to where this discussion was heading. 'Y'know when you go for a shit...' Alex whispered in part so that dad didn't hear and also so that no-one else would hear either. 'I seriously don't want to hear it Ale' I responded with a slightly louder voice to help and hopefully perturb him from continuing. There's only been a handful of times when Alex and I had attended some very high-class venues for competitions, most of them were in town halls or in sports hall venues. The swankiest place we'd competed at was the Blackpool Winter Gardens with its grand and historical significance in the dancing culture, our exposure to anything of a "higher class" was always only ever through the medium of YouTube and the various international competitions we'd see in videos. Now, here we were, in one of the most "high-class" events we'd attended to date, the V.I.P area of the Coventry Football Stadium, with its arrangement of large dining tables, sleek and shiny interior decor and the grandest chandelier hoisted above the dance floor space, that you'd ever seen. And what was Alex doing? He was about to, in-depth describe his recent bowl movement to me, 'classy, real classy' I thought. Alex then continued 'no, no, no, let me finish, you don't know what I'm about to say!' drawing closer to me again to ensure we'd have a "private" discussion. I kept my gaze at the incomplete entry form staring back up at me as he continued, 'Y'know after you've taken a massive shit?' Alex said, 'And you go to flush the toilet?' I looked back to him, our faces inches apart again, 'yeeeees?' I replied, I had literally no clue where he was going with this, there wasn't any form of set-up from a joke he might tell, and his face was genuinely concerned, so I bit my tongue and listened. 'What does it mean if the water in the toilet shoots up when you go to flush?' I stared back at Alex, a little taken back, the conversation could have gone in any direction at that point, but I didn't expect to hear him say that. 'What does it mean if the toilet does that?' Alex asked again, 'Ale that's not a toilet, that's a bidet' I replied now stifling a laugh so as to not embarrass him further. 'Ah' Alex said, looking off to the side (towards the direction of his misdeed) his eyes then coming back to meet mine once again, 'I think I've just taken a shit in a bidet then'. 'You've what?!' I exclaimed now releasing the stifled laughter I'd held anticipatingly before, 'you've done what?!', 'shh, shh, shh' Alex now ushering me to keep quiet his hands lifting to my face to keep me quiet. I looked back to him 'what are you going to do?', with a shrug he turned to the table and whipped out his phone, 'nothing', 'nothing? What do you mean nothing?' I was now facing him still laughing at the entire situation, a bit of a switch having now taken place compared to a moment ago. 'What do you expect me to do?' Alex replied, it was a valid point, what COULD he do. It's not like he had a pair of rubber gloves handy or anything and besides, he was going to be dancing his EADA Youth Latin event soon, so whilst something SHOULD have been done about the situation, nothing could be done from our side. Well apart from maybe alerting one of the staff members of the venue, we could have maybe done that, but I assume Alex was too embarrassed to mention it to someone else and despite now being an accessory to the situation, I sure as hell wasn't telling anyone (at least not for a while, until after the event was over). Whilst I continued filling out our entry forms, Alex sat beside me, both of us giggling away at the circumstance, dad asked to both of us 'what's so funny?'. Alex and I looked to each other then back at dad and in unintentional unison we said 'nothing', and we both leaned over to complete the entry forms together. Alex's EADA Youth Latin event was due to start soon, and he still wasn't ready, both our respective partners at the time (Alex dancing with a lovely girl named Gabbie and myself dancing with a petite girl named Debbie) had both arrived in at what seemed to be the same time and who were both heading to the changing rooms together to change for the competition ahead. I got up from the table with both entry forms in my hand and made my way back to Michael to collect the numbers we'd be issued for the day's events, Alex was following in toe, closely behind. As we snaked our way through the various dining tables approaching Michaels table, I said to Alex to go on ahead and that I'd catch up with him. 'I didn't think you'd be coming back' Michael joked to me, confirming, and listing all our entered categories on a sheet which would be delivered to the organisers. I showed him Alex's and my EADA cards (a requirement of validation if you were to enter any EADA competitions) and he handed me back two numbers which he'd randomly chosen to ensure Alex and I didn't dance in the same heat for the Amateur and Pre-Champ categories. As I turned and walked away towards the open double doors which would lead down a long corridor and the changing rooms, I saw Alex, standing there, waiting. 'I thought you'd gone on ahead' I said as we met, the smile on my face creeping across from the enlightening conversation before. We then turned and began walking down the corridor towards the changing rooms, a little into the walk, Alex slowed down, his eyes gesturing to the semi-open door of the disabled toilets. Looking in we saw two cleaning ladies, a burly looking lady, who was tall and broad standing judgmentally at the bidet that Alex had recently desecrated, a stern look plastered across her entire face, and on her hands and knees, scrubbing away, was a more petite and frailer looking lady, wearing marigold gloves. 'This is absolutely disgusting' the petite lady on all fours scrubbing away said, the stockier lady behind confirming her displease-meant by retorting 'filthy, absolutely filthy'. Without hesitation Alex then approached the open door and leaned in, the two ladies now staring back to him, and he then boldly exclaimed 'has someone? Oh no! that's disgusting, I can't believe someone would do something like that', I was in complete shock, I couldn't believe he had the balls to actually conversate about the whole situation, considering the fact that he was the evident culprit in it all! 'I know love', said the larger lady, 'if you need the loo, you'll have to use the gents down the hall there' and she pointed out the room in the vague general direction of the male toilets. 'Thanks so much' Alex replied, and he then continued to walk down the hallway to the changing rooms, a strange sense of self-confidence beaming from his shoulders, all the while I stood there, speechless, and very amused, watching him disappear into the male changing rooms.

I've told and re-told that story a hundred times, it's one of the escapades that sticks in my mind as a poignant snapshot of Alex and I's grand adventures of dancing the National circuit all across the country. There are a million other stories and scrapes we've experienced, but that's always been a personal favourite of mine, I think firstly because it didn't happen to me, no doubt I'd have very easily warped the situation if it was my own experience. But I think it's because it was such a contrast, we were working so hard in our dancing, the training, the lessons, the competitions we wanted to improve so badly that we'd have done everything and anything to enter the realm of the top dancers. The event at Coventry was something of a bridge to that form of experience and I guess it was made all the more funnier because of the stark contrast of Alex's "situation" and the grandness of the event and its proceedings. There were a lot of top-level dancers who attended the competition, all with something to prove and aiming to collect more EADA ranking points. We'd gotten pretty popular and familiar with a lot of the other competitors, not just in our respective field, but right across the board, in the younger categories and "senior" categories as well. Which I guess just added weight to how funny everything was, needless to say, I jibed Alex quite heavily about the incident, recounting it to dad in the front seat of the car later, on the journey home with Alex fast asleep in the back seat. Then the next day to mum when we saw her and next to David and the "Stagman" on Wednesday. I'm not sure exactly, but I think this was round the time that David would, in jest, call Alex a twat. It was a term that David had started to use, possibly because retaining a consistent dancing partner seemed an elusive task for Alex. Probably because the hilarious jokes Alex would say each week like a weekly stand-up night had everyone in stitches, or possibly because of the various forms of escapades we'd end up in painted a very colourful canvas of him. In any case, it was something that Alex would unfortunately hear on a regular basis, the term twat being labelled to him, which, like water over a stone, would gradually ware away on him, but we'll get to that soon enough. The competition in Coventry was the one and only time that particular event ever took place, it never appeared on the dancing calendar again unfortunately and so I think because of that, it holds a special form of significance to me, the fact that we were able to dance in such a prestigious looking venue, gave me a gleam of hope that all the hard work, the toil, the sacrificing, it was all building towards something great, I just had to keep on going. Plus, Alex took a shit in a Bidet there as well, that's also another reason why this story sticks with me.

Chapter 5 Beach Bods

When it comes down to acquiring EADA (Eee-aah-daah) points for Amateurs and Youth dancers, there's always been five big competitions in the calendar year to keep an eye on. These would include (in the order which they occur in the year) The UK Open Championships, which takes place at the B.I.C Arena all the way down in Bournemouth, The British Open Championships which has its history rooted in Blackpool. There's the UK Closed Championships which was also held in Bournemouth but instead utilised a venue known as the Pavilion (which was situated just across the road from the B.I.C). Then there's the International Championships which takes place in October, and which would be hosted down south, with qualifier rounds taking place in a huge sports hall venue in Brentwood and the main Championships being hosted in London's prestigious Royal Albert Hall. Lastly there would be the British National Closed Championships which took place in November, this would be the biggie that every competitor in the country would want to attend. These Championships all had their own glory and satisfactions surrounding the attainment of winning (being labelled as the British Open Champion has a nice ring to it). But for British competitors, especially those of us looking to attain more points in an effort to climb the leader board, these competitions could make or break your progression. Big events such as these were all double points, if you won or did pretty decent, you'd get double the amount of your regular value. It would be some time before I would personally participate in the UK Open Championships with its iconic blue staircase, of which every finalist in history has walked down. A huge honorary experience if there ever was one and attending the regularity of the International Championships was a little way off too. When Alex and I used to compete as Pre-Champ level dancers the inclusion of events such as Champs Of Tomorrow, hosted in January was added to the calendar as well as Stars Of The Future which took place in June all the way down in Brentwood. These events were supplementary to the lower-level dancers who wouldn't or couldn't partake in dancing the main "Big Five" events on the British calendar. To Intermediates and Seniors, Juniors and Juveniles, these additional events were two of the biggest supplementary events they could compete in, along with the British National Closed Championships (for some) and the UK Closed Championships. When it came to the Calendar year, Alex and I always included the "Big Five" irrespective of whether we would actually be attending them or not. The usual big events which we would participate in would be (in the order they appeared on the calendar) Champs Of Tomorrow held in the Blackpool Winter Gardens Ballroom in January, followed by Stars Of The Future which took place down in Brentwood's sports hall venue, the very same location where the International qualifiers would take place. Closely following that would be the UK Closed Championships down in sunny Bournemouth in July, dancing at the Pavilion and ending the highlighted events with us rounding off the major Championships for the calendar year with the British National Closed Championships in November at our home away from home, Blackpool. We wanted so much to participate in the big International and Open events happening in the year, but as Pre-Champ dancers we knew there'd be no point. We'd easily have been knocked out in the first round, we needed to get better before we'd even be able to think about taking part in those types of events. We'd become quite proficient at competing the Champs Of Tomorrow event and the Stars Of The Future event, acquiring the odd few points from the EADA events which would occasionally happen at the Stars Of The Future competition down in Brentwood. And dancing the Nationals for us was like second nature, we knew we had to make the effort, nationally speaking, even if at times we knew and felt outmatched in our personal efforts. But dancing the UK Closed Championships was a newer experience for us both, our teacher David had insisted that we should ensure we took part in the competition, firstly because there would be Pre-Champ events taking place alongside, 10-Dance events and Amateur and Youth Events, which meant there was plenty of dancing opportunity available for us both, essentially, we'd be able to both dance, eight events! So, it would have been a dumb idea not to do it, plus the fact that the Youth and Amateur sections also had double EADA points available, had meant that the decision to go down and compete was unanimously favourable.

Driving down to Bournemouth was always a mammoth task, with the journey from Scunthorpe all the way down to Bournemouth feeling like a global expedition. If you're not sure where I'm talking about, Bournemouth is a location at the very bottom of the British island and traversing there, all the way from Scunthorpe would total around six to seven hours, one way. There was no way Alex and I would be making that journey on our own, mum and dad stressed the fact that too many things could happen to us on the way down and when you were to think of the not so great condition that the Fiat Punto's we both had (I'd gotten a Black Fiat Punto when I passed my driving test and Alex had acquired a red one a year later, the copy cat!) meant that the degree of scepticism surrounding our ability to make it all the way down to Bournemouth and then back again (making it a twelve to fourteen hour round trip) highly suspect. So, mum and dad would drive us down in their navy-coloured Vauxhall Vectra, the car loaded up to the fullest with dance gear and luggage, with bags and cases in the boot and wedged between Alex and me in the back seats and footwells. As a family, growing up, we'd frequented places like Lanzarote and Grand Canarias for an annual family holiday, Mum, Dad, Alex, Lynda and Me would all travel alongside one fortuitous other (as it was cheaper for mum to book a holiday using even numbers of people rather than odd numbers) to one of these fun in the sun locations, the last of these holiday's we took together, was around 2006, to the Las Palmas resort in Grand Canarias. That was a fun holiday, there was only mum, dad, me and Alex that had gone away together, the small group of us making it even numbers had worked out cheaper, and I think Lynda was busily engaged in something that prohibited her from coming along. As soon as we arrived, I dumped my case in the bedroom and walked all the way from the hotel down to the beach, on my own, donning shorts and a loose t-shirt, the warming heat from the sun acting as a sort of chaperone to my quest. The walk down to the beach for me was around twenty to thirty minutes and when I say down to the beach, I literally mean down to the beach. The steep hillsides and tight bend corners on the roads seemed something reminiscent of an old country road, where white tiled pavements would encouragingly guide you along to your destination along with the acoustical sound of my sandals flapping on the tiled pavements. The interesting thing for me personally, was that whenever we went on holiday to places like this, I would be taken aback by how welcoming the locals were with me. With my dark hair and dark eyes and a tinge of an olive skin complexion, walking around in places like that (and at a later stage in my dancing, Italy as well) meant that I was always greeted and spoken to by the locals. So, having experienced this a number of times, I decided early on (like when I was twelve or something) to learn a bit of Spanish. I don't speak any Spanish, I'll plainly put that out there now, my Spanish speaking competency is minimal (despite having a GCSE in it) just the basic greetings and stuff like that, so I'd have enough to make pleasantries with people, but not enough to actually communicate efficiently about extensive topics with someone. After arriving at the beach and greeting many of the locals I'd come into contact with on my pilgrimage to the sea, using mild pleasantries and basic phrases to fill the conversations and somewhat reiterating to them all 'Voy a la playa' with a gesturing point towards the sea. The occasional local would help to explain, in depth, how I should get there, which would in turn resort to me giving a pleasant 'Gracias' as I continued to walk the almost straight line to the beach which was clearly and helpfully signposted in both Spanish and English. After spending time down by the seafront and at the beach itself, soaking up some sunshine sat out on some rocks which jettisoned out into the sea, the sound of the lapping tide trying to subtly dull the screams and tantrums of kids nearby. I then sauntered back up the hillside, back to the hotel complex, relaying to the family my personal excursion and "scouting mission" and highlighting to them that I'd found the way to the beach and that it was only about twenty to thirty minuets away. We'd all traverse down there sometime later in the week, whether it was the next day or the day after, I'm not too sure. But it was a short enough time span to allow for the locals who'd spoken to me on my first little visit, to recognise and shout 'Hola!' whenever I walked past whichever bar, shop or bus stop they happened to be situated. It felt a little like I was a local who was now in the company of this "English looking family", whom I was now leading to the beach like some type of native guide, the kind you might see in adventure films where some native local is guiding would be trepid explorers through a dangerous jungle. The only real danger in Grand Canarias would probably have been from a little bit of heat stroke or something. 'Everyone thinks he's from here, he blends in so well' I'd hear mum say for the duration of the holiday, it was something I'd always hear growing up whenever we went away abroad, but it became a more noticeable phrase I'd hear repeated on our annual excursions when I was a teenager. The rest of that trip in 2006 consisted of me drinking tequila like it was water (a thought that turns my stomach just thinking about now) watching numerous holiday "performances" which involved but wasn't limited to, an animal and reptile show, a "comedy" night (a loose term for the lady who was doing it, as she sounded more like she was complaining and demeaning the male populous, than actually telling jokes) and a hypnotist who may or may not have hypnotised me, making me perform lap dances on some of the guests and sneaking and rolling around like a spy to the sound of the James Bond theme music. Listen, if I don't remember it, then it didn't happen, ok?! Although the next day down by the pool contradicts that statement as the parental farther of a young family who I'd clearly been lavishing myself over under the guise of Hypnotic influence the previous night, certainly remembered it. The eye contact we made the next day by the pool, showed a fear element I'd never seen in someone who was six foot three and broad as could be, his whole family laughing at our personal misfortunes as we embarrassingly avoided eye contact. We'll blame it on the tequila, how about that?

After the holiday in 2006 we never went away again, not because of some nefarious reason or anything (although I am personally sceptical of hypnotists now). It's just that the dancing became a really big focus and priority with more important competitions (and expenditures) which in turn resulted in us needing to prioritise the dancing and its entailments more than having enjoyable family trips together. Going to Blackpool in November and later, the inclusion of Bournemouth, would act as our substitute holidays. That drive to Bournemouth was long, the seats becoming increasingly uncomfortable with every hour that passed on our journey way down south. We'd stop off once or twice at some pre-assigned service station for toilet breaks and maybe for something to drink or eat, but car journeys of any sort weren't allowed to stop every twenty minutes or so just because you needed the toilet (an understanding drilled into me from a very early age). That might be why I've always felt weird and uncomfortable stopping for a coffee or something when driving to some dance lesson (later down the line) or even now with the occasional weekend excursion away. In any case, I've gradually tried to get more comfortable with it, as it's not just me in the car anymore and it's ok to treat yourself to a quick fifteen- or twenty-minute break when travelling around. The Bournemouth summer dance festival would later be termed "mum's holiday" and with dad sat up front acting as her co-pilot (as mum was usually the one who would be driving us all down there) he would guide her with reference to his maps and the Satnav.

Our usual stay-in down in Bournemouth was the Premier Inn and was about a twenty minuet walk away from the Pavilion venue we'd be dancing at. The usual routine we all had was that we'd travel down on the Wednesday, using the remainder of the day to decongest from all the time spent bundled up in the car. We'd grab some food at a Wagamama's (because Lynda had introduced us all to it from her Uni time in Nottingham and so whenever we saw one, there would be this awe and wonder at going and having a taste of this newfound Asian experience). Bournemouth is a lovely little seaside town and in the summer period of July, it really comes into its own as a great place to kick back and relax. Every year after arriving at the Premier Inn where we'd all be staying at, mum, dad, Alex, and I would then venture on through the town in the beautiful sunshine weather, it really was like we were on a type of holiday experience. The UK Closed Championships would be an event that would take place over four days, running from Thursday through to Sunday in early July and so after making our way to the Pavilion box office on the Wednesday, to collect our tickets, which were always pre ordered in advance by dad and purchasing a programme too, of which Alex and I would spend the remainder of the evening scouring through, turning each page to find out what days (every day for us both in those earlier years) what times and what numbers we'd have for each of the various entered events that would be taking place over each of the individual days we'd be down there for. After sauntering around the town and grabbing something to eat for dinner, we'd all make our way back to the Premier Inn where mum and dad could finally kick back and relax and where Alex and I could go through the programme to see who else was attending the event and who we'd be competing against in each heat we found ourselves in. Would we be in the same heat together? It was never always clear as we had no direct control over whether or not we'd end up dancing in the first heat against one another. It was always a lot more fun if we were in separate heats as not only could dad video tape our dancing a lot more easily, his fast switching and shaky cam footage from those years ago flooding back into my mind as I type that. He wasn't bad at videotaping us, don't get me wrong, but let's just say that Steven Spielberg won't be getting in contact with him anytime soon, dads "signature move" whilst videotaping us was when he would film an empty space for a few seconds before then darting to whoever was on the floor dancing. It was only years later when Alex and I would attend competitions together alone and I would video his dancing that I realised why that would happen. Dad would have been watching us dance with his own eyes and not through the lens of the camera, a nice thought when thinking back about it, even though if it was annoying as hell when trying to analyse the footage afterwards for improvement. Being in separate heats for our competitions also meant that we could support and cheer for one another as well from the side lines. That element was always interesting to me, there were one or two other brothers who competed against us both as well, but Alex and I supported each other like it was our own dancing out on the floor, the other relations didn't have that same boisterous energy, that same enthusiasm for one another. It strongly felt like Alex, and I were in this together, a dynamic duo, each of us pushing the other, not just in the actual dancing itself, but motivationally from the side of the floor as well. Hearing Alex bellow my number as a spurred-on form of encouragement whilst I danced my Quickstep in the first heat, stitches in my side, the tail suit feeling more like a strait jacket and the feeling of fatigue and ache creeping in all over, would always give me some form of unmatched boost, a pick me up that allowed me to continue fighting and pushing through whatever I was feeling at that moment. Likewise, the sentiment was always returned, when Alex would take the floor for his last dance in the segregated heat, I would quickly towel down the sweat from my face and grabbing a quick swig of water. To then promptly take up a position by the side of the floor alongside other competitors and audience members who would be watching, cheering, and shouting, I'd be shouting and cheering so loud for his number, just as he did for me. I think that was hard for people to ignore (not only because we sound like a fucking foghorn when we're cheering) but because we were so passionately supportive of one another. I think it was hard for people not to feel some form enamoured interest for us as well, which would later materialise in the semi-final rounds where heats would be merged into one and Alex and I would contest against one another for getting through to the final and then soon afterwards; for a placing in that final. They were good times, simpler times, no politics (at least not actively in our personal awareness) no dramas, it was all about progression, all about acquiring points, it was all about the dancing.

During the festival in Bournemouth, the days, and times where Alex and I would be competing were always organised in some form of "slotted segment". This meant that you didn't have to be at the venue at something like 8:00am in the morning, where you'd then be expected to dance and wait until something like 11:00pm, where the event would draw to a close with prize presentations and the National anthem. Instead, on most days, you'd be in the venue for maybe four or five hours dancing through your specified categories, this meant that you could then spend the rest of the time doing whatever you wanted. There was the occasional day where we'd have to be there all day, dancing so many categories and various events, especially in the earlier years we participated in the UK Closed Championships. Meant that there was always going to be the odd occasion where an overlap of sorts would take place. Staying at the venue for a two and half hour "gap" was a better idea than deciding to change, collect and carry everything back to the hotel, where you'd then just find yourself sitting around for an hour, only to then collect everything back up again and trudge your way back to the venue. Sometimes, it was just easier to stay at the venue and wait it out by socialising with the audience and watching the other rounds consisting of maybe the senior categories or the beginners and novices, as well as chatting to all the friends we'd made on the competition circuit in our own divisions. The times when we would essentially do a "half-day" were always the best as we'd have chance to actually enjoy some of the nice weather down in there in Bournemouth. This aspect was more emphasised when Alex and I no longer needed to compete in the Pre-Champ division and would therefore have a little extra time to ourselves, strolling through the park area where a hot air balloon; which would carry people upward to see the entirety of the surrounding landscape and of which was situated alongside small wooded areas and a little waterway, seating areas spaced out around the entirety of the park area and a mini golf course too. The mini golf course was fun, you see it was always a rare situation where me and Alex would be allowed to "have fun" when out and about, there was always a form of dissuasion from anything "not approved of". Minigolf is not dangerous in the slightest and it was through the requested peer pressure of our competitive friends (who were lining up to play a round of mini golf all together) that mum's resilience reluctantly caved. Mum and dad decided to wander on through the town and left Alex and me to play mini golf, requesting that after we were finished, that we should go find them to get something to eat all together. Amongst the little group we were a part of now, was Jonas and Jasmine, the current Youth Champions in Ballroom, Latin and 10-Dance. We were really great friends with them both, seeing them regularly at all the usual competitions as well as the big championships too. Jonas was a slender and tall Lithuanian guy with light features and a wicked humour, Jasmine was a sweet English girl who had dark hair and a freckled complexion and who coincidently lived in Bournemouth. They were the Youth powerhouses at the time, and no one could touch them in the EADA leader board. Having seen them multiple times at various events across the country, inevitably, we became friends with them, sharing anecdotes and jokes at the long and drawn-out Sunday competitions and cheering for each other at the bigger events where they'd make multiple recalled rounds ahead of us, but who also, in turn would support us in our own earlier heats of the Amateur division. Jonas handed me and Alex a golf club each and a very worn golf ball which had seen much better days. We joked and laughed with everyone, truly having a great time and feeling somewhat "part of the gang". In the group were other top level youth dancers who danced in the separate Ballroom and Latin fields and the talk moved from jokes and anecdotes to dancing related topics as well as to the odd element of dance politics. We were, in many ways, associating with the future of Ballroom and Latin dancing. If you liken back to history with stories of earlier pioneers who ventured on great quests or great thinkers who would congregate to discuss the ideas of the times. That's what it kind of felt like to me, it felt like a culmination of various talents, all joking and having fun, with occasional dance related topics and elements thrown into the mix. We must have been over halfway through the minigolf experience when Jonas turned to Alex and me, 'you know we should not bother to play golf when we all turn Pro' Jonas said in his eastern European accent, his smile communicating an undercurrent thought he was having as he spoke to me and Alex. 'What do you mean?' I asked, intrigued to know where Jonas was heading with his statement. He paused and looked back, possibly to scout out if Jasmine and the others were still struggling with the putting section at the end of the course, we were all on. Looking to the end of the hole we were on; the group were all standing and laughing at and with one another, as each one took their turn to try and put their ball into the hole. 'Well, all the top Pro's go and play golf together, right?' he continued, Alex nodded back in agreement, 'so, instead, we should all play croquet' he said with a laugh. 'Yeeaahhh' I replied in agreement, the idea was bonkers, but it was still funny to imagine us all playing croquet instead of the expected game of golf like the rest of the top professionals. As we continued to play our round of mini golf, we would encouragingly try to coerce the rest of the group to join our rebellious little croquet gang in the pro division, with a lot of the other dancers in the group just looking back at us with a perplexed look. 'I guess they're not ready for the big leagues are they Jonas?' Alex joked, nudging Jonas in the arm with his elbow and we all laughed at the future prospects surrounding our "professional" Croquet game.

After finishing up with our game of mini golf a few people from the group dispersed, Alex and I also had to go, we needed to find mum and dad, much to the dismay of Jonas and Jasmine who wanted us to stay with them and hang out more. With a reluctancy, Alex and I said our goodbyes and headed off into the town in search of mum and dad who had incidentally messaged to say they were waiting for us at the Wagamama's restaurant just across the road from the Pavilion. Regrettably leaving Jonas and Jasmine and a couple of the others who had all remained at the park, all of whom were now in the midst of deciding whether they would take a ride on the hot air balloon or not. It's interesting to me as I look back at the times in Bournemouth, it was the type of event that felt the closest to taking a holiday but with all the surroundings of the dancing as well. It seemed that everyone (dancers) was able to relax and enjoy the weekend and its summer weather and to only jump in the saddle of the dancing and competition events when needed. Like when you watch your favourite TV sitcom or something and there's that episode titled "beach day" or something, seeing friends and other competitors essentially soaking up the sun, having fun, eating food, and playing around at the beach. Traversing to Bournemouth would turn out to be a regular occurrence for us after our initial introduction to it all, with the usual format of mum and dad driving us down on the long, long journey. Alex and I all cramped up in the back seat with additional cases and bags wedged in between us and in spaces you'd think weren't possible to fit anything. Sauntering through the Bournemouth town was a nice luxury that we'd not commonly have the opportunity to experience, with me and Alex striding through the town pointing out all the local shops and the top of the hot air balloon which we could see, located in the park area. Occasionally we'd have to stop and wait for mum and dad to catch up to us, you see dad was in his mid to late sixties and obviously couldn't walk as well as two young nineteen, twenty somethings and so mum would be walking alongside him, arm in arm, it's a nice image I've held in my head of them together, the both of them making their way steadily through the town together. I've honestly not been able to recall a lot of instances where I can remember mum and dad having time together like that, sure we'd been on holidays before. Our excursions to Lanzarote and the Canary Islands being evidential of that, but a lot of the time there were things happening which resulted in one or both to be preoccupied with something else. I'm sure they've personally had some wonderful and memorable moments together, the occasional anecdotal story being relayed back to the rest of the family, which on reflection, provided a snapshot of their time together. So, when I think back to the times of being in Bournemouth and the summer festivals, the memory of seeing mum and dad together like that is a memory that acts like a tabulated and highlighted moment of those experiences.

Whilst I'm on the subject of recounting to you exploits from Bournemouth, let me tell you about Alex's invitation to a Pride festival.

You see Alex and I liked to do our own thing at Bournemouth, the problem was that dads hands off approach to parenting meant that mum's more disciplined and regimented style was more "the lay of the land", if Alex and I wanted to do something or go somewhere, the confirmation and question had to go through her. And normally, well, normally the answer was a resounding 'No!'. However, when we were a lot more grown-up mums tight grasp on our personal freedoms would eventually loosen, allowing us more and more moments to do our own thing. We'd be permitted to see friends, go shopping, visit the cinema whatever really. Anyway, at one particular Bournemouth summer dance festival, after meandering through the town and visiting the odd shop and taking in the seaside scenery, the family was heading back to the Premier Inn where we were all staying. Strolling back up the inclined hill in the shopping district in the centre of the town, a shop to the right caught my eye, its white exterior and signage with black bold lettering to accompany it stood out contrastingly with the reflective glow of the sun bouncing off from it. It was a Top Man shop, a frequented establishment I'd look to spend my time browsing through in my younger years, nowadays however, not so much. I turned to see where mum and dad were, the summer sunshine beaming down on my shoulders trying its hardest to penetrate my white t-shirt. Ha! Penetrate... Anyway. 'They're all the way down there' Alex said, standing next to me and pointing in the direction of an arm in arm couple making their way up the inclined town centre. Mum looked to where we were standing and I gestured a somewhat abstract form of signalling towards the shop that had piqued my interest, in an attempt of highlighting to her that Alex and I were about to go inside. We knew they'd take a while getting to where we were and even if they did arrive at the shop, dad would most likely appreciate the rest on one of the nearby public seating benches. I made my way inside, Alex following quickly behind, the smell of the women's section of the shop and the cooling air conditioning greeting my senses first, whereby a couple of nearby ladies who were perusing the rails by the door along with a cashier, were now all looking across at us. It was almost with the type of look that conveyed that we were evidentially, foreigners who had just illegally crossed a prohibited border or something. I reached for the handrail of the nearby staircase and shot up the stairs away from the judgmental stares we were receiving and headed to the men's department, skipping two steps at a time as I did so, with Alex following behind and walking somewhat more normally. A young guy was arranging a series of cloths on a rail at the top of the stairs (we'll call him "Steven" for the purposes of the narrative) he was tall with that messy but cool looking hair style that only certain people can get away with. Whenever I'd tried to personally acquire that look, it never worked, I'd just end up conveying the appearance of someone who had just lazily woken up and gotten straight out of bed, or the look of someone who had escaped from a particular kind of bus and or institution. "Steven" wore a tight looking black T-shirt; I say tight looking because either, he'd purposely worn a T-shirt which was one size smaller to emphasise his muscular physique. Or he was possibly and quite literally that jacked that not even a frail T-shirt could prevent his protruding muscles from bulging outward. Stevie greeted me with a nod, and I moseyed off to one of the fixtures to the side to browse through the jeans which were displayed as having twenty percent off. Alex arrived up the stairs not long afterwards and after glancing across at this muscular assistant, he looked behind him to where I was situated and shot me a "telepathic" look, conveying something to the effect of 'he's big isn't he?' to which I then had to immediately turn away to stop myself from laughing. You see, it wasn't necessarily WHAT Alex was implying with his look that made it so funny, it was more, the overt way he looked right at Steve and then straight to me. There was no filter, no subtlety and if Steven was still looking at Alex and paying attention, he would have realised I was behind him, and would have known Alex was inferring something about him. Fortunately, that wasn't the case, good old Stevie-boy must have busied himself back to his rail after Alex had looked away from him and "telepathically" spoken to me. Alex and I separately browsed the various rails and stands displayed all around the shop, all of which were arranged in an attempt to hopefully showcase the shops appealing wears, one item in particular caught my attention though. It was a fedora, a white fedora to be exact, 'Ale' I whispered in a loud enough tone, trying to get his attention, 'hey Ale, come look at this'. Alex, turning away from the elevated rails running along the back of the shop where he'd been browsing a selection of T-shirts, scouted the shop to find me. I plucked one of the fedora hats from the pile stacked on a table where a mixture of other hats were positioned and I placed it on my head, exhibiting a prideful facial expression of 'ah, what do you think?' the smile on my face showing a sense of personal self-satisfaction at my new discovery. Alex sauntered over 'yeah, that looks good' he said looking at the rest of the hat assortments strewn over the table I was currently stood next to. 'I was thinking it would be good for shows' I optimistically said to him, Alex looked back at me, and I continued 'you know, like when Brian Watson did his Jive at the World Super Stars Dance Festival (WSSDF for short) 'ohh yeeeaahhh' Alex responded in agreeableness his realisation to the idea in my mind and my reasoning for picking up the hat now coming full circle. 'I'm getting it Ale, it'll be great for when I eventually do shows' and I removed the fedora from my now slightly messy hair, a pale imitation of Steven the sales rep.

As Alex and I ventured into the Youth division (Ages 16-20) YouTube was beginning to become a recognisable and widely used website and Alex and I would sit for hours at the orange custom made (by someone else) computer I had, watching countless videos from the World Super Stars Dance Festival (WSSDF). We'd watch all the top professionals at the time in both Ballroom and Latin and we'd watch uploaded videos of professionals from the past. This was the time where I would watch William and Alessandra competing and dancing shows, absorbing anything and everything I could from what I could see from the screen. Alex used to enjoy watching Brian Watson and Carmen, a top professional Latin couple and I would sit and watch with him the show pieces they'd put together. On one particular show piece, Brian was sporting a trendy looking Fedora hat, embroiled in the characterised manner he was portraying himself with his persona and charisma. He looked so cool, and Alex and I grew ever more excited the more times we watched the video. 'That'll be us one day Ale' I would excitedly say as we watched the way he played with the crowd's attention and the characterised manner he moved both to the music and with his partner Carmen. The scenes from that cabaret came flooding through my mind as I stood there in that shop marvelling at that hat and without a second thought, I picked myself one from the pile and made my way to the counter where Steve was standing, to pay for it. After the ring of the cashier drawn signalled the end of the sale of my newfound purchase, I glanced over to Alex and told him I'd wait for him outside. I made my way down the angular staircase of Topman, my very light, white bag in my hand containing my new hat and after avoiding eye contact with the any of the ladies in the shop downstairs, I somewhat skipped outside to where mum and dad had been waiting. 'What have you got there?' mum asked, standing beside dad who was sitting on the public bench beside her, I gleefully whipped my new hat out from the bag and placed it on my head, a grin beaming from ear to ear as thoughts of doing shows with this new hat began to creep into my mind. 'That looks nice son' the encouraging compliment from mum adding a little more self-satisfaction to my newfound purchase, and I took it off to remove the price tags, stuffing them in a nearby bin along with the white bag I'd been given. As I turned to face the front of the shop, myself, mum, and dad now waiting for Alex to emerge like a prize on a quiz show. I felt the warm summer sunshine on my shoulders again, glancing down I saw the beaming sun casting an almost gangster-like shadow on the ground, which came from my newly adorned fedora. It wasn't long before Alex appeared brandishing his own purchase, his personal satisfactory grin spread across his face, as soon as he had arrived, we all began our continued journey back towards the Premier Inn. Alex and I walked onward, the distance between us and mum and dad (now arm in arm again with one another) gradually increasing again. 'So, what did you buy Ale?' glancing to the side to catch a glimpse of Alex delving enthusiastically into his little White Topman bag, his excitement couldn't contain how eager he was to show me his recent purchase. 'I bought this!' Alex replied, presenting a black fedora, and holding it up in front of himself like a golden chalice, to which he then immediately placed on his head. 'You bought the same hat as me?' I asked, now feeling a little less enthusiastic about my own purchase and slightly annoyed that he'd decided to copy me. 'Yup!' Alex's response holding no restrain from his own personal contentment. A common experience growing up with Alex has been that both of us would be found wearing the same clothes quite a lot of the time, I guess it must have been cheaper/ easier for mum or dad to organise our clothes that way, when growing up. We'd have the same coats, the same t-shirts even the same bikes at one point, so I guess when I saw him brandish his new hat, the very same as mine, it almost felt like a blast from the past where we were suddenly the same again. I shrugged off my personal dissatisfaction in his purchase and complimented his new look, 'are you going to be wearing that for own shows?' I asked, moving the conversation away from my personal irritation. 'Yeah, I was going to wear it when I do Jive like Brian did', Alex happily replied, 'Nice' I retorted, a small response which inevitably ended the conversation on the subject, and we continued to walk up the town centre, eyes of the general public now watching us both. As we neared the top of the incline, the sound of techno music could be heard being played, ahead of us was a barricaded and fenced in area where some form of concert was taking place. Laser lights and smoke machines operating in full conjunction with the "festival" taking place inside. No sooner had we approached the entrance to the musical festivity happening inside, had a young and spritely looking "gent" bounced his way- out, leaflets clasped in hand which he held close to his personage. If this guy wasn't gay, then he certainly didn't hide it very well, pink and blonde short spiky hair with coloured glitter covering his face, denim shorts which were more short than denim, a bright white tank top with colourful beads and feather wreaths draped all around his neck, this guy was camper than a row of tents and as soon as he saw us, he made a B-line straight towards us. 'Oh shit' I thought as I moved myself behind Alex and over to the left-hand side in an effort to place myself the furthest away from our newly arriving spectacle and incidentally resulting in Alex being the closest to him. 'Hiiiiiii!', the exuberant flamboyancy oozing from every fibre of this guy's being, with a stern 'hello' Alex replied, a little guarded and possibly a little concerned. 'Love the hats boys' as he scanned back and forth between Alex and myself, 'where is this going?' I thought to myself as I glanced back to see if mum and dad had gotten any closer to us (they hadn't). 'Errrm, are you going in?' our new arrival enthusiastically asked, gesturing to the Pride festival taking place beyond the entranceway, feathers and glitter and techno music serving as additional visual accompaniments to the overall camp vibes gushing from the festival and he whipped a flyer from the stack he was carrying and gave it to Alex. I've always found Alex's personal awkwardness in moments that are like that, to be extremely amusing, when Alex is in a situation that he might not enjoy or he might not understand fully, he's pretty good at figuring out the correct way through the circumstance. But when he's in a situation where he has no knowledge or resource to draw from, the outcome is incredibly funny to me. Anything can happen and (usually) anything DOES happen, with regards to our new flamboyant friend, Alex took the flyer, looked the guy dead in the eye and gave him a firm and direct 'no' before then continuing to walk onward. As soon as he'd begun to walk away the colourful concoction amassed in this guy suddenly switched his attention to me, and I very sheepishly followed Alex in tow, laughing a little as we walked onward to the Premier Inn, we were staying at.

When Alex and I danced in those earlier years of the UK Closed Championships, the days and breaks in between the various events seemed very brief, but as we got a little older and ascended from the Pre-Champ division into just dancing the Youth and Amateur divisions. The spare time we both found ourselves acquiring, allowed us both to have more opportunities to relax and to enjoy the weekend break down in Bournemouth. With the competition festival taking place over a type of extended weekend in July, the lovely British sunshine weather shining through on most, if not all, the days we'd be away for. It was inevitable that a trip to the beach would take place, we didn't get chance to enjoy that aspect too much, but it was nice to have a chance to soak up some sun and get down onto the sandy beach whenever we could. After walking around the town with mum and dad on an early Friday Afternoon we all browsed the little boutique stands down by the seafront, the weather was nice, it was like we were on a holiday abroad again (minus the hypnotist). As the sun shone down, I looked out to the sea, you could see the reflective light bouncing and gleaming from the folding waves and the screams and laughter of people down by the beach which clearly signified that today was a summers day. I love the sun, some people are winter people with snow and frozen icicles hanging from a roof, others are autumnal people brandishing pumpkin spice lattes and thoughts of scarves, jumpers, and soup. Me, I love the sun, summertime is my time for sure and if there's ever an opportunity for enjoying some sunshine and topping up my vitamin D, then I'm all in. After browsing the pop up stalls which led towards the park and its numerous attractions and features, I turned to Alex, 'hey, why don't we organise getting some beach towels from somewhere and take a trip to the beach?' We wouldn't be dancing for another five hours, as our 10-Dance competition was split over the entirety of the day, we'd danced our Ballroom section earlier in the morning and we were essentially "hanging around" until the Latin segment would take place later in the evening. 'But we don't have any with us' Alex replied, he might have had other ideas of what he might have wanted to do with his time, but perhaps my suggestion piqued his interest. 'Don't worry about that, I think I saw a Primark in the town centre, we can just pick some up there and go back to the beach', I was excited to think that we might actually be able to have a little time by the beach. 'Let me go ask mum' I said, already making pace to catch up to where she was with dad. Like a peace treaty negotiation, I bartered some arrangements with mum and by what time she'd expect us back at the Premier Inn and after a quick hug from mum, I raced back to Alex. Whenever me or Alex managed to get an agreement from mum, it always felt like we'd just closed some sort of high stakes deal or something, something which felt like a slight accomplishment. 'Right, here's the plan' I really couldn't wait to get to the beach, 'we'll quickly grab ourselves some towels from Primark and then we'll find somewhere to chill on the beach for a few hours, mum wants us back at the Premier Inn before 3:30pm, so that gives us about three hours'. Alex seemed a little more excited now, we'd both been knocked out of the semi-final round of the 10-Dance Ballroom section earlier that day and we both were in need of something to help perk our spirits up, after relaying the plan, Alex's face began to show a little smile and we began to make our way back into the town centre to grab ourselves some towels. Both Katherine and Nat (our dance partners at the time) were spending the time in between sections together, I think they'd gone shopping and for coffee together and that meant that Alex and I were left to our own devices. Emerging from Primark we were both brandishing some brand-new towels, I was sporting a royal blue towel which adorned green palm leaves across it, and Alex, he was wielding a red and orange combo (which I may or may not, but most likely may, be in personal possession of now). We'd both managed to take our gear back to the Premier Inn and change into some more summery clothes after our semi-final knockout, I was wearing some long white and orange shorts with a white tank top, ankle socks and trainers and a lovely pair of aviator sunglasses. Alex (contrastingly) was wearing a grey tank top, long blue shorts, trainers, and white socks as well as his own pair of sunglasses. Alex has never had any shame of wearing sandals and socks or trainers and socks in combination with summery shorts, the "classic" British summer attire being his proffered choice of attire. After making our way back down to the beach we scanned the area looking for a vacant spot to roll out our towels and relax. Because of the cloudless sunny sky and the lack of wind, it meant that anyone and everyone was out on the beach, swimming, playing games, laughing, and sunbathing. Eventually, Alex and I managed to find ourselves a little spot to relax and after organising our towels, we sat ourselves down. The weather was hot, and I decided to remove the top I was wearing as well as my trainers and used them as a type of makeshift pillow, Alex, witnessing my genius at play, followed suit and we laid ourselves back in full acceptance of the sun's punishment on us.

Now here's the thing, when you compete in Ballroom and Latin dancing, there's always a "type of look" that you need to have, a lot of that "look" is taken care of with the attire you find yourself wearing, materialising in the form of suits, shirts, trousers, and dresses. The hair, make-up (mainly for the girls, although the guys do have a little something put on them as well) and subjective to whether you're dancing Ballroom or Latin, a clean shave (not as important for the girls that one, although…). But the other ingredient, which is commonly used, is spray or bottled tan, dancers tan themselves to give that European and Mediterranean visual, that flavourful and eye-catching quality. Tan is useful in many respects because aside from adding a huge advantage from a visual perspective, it can also cover the red face situation you'll experience after fiercely dancing your heart out. There had been many occasions when mum would have someone come to the house with one of those pop up Boothie things, of which Alex and I would be required to step into (wearing only our underwear) to undergo the experience of fumigation in an effort of covering our contrastingly, pastier complexion (more so Alex than me). But as we got a little older, we realised that it wasn't necessary for us both to have a full body tan, firstly because in both the Ballroom and the Latin, we wear trousers, so there's no need to tan anything from the waist down and secondly most of our torso and arms are also covered, due to the shirts and suits we wear. This meant that Alex and I would use a bottled tan solution, to tan our faces, necks, hands, and a large enough surface area of our torso which would be exposed when we would wear our Latin shirts. This detail was completely forgotten about down on that beach, Alex and I laid, basking in the sun, with small select patch areas of our bodies covered in very, very dark tan, which would contrastingly highlight our much paler complexion. As we soaked up the heat from the sun, we talked about the dancing, about the events earlier in the day and our semi-final knockout and about our intentions heading into the rest of the competition with the sounds of people running, playing, and laughing in the background. It was only when I perched myself up, to more properly engage Alex in a deep dance discussion we were having that I saw in his reflective sunglasses the visual appearance I personally had. 'Oooh, my face looks super brown!' I thought, not realising that my darker complexion was a result of the fake tan solution I'd plastered over myself, earlier that morning. It was only as I looked at the rest of my body in the reflexion of his sunglasses and saw my torso that I realised that the tan pattern on my chest, this very, very dark V-shape pattern acted as a geometric segregation to the rest of my paler complexion. Alex was no different, he was also displaying a prominent tan marking on his chest which compared to his much paler complexion made him stand out like a sore thumb. Who knows what everyone at the beach thought when they saw Alex and me laying on our beach towels our faces, necks, hands and a V-shape marking all tanned to the colour of a mahogany bench, whilst the rest of our legs and arms were a milk bottle white colour. In a nutshell. We looked like twats and after only an hour and a half of laying down on the beach, the self-consciousness of our physical appearance got the better of us and we put our T-shirts back on, rolled up our towels, put our socks and shoes on and left. The laughing sounds emanating from people nearby helped hammer home the fact that everyone who had seen us was just laughing at us and we left the beach a little embarrassed.

Those competitions down in sunny Bournemouth were always a form of highlight to me, they were never as important as the British Championships in Blackpool, but that didn't detract away from their significance and how important it was to be dancing at your best. But also, the holiday like feeling you had when you were there, the various interactions with other competitors, it all just made the competition season seem a little less intense. As soon as the UK Closed Championships would draw to a close everyone would be training in preparatory build up for the International Championships in October. The fortunate thing for Alex and me was that after the Bournemouth event, a lot of competitors went on holiday and did other things which pulled them away from the national dance scene, people wouldn't frequent their lessons as much and that meant that Alex and I could close the gap in our daily training efforts as well as acquiring points in the EADA ranking competitions. Bournemouth would help us both gauge where we were on the national pecking order, and we could use that realistic feedback (regardless of how brutal the factuality of the result was) as catalytic motivation which would help fuel our drive and determination. Everything we did moving forwards from the Bournemouth summer festival had us moving towards the National Championships in Blackpool in November, we'd have four and half months to get into the best condition we possibly could, in an effort to make a dent in the National Championships themselves, but more importantly, to acquire EADA points, it was always about the points, if we could acquire more points, we'd climb the National league table and we could maybe even go to the World or European Championships. Everything was set, the targets were clear and with newfound determinism Alex and I confidently packed the car with mum and dad at the close of the event, ready to make our pilgrimage back home. We were ready to get practicing again, we knew there was a long way to go still, and we were excited about the hard work ahead. With the sun shining down brightly on a Monday morning I sat in the back seat of the car, the various bags and cases wedged between Alex and me again and I found myself staring out the window, as I always did on long car journeys. I was imagining the recalls I was hoping to make at the National Championships, I was running through the experiences of the recent UK Closed Championships which helped add fuel to my burning desire to improve and to make some recalls at the Nationals. Most of all I couldn't wait to get back to training in the living room, that sanctum sanctorum where my toughest forms of training would take place and a safe space where I could try out new ideas. With the scenery surrounding Bournemouth slowly disappearing into the background, I put my earphones in my ears and listened to the dancing music I'd amassed, visualising various elements I'd seen from other competitors who had made the top finals, from the professionals who had danced over the weekend. I was inspired and I was determined, with melodies playing in my ears from various dances, I pictured myself at the Nationals and the cheering crowds who would be supporting and watching me dance. I was determined to make a dent and the inspirations from Bournemouth helped fuel the passionate visualisations I had about competing the National Championships.

Chapter 6 Ducking Lost

'What do you mean this isn't the right place?!' Alex's frustration could be heard by every animal and insect in the nearby vicinity out in the countryside. We were on our way to a very crucial, very important EADA (Eee-aah-daah) competition in Oxford and just like most of our dancing escapades, we'd gotten lost. Usually this wasn't too much of an issue, we always set off an hour earlier than we planned to in an attempt to accommodate for just this type of thing. However, this time we were in deep trouble, we were in the middle of the countryside, the middle of nowhere, in mid to late July in 2010 and my first round of the Ballroom section to the EADA 10-Dance event I was dancing in was going to start in an hour and a half. I was panicking, I still had to enter all the events I'd be dancing in that day, get changed and find Nat (my dancing partner) so that we could warm up together. The worse thing about all of this was the fact that this was a new event for Alex and me, we'd never been to this competition before and so we had no real idea where the hell it was. The last time we competed in Oxford, we travelled to a sports hall venue which was set out in a similar fashion to how we saw some of the big IDSF (International Dance Sport Federation) events, that we'd regularly see on YouTube videos. But that comp was removed from the calendar and there didn't seem to be indication of an Oxford competition in the near future either. But when Alex and I looked at the listing for 2010, there it was, mid-July, EADA Ballroom and EADA 10-Dance events, all the way down south in Oxford. It was crucial that we did that event, firstly because there points available, but secondly, because most of the other Amateur competitors wouldn't bother going to some of the following events right after the UK Closed Championships, which were held in sunny Bournemouth in early July. But we did, we'd frequent any and every competition we could, knowing how "lazy" some of the other competitors were in that regard meant that all Alex and I had to do was attend every and any event (or as close as we could) during that summer period and we'd make some serious headway with the points we'd eventually rack up.

In 2010 both myself and my partner Nat were poised to make some serious headway in the 10-Dance category. You see, earlier in the year we'd assessed how the dancing in 2009 had gone, we knew we needed to step things up and we made a plan of how we could do that in both the lessons/ training environment as well as the competition environment. Nat was a fantastic partner, she never complained at how difficult the work was, I'm sure she wouldn't have ideally wanted to be aching and sweaty after most of the training sessions she endured with me, as most girls hate the thought of that. But she just cracked on and got stuck in with every element of the ridiculous training I had set us up for. When we sat down at the beginning of the year in 2010, we began assessing how the previous year had gone, we'd danced in a whole bunch of various competitions, winning a handful of various events, and making some pretty good recalls too and so, because of all this, I decided that we would only dance in the Amateur sections of any and all competitions for 2010. When we sat down together, I told Nat that we should ideally do two competitions a month and where it's possible, we should push to do a third one. I remember Nat sitting beside me in the old school hall where our lessons took place, her fluffy pink pen in hand, ready to take notes and write down anything that we were talking about. With my printout sheets in hand, I began showing every and any event taking place right across the UK which I had collated with dad and looked at which ones I thought we should ideally do together. Nat was certainly not afraid of the hard work involved, the lessons and training was seen somewhat like a 50/50 split, as it took us both near enough the same amount of time to travel to the studio. The competitions were relatively the same, some comps were closer to Nat (such as the ones in Manchester) and others were a little farther afield, particularly if they happened to be the listed competitions down south. Because we were from the North, it was somewhat expected that we should dance near enough every northern competition that there was. The comps taking place in Sheffield, in Manchester even right over to Liverpool with anything everything in between, were all events we should have been dancing. This was primarily because these types of events were seen as "on the doorstep" and should ideally be attended if we wanted to seriously compete. However, the competitions further down south and even over in Wales were the more challenging ones for us to get to, primarily because of the distance involved in travelling to these other events. In some ways this worked out favourably for us though, as not many northern competitors would travel the long distances to these events, but we would. After making a plan of what we were going to do, we headed into the studio space to warm up and practice, ready for a full day of lessons and training.

The training was very tough in the studio, and it was a self-imposed structure made by Alex and me. Alex and I had become good friends with some Russian brothers, Sergey and Lev, who were also having lessons in the studio. We'd spend ages talking with them about their experiences back home in Russia, the types of training they'd experienced, especially so after the summer period where they would return home to the "motherland" and attend what was referred to as a "summer training camp". When they got back into the studio after their experiences over there, Alex and I would Q and A them about any and every training method they'd experienced and try to find clever ways of asking what they'd learnt in their lessons. We desperately wanted to experience the disciplined environment from foreign studios for ourselves but without a stockpile of cash available to us, the best we could do it was to learn third party, via Sergey and Lev. One of the training methods that they told us about was referred to as "Finals Training", this was essentially a combination of dancing a five dance final to an entire piece of music (a five dance final is when you dance your five dances in either Ballroom or Latin, simulated as if you were in a competition i.e. dancing all out) and then immediately switch into a variety of exercises which included star jumps, sit-ups, push-ups, planks, and "pistons". By the way, a piston is where you balance on one leg with the other leg outstretched in front of you and you then flex and extend that leg you're stood on, without letting the outstretched foot touch the ground, all whilst also remaining on the ball of the foot your currently stood on. And as difficult a task that, that was to explain, that's how difficult it was to execute, at least initially. After the first wave of this structure was finished, you'd then strap weights to your ankles and repeat the entire thing again, the dances to full tracks of music (usually around three minutes) and then the drills of exercises. After that was done, you'd repeat it all again only this time the weights were on your arms. After torturing yourself with that, you'd then do it a fourth time with weights on both your ankles AND your arms. As soon as you'd completed the fourth round of it all, you'd find your body completely wrecked from the constant strain of hauling yourself through repeated dances and then punishing your body with a slew of exercises. You'd then round off the training session by taking yourself through one last final, free from all the weights, making it a total of five repetitions. And if you were a ten dancer (like I was) then you'd have switch and do it all over again, only this time in the Latin. We tried doing this training in the studio once, but because we couldn't control the music being played (as other lessons would take place) it made it very difficult for us to do this form of training. We'd additionally been deterred from doing it in the studio because of the jabbed comments from our teacher David, remarking how we looked like idiots and creating a feeling of self-doubt and embarrassment and so, as a result, Alex and I resorted to doing the "Russian Training" as we liked to call it, back home in the living room, away from the people who didn't understand what we were trying to do. However, in an effort to still maximise the potential from the lessons and training as well as the general practicing that I'd be doing in the studio, I still decided to wear weights on my arms and legs. This element really helped me I think, as I would take them all off at the end of the day to do one last little bit of practice, unhindered. When Nat came on board, she didn't hesitate to get involved with the ridiculous training I was doing, we'd done something in our practicing early on in our partnership, which had resulted in me saying how I thought she was too slow, Nat's response took me back a little. She asked me what she needed to do to improve and so I said that she should also be wearing weights on her ankles like I was doing. Without hesitation she agreed to wear them, and we were ff to the races. I always lead by example in those cases, I never forced Nat to do that form of training, I just led by example. By adopting the training method, myself, I'd hoped she'd also want to do it, fortunately, she did, she was fully on board with the level of training I wanted to do and when I talked with Sergey and Lev about their Russian experiences, Nat was right there with me listening and learning.

After a short time of experiencing lessons in the old school hall where I'd first entered a few years prior, essentially meeting and walking my new path in my dancing career. David and Helen told us that they were switching locations, there was a scout's hut which was situated just around the corner somewhere and the lessons were all being moved to that location during the daytime. The only issue was that the scout hut location could only be used until 5:00pm, which meant that the remainder of the lessons which they would teach, would happen in another different location. Initially, that switched location was a local school hall, the head teacher of which happened to be the father of a girl named Jenny, a sweet Italian girl who danced with a young boy from Cannock. He agreed with David some terms for times etc. and the teaching began in this alternative location from 5:00pm onwards. The benefit that Alex and I found with this location, was that it had an additional studio space (that you had to walk what felt like an hour to get to) which we were fortunately allowed to use. This was a big game changer for me and Nat, now we could do finals training together in a studio space and that's exactly what we did, we'd use the additional studio space to blast out finals, work through training and exercises as well as run through practice drills together. That time was fantastic, and it was especially nostalgic to me when Alex was in the training space as well with his partner Katherine. All of us working hard, making improvements, and pushing one another, It was really great to have that. All the hard work we were doing in there, was then materialised into the various dancing competitions we'd next attend. If we had a comp in Manchester, no problem let's build up for that, now there's one in Birmingham, back to the grindstone we go! It was a conveyor belt of progression which was in turn, fuelled by the desire to climb the EADA leader board. Every competition that was agreed by Nat and I was strategically selected, we'd used 2009 as a test ground for the structural idea of it all and had additionally used that time for the couple to get a solid training structure organised. 2010 was where we'd really push to make some strides and our competition selections were where it counted the most. I'd managed to work out that if we could statistically rack up points just by making occasional finals but regular appearances at a sizeable selection of events, then we should just about manage to break into the top ten in the 10-Dance category. And if we're lucky enough, maybe even make a dent in the specialised amateur sections of the Ballroom and in the Latin too. I loved dancing 10-Dance (10-Dance referring to an event where competitors are required to dance all dances in both Ballroom and Latin in one section) I loved dancing it because I truly felt like I was able to push myself to my limits and find new ways of breaking past them. I'd of course still compete in the regular Amateur Ballroom or Amateur Latin events as well, but I really enjoyed dancing all 10 dances. That's been an interesting thing over the years, many people would ask me, 'What's your favourite dance then Ian?' and honestly, I thought it was a weird question, primarily because I loved them all, but being constantly pressed into making a choice by people not satisfied at hearing me say that with their refutable 'no, no, if you had to choose, which one is your favourite?' I would regularly find myself answering the question by stating what I was known for dancing well at, at the time. Which when you think about it, somewhat avoided answering the question and which would fortunately draw a close to the interrogation I'd been unsuspectingly receiving.

As Nat and I tallied points for the various events which I'd worked out earlier in the year. I told her that I thought we should really push during the course of June, July, August and September, to do three comps in the month if we could.

It would be a lot easier for us to acquire points during that part of the season because most people were going on holiday or having some form of break for themselves. With the British summer weather coming into its own at that time of the year, many dancers would definitely prefer to be out in the sun and having days out together, rather than going to a competition, wearing restrictive suits and dresses. That's where we would double down and acquire more points for ourselves and after seeing that right after the competition in Bournemouth, right after the UK Closed Championships. There was a competition in Oxford the very next weekend, we marked it on our calendar as one not to miss. After the UK Closed Championships had ended, Alex's partner Katherine had gone on a family holiday, which meant that the arranged competition in Oxford, was just going to be danced by Nat and me. This unfortunately meant that Alex was going to be assigned both the designated driver and the cameraman for the day. He was ecstatic, clearly. After plugging in the Satnav system, we were using (which was connected to the cigarette lighter of Alex's red Fiat Punto) and after I'd inputted the post code for the venue where the competition was taking place, we began our three-and-a-half-hour journey down to Oxford. My dancing gear and bags were all in the back seat of Alex's car (hopefully) to make the loading and unloading easier and as we hit the M181 leading us out from Scunthorpe towards the motorway, we cranked up the stereo with Alex's music selection. Generally speaking, the journey down to Oxford was uneventful, we met the usual forms of circumstances which consisted of dozy "Sunday drivers" sitting in the middle lane of the M1 Motorway, the frequent Audi, BMW or Mercedes giving Alex's red Fiat Punto a Hemorrhoids check, as well as encountering the frequent stretch of road works strewn along the Motorway, which, because of those yellow cameras at the side of the road, would require you to drive at a steady 50mph. Eventually though, we made it into the scenic and very picturesque countryside of Oxford, the only thing that was really missing was postman pat driving along in his little red van. Although in all honesty I think if we had run into old postman pat, he wouldn't have appreciated the My Chemical Romance CD blaring from the cars stereo system. It was after Alex had made a right turn and put us on a single lane road which winded around an inclined hillside, picturesquely situated overlooking the nearby countryside, that we heard the worse sound we could at the time, the Satnav system stating to us that, 'You Have Arrived At Your Destination'. Alex and I looked at one another in surprise and then at the Satnav, which I guess if it could, would have been smiling back at us. When we looked back towards one another Alex, without restraint, blurted out 'Bullshit!', I laughed in agreement with him, 'the place must be around here somewhere I said'. But as I glanced at the time on the dashboard, panic began to set in, I couldn't see any sign of the venue we needed to be at and it was becoming ever more clear that we were no way near it, we only had an hour and a half to find it and for me to get myself changed ready for the Ballroom section of the competition (an arduous task in and of itself because of the nature of the tail suits we had to wear). I twisted myself round to grab the Dance News newspaper from the back seat of the car and scanned the back section looking for where the competition was listed, surely the postcode I entered wasn't wrong was it? Had I directed us to the wrong competition? 'There!' I exclaimed 'I've got it!' As I called out the post code, Alex entered it into the Satnav system. The worst situation came back, the red arrow (Alex's car) was sitting just under the blue arrow (the destination). 'How the hell does that work?' I shouted, I was frustrated, I hate being late for things, especially when it's important to me. Not only could we not figure out where the hell we were, not only could we not understand where the actual competition was taking place, but I was also scheduled to dance in less than an hour and a half. I got out of the car, which was now parked on the roadside overlooking the lush, green, English countryside, with the summer sunshine mercilessly beating down on the back of my neck and head. I whipped out my phone and began to call Nat, I needed to let her know where we were (the middle of nowhere) and try to form a plan for the competition. The main events were the EADA Ballroom and the EADA 10-Dance events and if we missed the first rounds of either of those, then the entire journey would have been a wasted effort. After telling Nat where I thought we were and apologising, I asked her where she was. 'What is it with you two and travelling this year?' Nat jokingly replied, earlier that year we'd experienced a number of travelling escapades, including but not limited to our accident in the snow, a few breakdowns on the side of the road and a brush against a curb which resulted in a nice £300 expense for a set of brand-new tyres. Nat had already arrived at the venue, she'd been there for about half an hour, I reached into the car through the open window and reached in to grab the Dance News newspaper from the seat I'd left it on, sprawling it out across the car bonnet. 'What post code did you use Nat?', as I found the event listing in the paper, my finger rolled down to the address section of the page and I followed the post code on the paper as she called it out to me. 'That's exactly what it says here, yet we're in the middle of nowhere, how's that happened?' I was a little frustrated and I think it came across in my tone, I was so confused at how we could have used the same address yet found ourselves in completely different locations. I leaned back into the car through the open window, the hot doorframe toasting my arms as I did so, 'Ale, what address does the Satnav say?' as Alex read back to me the last entry in the system, that's when it became all too clear what had happened. I'd used the first part of the address for the venue we were trying to get to (the one that would essentially, direct us to Oxford), and the second part of the address happened to be for an event happening a week later and was listed just below the Oxford competition. I'd mixed the post codes and that's why we were in the middle of nowhere! 'Fuck!' I barked, 'Ok we need a plan!' I threw Alex the newspaper and got him to input the new post code into the Satnav, meanwhile, I told Nat to enter us for all the events she knew we'd be doing that day. Normally, when it came to entries for the events at the competitions and championships, it was me and Alex who would organise our entries, the girls just had to make sure they arrived on time and were ready to dance by the time the specified categories rolled around. This time it was the opposite way around, Nat would have to do the entries and I needed to make sure I got my ass to the venue on time. I gave Nat my EADA membership number and after a little more exchanging, she made her way to the entry table to enter us. After Alex had entered the correct address, the Satnav showed that it would take us around 45 minuets to get there, we essentially had to get to the other side of Oxford and then find the actual venue itself. Time was not on our side and every minuet counted, as Alex began to organise a three to seven point turn on the little single lane, country road we had found ourselves on, I began to reach into the back seats. You see in an effort to save time (a funny statement given the circumstances which had now developed) I had put all my dance gear on the back seats so that it was easier for me to access (primarily as well, because Alex's boot was temperamental and didn't always want to open, despite having it looked at four times). In an attempt to save time when I got to the venue, I decided to get changed into my entire Ballroom tail suit in the front seat of the car. The initial problem with all of this (aside from being 45 minuets away from a crucial event which was scheduled to start within less than an hour and a half) was that it was mid-July, that hot sun beating down through the windscreen of the car added much more unnecessary heat into Alex's car and to top it off, Alex's car was on its last legs. A sad result of traversing here, there and everywhere from Liverpool, to Wales, to Birmingham even down to London, his car must have racked up a hundred thousand miles by this point (compared to the original twenty-five thousand miles when he first bought it) a resulting factor of his cars arduous experience was that his engine would constantly overheat. The solution to the overheating engine was to have the air conditioning on full blast with the temperature right up, this was aspect was never an issue on the long journeys in the wintertime as the heat from the engine acted as a nice contrast to the icy air. But in the summertime, with the windows rolled down, it was a killer. So not only did I have the hot weather outside to contend with, but I also had the heat of the air conditioning blasting into my face to manage as well, all whilst squirming and shifting in the front seat to squeeze into a full tail suit.

I think if the competition wasn't as crucial, then the mad scramble that ensued in trying to get there could have been avoided. But it was important, not only for acquiring points in some potential finals, but also because we knew the event wouldn't have as many competitors attending it. It was important that we got there in time for the first rounds of the EADA events, you see at this stage of the calendar year, Alex, and I and then Nat and I had planned every event we were attending up to that point and as a result, had managed to successfully acquire the points we were looking to get. Nat and I had done this so successfully, that in actual fact, if we were to make consecutive finals and manage a top three placing over the next few months of competitions, we'd manage to break into the top 10 of the EADA charts and maybe climb the table to reach the top 5 if we were lucky enough. That's why I was so irritated that we'd gotten lost, everything was to play for, and we were in the middle of nowhere on the other side of Oxford, if we didn't make it there then the following few events during and after September would be tough for us. We'd been training so hard all year, we'd had various lessons from guest teachers like Frank and Lynda Venables, Latin lessons from Alex Invanets and Mark Lunn. I'd maxed out two credit cards spending thousands of pounds buying various music CDs to put onto my training iPods along with a plethora of lecture DVDs and instructional DVDs from various world champions (with no real financial plan of actually re-paying any of that debt back either unfortunately). Those DVDs were heavily insightful (you'd hope so for the total price of nearly £500 per set) and Nat was always sat right next to me holding the small portable DVD player Alex had brought to the studio. We'd spend ages watching our competition footage back in an effort to evaluate what we saw and what we thought, as well as watch the lecture DVDs I'd "invested" in, picking up any new ideas to try out and implement in our own dancing. That's why I have so much respect for Nat, she never complained about the work, she just rolled her sleeves up and got stuck in. We need to put weights on and practice basic walks in Latin or basic content in Ballroom, no problem. Need to do finals training in the small studio space in the school we'd find ourselves in, let's do it! We need to sit and watch our dancing back on the DVD player to pull apart and analyse where and what needs some improvement, or to even learn some new ideas from the DVDs I had bought, Nat would grab the popcorn (full disclosure, there never was any popcorn unfortunately). This likeminded attitude meant that the improvement that Nat and I made together was somewhat exponential, we'd used the 2009 season to get a few ideas and routines into place and to get a better understanding of one another. This meant that when 2010 rolled around, we were able to push the potential of the partnership and see what it could really do, every competition was recorded on a handheld camcorder which would be watched back the following day by me and Alex (depending on whether or not he was dancing at the same event) and then that following Wednesday, Nat and I would sit down together and watch through the competition footage again. All these elements collated into a very systematic formula which was always geared towards improvement, it was a concoction which constantly pushed us both out of our comfort zones and forced us to make improvements where they were necessary. The competition in Oxford, was a pinnacle opportunity for all that hard work to culminate and be used in acquiring extra points where other competitors' laziness (by comparison of course) could be used as a capitalistic opportunity.

As soon as Alex completed his manoeuvring and the little red Fiat Punto was heading in the direction it had just traversed, the vocal sound of 'At The Road End, Turn Left' came blurting out of the Satnav. I was halfway getting changed in the front seat, I'd already stripped down to my underwear and had not long since put on my shirt which required separate studs to be inserted into the little holes at the front, instead of using buttons. I'd managed to put my cufflinks in the sleeves of the shirt and the main collar studs which fitted both at the front and back of the shirt, were in their designated holes. To this day I have no idea why Alex thought this, but as a guess, I assume all he heard from the Satnav was turn left. Alex would have been as stressed as I was, we'd constantly talk about our dancing with one another on our weekly excursions to the studio down in Wolverhampton. The talk of what we were working on, some of the recent major championships and the top-level dancing we'd witnessed along with details surrounding the EADA events, were always the hot topics. Alex knew how important this Oxford competition was for me and Nat, we'd planned it all earlier that year and Alex and Katherine were to try and match what we were doing when and where it was possible to do so. So possibly, due to the stressfulness of the entire situation, the heat of both the sunshine outside and his run-down Fiat Punto engine making things feel more intense, Alex suddenly darted sharply into a left turn, which slung us onto a very narrow, very bumpy side road. I was halfway through putting on my Suit trousers at this point and as he sharply banked into the left turn, I rolled right into him, my face pressing right into his shoulder, my hands were busy trying to pull my trousers up as quickly as I could and the sudden turn that Alex had made, had flung me over to his side of the car, my face acting as the only method of stability as it squashed into his shoulder. I think by this point it's safe to say that whilst I was in the midst of changing into my suit, I didn't have the use of a seat belt acting as the required safety element of any car journey, a big no, no of course, but I had to get changed and I had to save time. As Alex trundled his car down a very uneven and exceedingly bumpy country road (a road which would have predominantly been used by tractors) I felt the crunch of my hair (literally, as it was caked in hair gel and hairspray) bound up and down off the ceiling of the car. A consequential factor of not wearing a seat belt I guess, I repositioned myself back into my seat trying to compose myself and to stop myself from laughing at what shenanigans were taking place. It was at that point that the car began to be attacked by the hedges which were positioned either side of the "road". They were narrowing as the road continually progressed onward and with a panic Alex and I grabbed the handles on either side of the door to frantically wind up the windows, a variety of twigs, leaves and other assortments receiving an unintentional pruning with their remnants landing inside the car as we did so. Eventually, the car made it into a clearing, I was covered in foliage, Alex too, as I dusted myself free of the new acquired debris, I reached into the back seat of the car again, this time to grab my jacket and my dance shoes. This was turning out to be such a weird day, first we get lost, next I have to change in the car whilst Nat enters us in the competition and now, we've been attacked by a row of hedges after Alex's Lombard rally detour. As soon as we had cleared the hedges section of our quest and made our way over a ridge like hill, the car constantly having its suspension tested by the uneven dirt road and Alex and me once again winding down the windows to try (in vain) and get some cool air back in the car, that we then faced the next obstacle in our journey.

I think if I had to use one word to sum up my experiences of dancing in those "Golden Years" it would be this. Persistence, I know for myself, I was extremely persistent in my pursuit for improving my dancing ability, I was persistent in the competitions I danced too. Anytime I was on the floor, I always gave it my all, nothing was held back, I always felt like I had something to prove, something that kept pushing me in my lessons, something that allowed me the capability of waking up every single Saturday morning at 5:00am, getting in the car at 6:00am, driving all the way down to Wolverhampton for an 8:00am start to my lessons. Which would be slightly spaced out, allowing me to train and practice with Nat. Before then having to jump back in the car and drive all the way back to Scunthorpe and go straight to work at the local Tesco Extra store, where I would find myself hauling various cages and pallets of stock off trailers in the delivery section of the shop which I worked at, until 10:00pm, only to then end the day when I got home to crash out. Before then waking up to the sound of my alarm blaring out the next morning at around 8:00am or so, depending on how much time was needed to get organised and prepped with the dance gear, which would be loaded into the car before then travelling to whatever competition I was attending that weekend. Determinism could one word to describe that endeavour, maybe even passion, but I think if I honestly had to think about why I was bothering with any of it. Why, despite the various forms extremity that it all entailed and why I would choose to blindly ignore all the odds that opposed me. The lack of money, the lack of political favour, the lack of knowledge, everything. Why would I bother to keep on going? That can very easily be summed up in one simple word, Persistence.

Anyone who knows me will attest to the fact that I am very competitive, the dance competitions and the prospect of climbing the EADA rankings was a great outlet for all that. But ultimately, I'm very competitive against myself, sure I want to win, who doesn't right? I'd loved to have been labelled the Amateur British Champion in those days. But I also know that the accomplishment of that title would mean nothing to me. I didn't care so much about the winning aspect, I mean, I always aimed to win of course, because, well. Why else would you compete if you have no desire to become the number one in the competition/ Championship? But when it all came down to it, I was fiercely and brutally competitive against myself, I still am, I think. There's always something I can do slightly better, something that I can understand better than I did the last time I experienced it. I enjoy learning, especially now, and it wouldn't matter to me whatever type of details that might happen to be, whatever I'd be required to learn, I enjoyed it all. At the time of writing this, I've recently been completing and organising a series of "Latino Rhythm" books. Books, that help you learn some of the basic steps in Salsa, Bachata, Argentine Tango and the like and a book that can help teach any beginner level dancer how to dance Ballroom and Latin. I felt quite good about them all after I'd written them to be honest, feeling a little self-satisfaction at "becoming an author". But then that competitive itch creeped in, I felt I understood the books that I had written (you'd hope so considering I wrote them). But were they good enough for the everyday person wanting to learn a little more about the dancing, did they actually help someone understand how to go from zero to a confident seven in their understanding? The short answer was no, despite all the extensive detail involved in the books I'd made, there were still things I needed to iron out with them and so that means a second addition is on the way. The reason why I'm saying all this (aside from a shameless plug of course) is because I am persistently competitive in anything and everything I personally do, whether that's been in my dancing career or something as simple as making a pasta dish in the kitchen. When it came to the competition floor there was initially some form of hesitation and slight trepidations that crept in when I was on the floor. I wouldn't go so far as to say I felt inadequate when I competed in those earlier years, but I knew that I wasn't really ready to contend with the top-level, not yet anyway. That all changed after Nat, and I danced our first National Championship together in 2009. For years I'd gone to the Nationals, the final rung of the competitive ladder in the competition season for all the national competitors. The main event where all of the best dancers in Britain would come together and battle it out for supremacy in front of the former World and European champions of the past and top-level finalists from years gone by. After dancing all week in the various Ballroom events we'd entered, Saturday was the day when the Amateur Latin Championships would take place. Nat and I had been wiped out in the early rounds of all our Ballroom categories and so everything was to play for in the Latin, no holding back, we had to give it our all. After dancing the first two dances in the first round, Nat and I felt good, we felt we were dancing our best, after a quick drink of water and towelling down any sweat from my face, the following heat concluded their second dance. We were in the third heat out of four so there was a little gap period where we could both re-group and "get in the zone" before our next dance would start. Alex was in the first heat with Katherine, so I would elbow my way through the crowd of competitors waiting on the side-lines to go onto the floor, just so I could get a front row view of him dancing and to cheer for him when he danced past me. It wasn't long before heat three was announced and it was the Rumba, now usually I would have personally positioned Nat and I in the centre of the floor for our Rumba. It's a static dance which means it doesn't tend to progress anywhere (or at least it shouldn't) and because the judges tend to all stand in front of the stage, the most optimum position to be on the floor for that dance is the centre of the floor. That way you can maximise the potential of the judges seeing your number and potentially increase your chance of getting marked back into the following round. As soon as Nat and I walked onto the floor it became clear that taking that centre spot on the floor was not going to be possible, there were far too many people in and around that centre floor space, I only had a few seconds to choose a spot to start our choreography before the live band would start to play. Hastily, I quickly positioned us to the far right of the floor and turned to walk away from Nat ready to commence our opening segment of our Rumba choreography. Not a great position to be in, we would surely be missed by the judges, who would no doubt be trying look through the sea of competitors right in front of them all. Our opening section of our choreography always started away from one another, this was not only a "story" element we'd used to portray our dance (the couple starts away from one another and ends together) but also because we were quite a small couple and so we needed to utilise the space factor of the floor to make ourselves look a lot bigger whilst we danced. The annoying thing about our commencing position was that, annoyingly, in big international events, the more arrogant international competitors weren't deterred from blocking us both by standing right in the middle of us both or even walking straight through where we were positioned. As I walked away from Nat, things seemed to go from bad to worse though as, walking on from the corner of the floor, was none other than the current British Amateur Latin Champion, Neil Jones, and his partner Katya (yes, the same ones from strictly). They were poised to win another British National title that evening and move on to becoming the Amateur World Champions by the close of that calendar year. Neil and Katya were easily going to make the final and because they were the current champions, they were "given a pass", which meant that they didn't need to dance the two earlier rounds that Nat and I had to, it was round three in the Rumba when Neil and Katya took up their position at the far right of the floor, exactly where Nat and I were positioned. 'Great!' I thought as I turned to face Nat, 'now everyone's going to be comparing us both and it's clear I don't stand a chance against him'. Before I could think about it any longer the band began to play the introductory bars of the Rumba and we began to dance our choreography, now seemingly in a head-to-head bout against Neil and Katya. Sat along the front row nearby were my teachers David and Helen who were shouting encouraging support as we danced by them, along with their daughter Dani, who was also cheering for us. However, as Nat and I separated into an open extended position, magnified by an extra spin I'd thrown into the routine to create a bigger contrast of spacing on the floor, as well as show off, that I then found myself back-to-back with Neil, the subtle glance over each of our shoulders raising the awareness to the situation.

On the competition floor you don't have long to make decisions, it's very much a do or die scenario, if you don't have a lot of confidence in yourself or if you don't feel able to carry yourself strongly on the floor, head held high, then unfortunately you look weak. As I stood back-to-back with Neil I felt the pressure of the situation, the crowd watching nearby will have seen the proximity, they'd have seen Neil and I slam into one another, our backs both creating and absorbing the force of the exchange. I scanned the front row where David was sat and saw that only a few seats down the row, that none other than Donnie Burns, the 14-times World Professional Latin Champion, an icon in the Ballroom and Latin community, was also present and watching. I composed myself looking for Nat, there was no way in hell I was going to look weak in front of someone so dignified and accredited in the competitive dancing scene. I danced a series of Cucaracha movements from side to side, using my shoulder blade to push Neil away from me, 'holy shit!' I thought as a I continued into a spin and lunge forward 'I just shoved the British Champion!'. I didn't have the time to see if Neil was affected by the encounter, the competition was still going, and I was determined not to look outmatched (despite the fact I actually was outmatched). With a close of the music, Nat and I presented to the audience, Neil and Katya presenting not too far away, and we made our way off from the nearby corner of the floor, the opposite corner to where Neil and Katya had decided to exit. I glanced over to see if there was any form of acknowledgement from Neil, but all I saw was the back of him as he left the floor. As Nat and I made our way around the back of the audience to grab a quick drink and towel down ready for the last dance, the Paso Doble, something came over me. There was a strange sense of confidence I began to feel, I'd just tussled with the British Champion, no, the soon to be World Champion and I was still alive, I hadn't messed anything up. I'd held my own and I felt good, I'd just somewhat non-verbally told him to Fuck off! With the way I shoved him with my shoulder blade and nothing bad had happened. I felt good, I felt strong and more importantly, I felt ready for the next dance. I powered down that floor in the Paso Doble that followed, a strong confidence exuding from every pore of my being, I attacked that dance so much that I developed 4 stitches in my sides and could barely breathe after I left the floor, leading me to collapse in the corner whilst the final heat took to the floor. Regrettably I didn't make the recall to the following fourth round, the competition was too strong, and Nat and I weren't good enough to make it. After the third round had ended, we made our way upstairs to the balcony where mum and dad were sat. Mum greeted me and Alex with big hugs, hugging Nat and Katherine for their efforts out on the floor with us as well. As I sat in the seats overlooking the ballroom during the intermission period after that third round, David sauntered past, both Alex and I were sat next to one another, with the girls sat on the carpet in front of us. David mentioned a few minor details for us all to use, in case we made it into the next round, but then he turned to me, immediately I had to ask him. 'So? What did you think?' a question that was always the first one Alex and I would ask to David and Helen whenever they saw us dancing. 'Not bad' he replied, he couldn't give us any real assessment to be honest because, well, frankly, there was no point. We couldn't make any real changes to our routines or learn any new technique in the following twenty-minute interval and so essentially a pat on the back was all you'd get. 'The Rumba got better as you danced it, and your Paso Doble was by far your best dance', before any response could be given to his statement, David vanished in the myriad of people passing through the back seating where Alex and I were situated. That stuck with me a lot, I'd switched my tactic on the floor in the moment that elapsed in that Rumba, I'd gone from being a somewhat apologetic dancer, nervous to contend with the best dancers, to being a determined and somewhat unstoppable one. It hadn't yielded any technical proficiency, but it had boosted my self-confidence in myself on the floor, which was only increased when I saw the results a week later. Cha-Cha and Samba were terrible, only a handful of marks in total, but Rumba had a few more and the Paso Doble nearly had half the panel of judges marking us. The following training sessions reinforced a feeling of persistence, if I can be persistent on the competition floor, in pursuit of more and more knowledge in every facet of training, never relenting or buckling under the strains I'd find myself enduring, no matter how difficult, weird, or abstract those training circumstances might be, then maybe, just maybe, I'll have a chance. Maybe, it'll all be worth it.

There had been other examples of when a "form of confidence" or should I say, nonchalant-ness, had resulted in a new feeling of purpose and that had emerged on the dancing floor, this time in the form of Alex and Katherine. A new event had emerged on the calendar in 2010, and it was extremely important for both Nat and I and Alex and Katherine to make an appearance at it. The new event was being held at Heathrow Airport in a very fancy looking hotel with a huge chandelier in its ballroom. Large circular dining tables adorned the room and competitors, and spectators would fill these tables in loom of the various events taking place. As the Amateur Ballroom event neared, the room began to fill with more and more competitors, our friends Sergey and Lev (the Russian brothers whom we trained with) even attended the event. The room was packed with people, and it honestly must have been the most amount of Amateur competitors I'd ever seen at a "Sunday comp". Because of the huge volume of competitors who had attended the event, the Amateur Ballroom section was split into multiple heats, dancers were split into three or four heats, in an effort to permit the judges ample viewing capacity of each contender and to allow the dancers a lot more freedom on the floor. (This idea was then contradicted when the organiser arranged for everyone to come onto the floor and dance a few bars of Waltz all together, between thirty and forty couples were told to squeeze onto the floor and the music played, you could barely place your arms into position, let alone move and yet people still tried to dance their choreography competitively. A stupid move by the organisers in an attempt to perhaps showcase how popular the competition was by highlighting how many dancers had turned up to dance the event, whatever the reason for it, it caused more problems which were completely unnecessary. When the actual competition started Alex found himself in the second heat, I was in the first, we both would stand on the front row of the crowd of Amateurs who had congregated at the bottom end of the floor. All with the intention of cheering one another on, as I took position with Nat for our first dance the Waltz, I heard Alex bellow as loud as he could for our number. The unbridled support Alex showed was always reciprocated and it was always a great feeling hearing your younger brother cheering for you.

After the conclusion of the dance and our presentations to the audience, it was Alex and Katherines turn to come onto the floor. As they took position, the music began and when they whooshed past where Nat and I were standing, we cheered for them as loud as we could, reciprocating the supportive efforts made by Alex and Katherine when we had danced by them. The competition progressed during each consecutive dance in this particular way, following the Waltz, was the Tango, where dancers fought across every Inch of the floor space that was shaped more like a square than a rectangle (the typical floor space for dancing on is usually rectangular and constitutes couples creating choreography that dances down "long sides" and "short sides" of the floor space). The Tango was a vicious one because of the lack of spacing and the quick, sharp bursts of speed and momentum made by the dancers on the floor. The Viennese Waltz soon followed the Tango and the lyrical and melodic rhythms of the dance carried couples around the floor and sporadically into the centre, to dance what is known as a Fleckerl (sometimes pronounced Fleck-er-al). The competition was certainly tough on the floor and when the Foxtrot came around, everything was to play for as dancers skilfully (more than the Tango at least) manoeuvred around one another in each of the ensuing heats, which in turn prompted the organiser to comment on the seemingly effortless and professional manner of floor craft was being used on the floor (despite the numerous wallops people received in the Tango, myself included, right in my fucking eye as well!). The last dance, Quickstep, was one to remember though in that first round, with Nat and I positioning ourselves ready for the start of our choreography in the first heat we prepared ourselves for the level of speed and energy about to explode around the floor. The crowds cheered so much in that room, and I remember distinctly seeing Sergey and Lev, Jonas and Jasmine, Alex and Katherine and a whole host of other dancing friend's cheer for me and Nat as we flew around that floor. After an extremely energetic performance where both Nat and I gave it our all, it was soon Alex and Katherine's turn to take to the floor and battle it out. During the exchange of competitors coming onto and leaving the floor, I'd made my way to back of the room quickly, where all the bags from Alex, me, Nat and Katherine had been kept, to towel my face and grab my bottle of water for a quick drink right before the next heat started their Quickstep. I didn't want to miss Alex's last dance and I wanted to be cheering for him as loudly as he'd done for me. With the sound of the music playing the introductory bars of Quickstep music for the second heat, I squeezed my way through the crowds to get a front row view of Alex and Katherine whizzing around the floor. In all honesty, Alex was never a bad Ballroom dancer, he had a decent enough frame and posture, and his personal physique matched the typical aesthetic requirement for Ballroom dancing (tall and thin with long arms). He always managed to dance a decent performance in his Ballroom dancing competitions, it's just that he had such a deep passion for Latin American dancing, that to him, Ballroom dancing was tiring and restricting (especially when being danced in the tail suits you have to wear). Foxtrot was his best Ballroom dance by far and because of the melodic way he injected energy into his Quickstep, his Quickstep dancing was pretty good too. Hops, jumps and flicks were all the slick combinations that were interwoven with swing and chasse groups in his choreography. As I'd already mentioned though, the dance floor was more of a square shape, than a rectangle and it was also a lot smaller than some of the standard floors you'd find yourself dancing on. I'd already found this out (as did many other dancers no doubt) as I'd had to "bend my routine around the corner" a "long side" of choreography now went down and around the floor, my "short side" was situated by the stage and in the grand scheme of things, the whole chorographical structure was way off. So much so that I think halfway through my Foxtrot, I lost where I was in my routine and somewhat adlibbed a series of steps that gradually dragged the couple to one of the corners, ready to start the routine from the beginning again. In any case, Alex and Katherine had made it work, I knew most of Alex's choreography from our training sessions and as he rounded the upper right corner of the floor during the Quickstep (in contrast to the bottom end of the floor where the Amateurs were all stood, including me and Nat) I watched as he danced two hops which turn (known as Step-Hop's) and danced a series of Chasses into flicking and landing movements. It's difficult to put into words the exactness of the movement but the gist is this, after dancing two Step-Hop movements which turn around, the couple then dances a syncopated form of chasse to the side (Leader facing the centre of the floor) the couple then flicks their foot out to the side and then behind themselves, before then landing on that same foot, this flicking movement is repeated twice, sometimes even three times and is usually orchestrated to navigate corners or position the couple for some form of "trick step". Because of the disorientating manner Alex found himself in due to the fact that he was dancing on a smaller floor size, he danced only one of these movements and then quickly switched into regular "Scatter Chasse" movements (where the couple dances two turning hops and a syncopated chasse, which is usually repeated to progress very quickly around the floor and uses a very high level of speed and energy which is combined with spring movements).

The majority of judges had positioned themselves around the perimeter of the floor, mainly in front of the stage (as they are somewhat prone to do, in dance competitions) with couples narrowly avoiding them due to the lack of floor space. Some had chosen to stand in the corners as a means of safety, and one such judge, a man named Alan Ford, was positioned himself at the top end of the floor, situating himself in the corner by the scrutineering table and the entries tables. As you've probably recalled me mentioning, you don't have a lot of time to fully evaluate a situation in the thick of a competition, you can only make quick decisions whilst you fight to maintain all the disciplines and attributes needed for top level dancing. As Alex switched tact during his choreography at the top end of the floor, he inevitably picked up speed again (as the chasse flick combos tend to slow you down). This meant he would travel a lot further and a lot quicker than he would normally do across the short side of the floor. Before Alan had chance to look up from his judging pad (where judges write the numbers of competitors chosen to make it through for the recall into the next round) Alex slammed into him with the full force of two people moving through the air. The entire crowd of Amateurs (again, myself and Nat included) all winced and a huge (ooh!!) was heard from our side of the floor as we all watched poor Alan fly right over the scrutineering and entries tables. On reflection of it all, it was hilarious to see as his judging pad and pen and the cart-wheel manner of his legs all flipped over the tables and landed in between the people sat on the opposite side of those tables. In such a scenario you'd expect the competition to stop briefly, but no-one on the stage had realised what had happened. With a quick glance over his shoulder, to check if Alan was ok, Alex saw Alan whack his hand on the table of the scrutineers to hoist himself back up again onto his feet rearranging his suit and tie and fixing his now erratic looking hair. Alex didn't hang around though; he knew he might get disqualified if Alan realised it was Alex who had just sent him careering over the nearby tables and he quickly danced a single step hop and pepper pot (another form of syncopated chasse movement) to fly down the centre of the floor and away from the situation. The second heat soon ended, and Alex didn't hang around on the floor to do the usual presentation to the audience, instead he led Katherine straight off the floor to sheepishly sneak away to the back of the room and to hide out of sight. Alan was fine, a little bewildered by the entire experience, but he was fine, and he resumed his judging duties for the third heat that followed. As strange as it may seem, (he says sarcastically) Alex didn't make a recall into the following round, Nat I did, but Alex and Katherine didn't, when looking at the marks a few days later, Alex saw that he'd gotten a mixed bag of results and that Alan had consecutively marked him through in the former dances but hadn't put him through in the Quickstep. I wonder why? Unfortunately for Alex, he needed only one mark to get through to the next round and it turned out that Alan HAD realised that it was Alex who had sent him flying and decided to not mark him through. Ultimately, the experience was hilarious, but I think what was most funny about it, was the fact the organisers had complimented the entire collection of Amateur contenders on their floor craft ability, to which Alex suddenly juxtaposed by sending one of the members of the distinguished judging panel flying over a table. The rest of the events which Alex and Katherine danced in weren't well received by Alan's marking, the remaining Ballroom events they'd entered and the following Latin events as well, all of them were danced in vain when compared with the manner of marks which Alan either gave very little of, or if required to place them for a final, gave Alex and Katherine a low placing in the final. The take home lesson? Don't barge into the judges on the dance floor, it doesn't work in your favour if you do.

Looking down at the bottom of the footwell in the passenger seat I was sat in, I could see the remnants of debris from our recent gardening experience, no sooner had I looked up, did I hear Alex exclaim 'Oh SHIT!'. The clearing we'd found ourselves on dipped and bumped with the uneven ground that tractors would clearly traverse down, with fields on either side of us now coming into view. Out from the right-hand side, like a scene from an old Looney Toons cartoon, waddled a group of ducks. They must have been only a few metres away from us, another herculean task acting as an obstacle which was stopping us from reaching our destination. I nervously looked at Alex, the sun glaring through the windscreen and making the suit I was now wearing feel like a fucking furnace, Alex looked back at me, his eyes conveying something sinister. 'We've got to get there he said' and without hesitation Alex slammed his foot on the accelerator, we both just stared forward, screaming as Alex's death chariot neared the innocent little group of ducks, all of which had clearly just wanted to waddle across to some other pond that must have been nearby. The last thing they were expecting was two lost lads from Scunthorpe, running late to a dance competition, to essentially attempt a little bit of murder. One duck, two ducks, three and four made it safely out the way, the fifth duck didn't, as Alex barrelled forward, we heard the dramatic thuds of the duck hitting the underside of the car. We nervously looked at one another, fearing that we'd just committed something atrocious. As Alex looked back in his rear-view mirror, I twisted myself around to look out the back window, had we just killed an innocent little duck? In a cloud of feathers that acted like the confetti you might expect to see on a game show, the little duck got itself up from the ground and shook itself loose from its experience and waddled on to re-group with its friends. 'Phew! That was close' my heart was in my mouth at that point, there was just so much to process, so many emotions. 'At least he's all right' Alex said in that calm, collected way that only a psychopath would be able to manage. 'Why didn't you slow down!?' I barked at Alex, 'you saw them come out from the field, right?' Alex just gave a slight shrug as he indicated the right turn which the Satnav was encouraging him to make. 'No-one got hurt, so no harm no foul' Alex then nonchalantly replied, we were now on track to the competition, the reassurance of the dual carriageway we had now found ourselves on was an evidential and supporting fact of that. My first round was due to start in around half an hour and we were now 15 minutes away from the venue, as Alex manoeuvred through some small streets, nearing the destination, we made a plan. 'Right, when we get there, you go on inside with your dance shoes, don't worry about bringing anything else I'll grab it all, you just get inside and find Nat'. Alex was clearly as stressed as I was, I hate being late and so Alex must also have been feeling the same way, after confirming the plan, Alex rolled into the carpark to the venue. I grabbed my shoe bag from the footwell along with my phone and wallet too and I darted inside, the evidence of twigs and leaves following me like a botanical trail, the remnants of our excursion through the countryside and leaving Alex to go to park the car. I rushed my way to the table by the door to the main hall we were dancing in and paid for myself and Alex, reassuring the ladies behind the desk that he was on his way in, and I rushed inside to find Nat. Earlier that year Nat had bought a fantastic new dress, it was a discount dress which had been worn as a sponsorship dress by a Dutch girl who had made the world finals, this dress was stunning, it was a beautiful pink and orange coloured dress with diamantes adorning it everywhere, the dress of a true champion. It really suited Nat as she had very dark hair and with the tan she'd be wearing, she would have a very European look about herself, which contrasted the very northern accent that she had when talking to people. A lot of people thought we were Italian because of this type of look that we had (plus a lot of people thought I looked like a guy called William Pino, who was actually from Italy, so there was a little bias there too). Because Nat was wearing this stunning dress, it wasn't difficult to find her, firstly because the actual hall in the venue was relatively small, especially when compared with some of the other venues we'd commonly find ourselves competing in. Secondly, she was wearing a very eye catching and colour contrasting dress and thirdly, because as soon as I made my way into the hall, she was stood by the bar near the back of the room, so she instantly saw me when I darted in. We greeted each other with a quick hug, and she handed me my number, which after finding a nearby chair, I relinquished myself from my torturous suit jacket and draped it over the seat in an effort to position the number as centrally and as perfectly as I could, before then pinning it onto the back of it. Alex soon entered, bags in either hand along with the bag which had all my outfits and "civilian clothes" tucked under one arm. We were off to the races, Nat had told me not long after I'd arrived that the competition was running about 45 minuets late 'no need to have rushed and nearly murdered a family of ducks then', I thought. It was later in the following week that I relayed to Nat the entire exploit that had happened with Alex and me, to which we laughed about later, well, we did after Nat had gotten over the shock that Alex nearly killed a duck.

The competition down in Oxford was important because like I've already mentioned, EADA points were up for grabs and not many competitors were turning up to the summer events, if dancers went to one event in July, then they probably wouldn't do anything until late August or September. That's what I meant by saying they were lazy, everyone worked hard in their dancing in their own way, but as far as attending competitions was concerned, after the UK Closed Championships, everyone was a lot laxer with their attendance. By the close of August all the hard work that Nat and I had done culminated and allowed us to not only reach the top five in the Amateur 10-Dance league, but to be placed fourth in the entire country. It was a really big deal; we'd climbed from somewhere in the mid to late teens at the beginning of the year and had achieved a fourth placing in the National rankings! We were not necessarily the best, there were other contenders who were a lot more skilled, a lot more accomplished that we had overtaken, we were just more persistent. Attending any and every event we could, racking up points from Semi-finals, finals, and the occasional top three placing, whether that was winning, coming second, or coming third, it didn't matter. We racked up so many points that we overtook some of the better couples and had landed ourselves in the fourth-place position, which all came full circle, the reward of all the hard work, the expenses, the late-night training sessions I used to do from 10:00pm to 2:00am nearly every night. It all amassed and presented me the reward in one phone call, a phone call I received on a Wednesday afternoon whilst in the dance studio having a lesson with David. I never had phone calls, I wasn't important enough and my entire life revolved around doing the dancing, so I had no-one who was ever needing to call me. When my phone rang with a number I didn't recognise, I made my way out of the studio leaving Nat and David standing in the studio hall and picked up the call. I cautiously greeted the other end of the line with a tentative 'hello?', who was this other person? A scam caller? Who was it and why had they just rung me, seemingly out of the blue? 'Hello, is this, Ian Whyatt?' the female voice on the other end of the line asked, she was from London, I could tell by the accent. 'Yes, this is Ian, who's this?' why is someone from London calling me? Was it maybe something to do with my credit card debt which was now massively overdue? (Primarily because I didn't have the money to pay it back), I listened in further. Nat had now joined me in the waiting room of the studio hall with David leaning at the door frame, 'Hi Ian, I'm calling from the head office of EADA...', 'holy shit!' I thought, 'why is EADA calling me?', I mouthed to Nat that it was EADA, and she moved closer as I continued to listen in. 'I'm calling because it turns out that our number one couple has fallen ill and can't compete in the upcoming European Championships, allowing the couple ranked in third place to substitute for them', 'oh no, really?' I replied as I continued to listen 'yes, it's unfortunate' the voice on the other line responded. 'The reason for the call Ian is because we need you and your partner Natalie to be ready to represent England, if our number two couple isn't able to make it, you are currently ranked fourth in the EADA charts at the moment and so if our number two couple can't make it either, then you're our next option' I was shocked, I'd worked so hard, Nat too, and now we were on the precipice of actually being able to dance at the European Championships, everything was beginning to come together. 'We'll follow up with you in a few weeks' time if we require you to represent us', 'thank you so much, absolutely!' and with a click of the phone she hung up. I couldn't believe it, I might actually be going to the European Championships, my phone slowly dropped down to my side, 'well? Is everything ok?' Nat asked, David now moved in closer away from the door frame he was standing by. 'That was EADA' I said, still in disbelief of what I'd just heard, 'they want us to be ready in case the number two couple can't make the European Championships, the number one couple can't make it so they've asked the couple ranked third to go instead and they want US to be ready in case the other guys can't make it either'. Nat gave me a huge hug, she was ecstatic to hear that news, it must have acted as a strong reassurance to her as well, something which allowed her to know that despite all the difficulty and various obstacles we both found ourselves experiencing, it was all beginning to come together. 'Jolly good' David said as he made his way back into the studio hall, Nat and I followed closely after, ready to power through the remainder of the lesson and the training for that day with a newfound fire and determinism.

Persistence was the driving factor of 2010 for Nat and me, persistence was what helped push us both in the competitions, I was so desperate to make something of myself, we wanted to climb the leader board and be Britain's number one, especially in the 10-Dance. Persistence was what pushed me to know more, to do more, to train harder than anyone else, if I can't beat the top-level dancers on the competition floor, then I'll just beat them where I know I can, in the work. I would find myself on Wednesdays with Alex down in Wolverhampton spending around twelve hours there, not all of it was training mind you, as we did have to travel to a different location at 5:00pm and we also needed to eat and take the occasional break and stuff, so I'd say that we had about nine- or ten-hours training/ lessons/ practicing. Saturdays would have us in the studio from 8:00am until around 2:00pm where I'd then have to change and drive back home to Scunthorpe before starting work at 5:00pm. Saturdays were more my training day than Alex's as he didn't always need to go on the Saturdays and he soon got a job that required him to be at work on the Saturday mornings, so more often than not, he'd be with me in the studio on Wednesdays. That meant that I'd get around another six hours in the studio on Saturday, and that's without counting the roughly four or five hours I was doing the "Russian Training" each night after everyone had gone to bed. Dancing was everything to me, I wanted so badly to make a name for myself, to become what I knew I always wanted to be, receiving inspiration from various World and European competitions and seeing shows performed by some the industries top-level dancers at the World Super Stars Dance Festival (WSSDF). All that time during the week only amassed to the physical aspect of the dancing though, Alex and I would regularly watch lectures from the BDC congress, which showcased the top-level dancers of the season, all of whom provided various lectures in Ballroom and Latin technique. The DVDs I'd spent an absolute fortune on, in the hopeful attempt I could just to glean any extra little insight from the top professionals, including Mr William Pino and Alessandra Bucciarelli as well, whom everyone thought I looked like when I competed (William by the way, not Alessandra). Persistence was the drive that fuelled me, and I'd confidently say it was a fuel that pushed Alex too, on the competition floor, regularly dancing against some of Britain's best, we learnt not to give any quarter, my National experience with Nell adding fuel to that fire. We wanted to be the best and, in an effort, to achieve that, we had to dance like the best. If the current British Champion was on the floor, then I'm not holding back, they need to prove that they can outperform me, there's no way I'm letting them just walk the competition straight into the final without a fight, no matter if it's a regular Sunday competition, an EADA ranking event or a major Championship, I'm not holding back. It is after all, a competition and I've always been a fierce competitor, ever since I was little, the feeling of constantly pushing my limits has always been exciting for me and it's what has comparatively supported that persistence in my attitude towards what needs to be learnt and done.

Receiving that phone call was the pinnacle of everything I'd strived to do, I'd aimed to prove to myself that I had what it took to train and compete at the top international level and that phone call was essentially the universe telling me, that I was on the right path (at least that's what I've taken away from the experience at least). I'd sacrificed so much at that point, denying myself a personal relationship so that I could spend more time and resource on doing my dancing, usually you find that most dancers decide to form a relationship with the person they are dancing with. My experiences as a junior level dancer and being the age of fifteen, had taught me that no matter what you might have in your head or how you personally feel about someone, not everyone feels the same way you do. A painful lesson I learnt from a girl I was head over heels for, who didn't feel the same way about me, and which had resultingly left me heartbroken from the entire experience. I'd see numerous examples of other dance couples during my youth career form partnerships with one another, embroil themselves in a romantic relationship, only to see that relationship decay, resulting in the partnership splitting. I knew that I needed a long-lasting partnership if I was going to make it as a top-level dancer. I just didn't have the resource, the money, the luxuries of a studio space 24/7, or the help of mummy and daddy (said in a posh and whiny voice) to make it happen. Every decision needed to be clear and concise, which meant every dance partner I ever had, was purely that, a dance partner, nothing more. I had no desire to constantly flip between one partner and another just because the romantic relationship would deteriorate, if we're dancing together, it's because we have the same goals and were both willing to do what it takes to achieve those goals. I'd also denied myself the luxury of retaining any form of money, the life of someone trying to make it in their life always seems to be walked along the cobbled stones of poverty unfortunately. Any surplus of cash that I'd suddenly found myself acquiring was immediately thrown into another outfit, buying more music CDs or lecture DVDs or (occasionally) paying off some of the credit card debt that I'd racked up. It all meant that I was never in a position where I had thousands of pounds stored in a personal bank account unfortunately, or that I'd made "wise" financial decisions with my income from the full-time job I had, which was used solely to subsidise the dancing with. I'd also had to sacrifice time with friends, pursuing the dancing to the extent that I had chosen to do, had also meant that the friends I'd made from work, from school and from college, had thinned quite extensively, there was always some reason why I was never able to see them, and it was always because of the dancing. My best friend Bruce (his real name is Chris, I call him Bruce sometimes because I remember once seeing a Monty Python sketch where everyone in the scene was calling each other Bruce and I thought, y'know what, the next person I see, I'm going to call Bruce, turns out it was him). Bruce had gone to Sheffield Uni, about an hour's drive away and he'd always said that if I had got chance to, that I should nip over and see him. Whenever he got back into Scunthorpe, we'd find a way to hang out, but I never got chance to see him at Uni, well… I did once, but I'll talk about that soon. Every time there was a possibility of me going to see him, the dancing got in the way, there some lesson, some competition that I had to go do which deterred me from seeing him.

The dancing had really become my life, it had consumed me, it was my identity, I wasn't Ian the happy go lucky, slightly cheeky chappy, I was Ian "the dancer". I'd find myself sneaking off into the warehouse at the Tesco store I worked at, practicing dancing moves and little tid-bits of technique. I once disappeared behind the back the outside warehouse where broken fixtures and other assortments were strewn, just so I could spend thirty minutes every day practicing a new move I was working on for my Jive. I'd position a half-broken mirror against the wall of the outside warehouse where I would repeat the move over and over again in an effort to get the feel of the action and develop its technique. Thirty minutes for like two months, every, single, day I was at work. Dancing had wrapped itself around me so tightly that I'd perceived the circumstance as a blanket, a blanket which protected my thoughts and feelings, drives and ambitions of the dancing. That phone call from EADA helped solidify the justifications for everything that had been sacrificed and everything I was doing, it wasn't always correct, but it definitely seemed to be working and it definitely seemed effective. With every up swing however, there's always a major down swing which follows it and my experiences of 2010, the highs, the gradual and incremental increases made in every facet of the dancing, was unfortunately leading me into a big downward trajectory, I just didn't know about it at the time, but don't worry, we'll get to that soon enough.

Chapter 7 The Old Damsel In Distress Routine

Standing at the side of the road, you really are able to appreciate and take in some of splendour the English countryside has to offer you. When it's pitch black at around 11:30pm at night, you don't tend to notice it as much, especially so, if that darkened landscape is accompanied by the aroma of urine, let me explain. The Wednesday training sessions Alex and I would experience always resulted in us accompanying David, our teacher, and a man named the "Stagman", to the local bar for a few drinks after the end of the days training and lessons had ended. When mum and dad would accompany us in those earlier years of lessons, one of them would be assigned as the designated driver (usually dad) which would mean Alex and I could enjoy grabbing a pint of something (usually a fruit cider). As the conversation at the table circulated through dancing topics, jokes made by Alex which would in turn involve the majority of the bar listening in and presenting Alex with an almost prompt open mic night, as well as other minor topical elements. The table was usually presented with a tray of cheap sandwiches, kindly whipped up by the kitchen staff and which nicely accompanied the various alcoholic concoctions everyone was ingesting. Later in the years, as Alex and I branched into travelling to the studio on our own, the table finding itself with two less occupants, but no less form of topics to discuss. This meant that every Wednesday, Alex, and I would alternate who was driving and who was going to have a drink. Every week would involve the same elements of discussion, sometimes Nat would join us, sometimes Katherine and her mum, and every so often our friend Jack would pop in, recounting some of his recent exploits in the international competition scene. Jack regularly had lessons with David (when he hadn't fallen out with him that is) and usually Jack would have a few things to tell us from when he was traversing abroad, dancing and training with the top-level dancers and teachers in the Ballroom field. Fortunately for Jack, his family was able to subsidise these exploits and so Alex and I would often press Jack about the new things he'd learnt and about his latest experiences. I recall quite distinctly in the studio one time, how as I was practicing through some little things in technique, waiting for Nat to arrive, when Jack came over beside me looking into the mirror, he was waiting for his partner to come out of the toilets and probably wanted the company. 'Hey mate', he started, 'y'know I just had a lesson with Andrew Sinkinson', 'oh wow Jack, that must have been awesome', Jack was fortunate enough to have lessons with former World Champions and world class teachers, and Andrew Sinkinson was just another name on the list of accomplished dancers that Jack had the privilege of experiencing. 'Yeah, yeah mate, listen I had an hour and a half lesson just doing box Waltz, like this...' Jack began to then move through the sequence of "boxed Waltz" movement known by every and any dancer. It was an exercise that I regularly practiced myself, working on co-ordination, balance and control through the legs and feet. 'You see that mate, Andrew told me that you have to move like this', I watched as Jack slowly moved through each facet of the movement, absorbing anything and everything i could. There was value in what Jack was telling and showing me, even if he didn't fully understand it himself at the time, regardless of whether or not he tried to portray the fact that he did. 'Oh, excellent man, is that what you're working on now then?' my response seemed a little futile, of course that's what he was working on, there wasn't any reason for him to tell me about it otherwise. 'Yeah mate, I am' and Jack turned to find his partner emerging from the toilets, ready to practice through some of the things they were working on before their lesson together. I turned back to the mirror contemplating what Jack had just told and shown me, like I just said, there was value in what Jack had just outlined to me and I continued moving through the boxed Waltz movement Jack had just roughly explained and shown, attempting to decipher the almost cryptic explanation he had given me. Before Jack had left me by the mirrors, he closed the very brief tip he was bestowing on me by say how he had spent £90 for that information. My mind dwelled on that fact, '£90 to just learn the boxed Waltz?', it's not that, that was a waste of money in my view, it was more the fact that in my mind, if you're going to a World Champion like Andrew Sinkinson, you shouldn't need to be doing that type of lesson. You should be working more on the finer elements of control, balance, maybe even some fancy chorographical elements. But boxed Waltz? No way? In that moment I made a determined decision, if I ever found myself in the company of a "top-level teacher" (quotation marks used because I'd like to see you define to me what a top-level teacher is, as not all the best teachers in the world have the most distinguished accolades for themselves). But if ever found myself having a lesson of that calibre, I wouldn't be doing the boxed Waltz, I'd be developing my movement, the actions, the quality and overall fundamentals, especially so if the lesson was £90!

Back in the bar and the whole place was in stitches at Alex's recent quips and jokes, David was wiping away tears from his eyes, the Stagman was giving a more restrained laugh with his arms folded, but mum was absolutely howling, which to be honest made Alex's jokes seem a lot funnier. Alex is always quick with a joke, there's just a certain way he tells them that make the whole experience of his comical quips just come across that little bit funnier. In the bar, with crowds of people emerging to hear his deliveries, Alex would nervously present his routine (a combination of jokes ripped he'd from other comedians) which would have the whole place laughing. Those Wednesday nights were always so funny and that was always before Alex and I would delve into whatever mishap had taken place that week, whether it was a travelling experience or something from the competitions, the air was always filled with laughter. After the night at the bar would find itself ending, we would all surreptitiously make our way outside, everyone making their way to their cars to then traverse back to their comfy beds. That was always easier for The Stagman and David as they only lived a maximum of ten minutes away, for me and Alex it wasn't as easy, after spending a total of twelve hours in the dance studio (again, not all of it was dancing and training) we'd then have spent around two more hours at the bar, meaning that by the time we got on the road to head home, the time on the dashboard would be glistening at around 12:30am, with a two to two and a half hour drive still to go, the journey made by only Alex and me was a long one. Whenever mum and dad had joined us at the pub, the journey back was never so bad, Alex and I would be sat in the back seats of their Vauxhall Vectra and after maybe ten to fifteen minutes of getting onto the road, we'd be completely conked out, fast asleep in the back of the car. When we eventually travelled together on our own, the Wednesday night journey back was always a long one. Every single time one of us was driving we'd say to the other, 'make sure you stay awake in case something happens', to which that person would then somewhat immediately fall fast asleep, leaving the other person who was driving, the sole responsibility of travelling essentially by themselves. With only the dull hum of the stereo playing to help keep that person awake as the other person sat in the passenger seat would turn the stereo down. Between us both we made it work, it was extreme and intense for us both, but it was worth it, having the privilege of training all day as a trade-off for a very tiring journey home was worth it if we could make tons of improvement. With a large can of Red Bull opened and ready to go and a few Pro-Plus tablets to act as additional caffeine supplements, the designated driver was geared and wired for the trip home.

It was never easy that journey back on a Wednesday evening and when you think about it, in actuality, it was more like an early Thursday morning. If I'm being honest though, when I say it was never easy, what I really mean is that it wasn't easy when I was driving, when I was a passenger, the time just flew by! But when I was in the driver's seat, I'd constantly have the reassuring assistance of the rumble strip and cats' eyes from the road, thudding into the tyres as I drove Alex's little red Fiat Punto back home to Scunthorpe. Because Alex's little car engine would always overheat, it meant that the air conditioning unit was always turned up to full and blaring out hot air into your face. This was a nightmare on the way home in the early hours of a Thursday morning, the soft music playing from the stereo plus the warm air from the engine was fighting hard against the combination of Red Bull and Pro-Plus and the cold air from the open window you'd have to have even if it was raining or freezing outside. It wasn't uncommon for me to have the occasional nod of the head, the cosy and warm car with it's almost lullaby stereo music drawing me in to fall asleep at the wheel. Fortunately, the road was always there to jolt me back awake. The benefit of driving back so late (if there ever was one) was that there was virtually no one around, meaning that the occasional drift across the lanes as I fought to stay awake at the wheel, was never too serious. I'm not excusing the fact that what Alex and I was doing wasn't dangerous or anything, far from it! If you're tired, you just either re-adjust your travelling time or stay overnight somewhere. But we were fortunate enough that no one was around at that time, because otherwise our journeys home would have been much, much worse. For some reason though, every time we would drive along the A38 heading towards Derby, there was always a certain spot along that road where the feeling of needing to pee just sprung upon you. My guess is that when mum and dad used to drive us down on a Wednesday, that, that was the place where we'd always stop so that dad, Alex, and I could relieve ourselves. There weren't any service stations along that stretch of road and any garages that you'd encounter along the way, were all closed at that time. The best you could ever hope for was that you could make it to the Tibshelf services, on the M1 Motorway and an hour, and a half away from the studio. That was a long time to hold in a pee and no doubt would have caused a kidney issue, so instead, whoever was driving would roll into the hard shoulder, the juddering of the rough white strip separating the lane of the road with the hard shoulder waking you up. To which everyone would then pile out of the car to got to the "toilet" (apart from mum of course). Anyway, I think because this happened every Wednesday, there must have been some subconscious signal that would go off near that spot on the A38, which resulted in you having to pull over and go to the "toilet" (essentially putting Pavlov and his dogs to shame I guess). The freezing cold late night would wake you up regardless of whether you were the passenger or the driver, but especially so during that Autumn and Wintertime of the year. I think that's why I personally don't like that time of year to be honest, some people love the snow and others love the windy brown and orange blankets of leaves in Autumn, I personally love the summertime, give me sun, sand, and sea any day. My personal assumption is that my personal experiences around this time of year haven't always been pleasant and so I guess it's kind of stuck with me that when the cold, wet and windy weather rolls in, that the day just feels a little longer. Which when you contrast that with the sunny, warm, and upbeat feeling of the summertime, makes the overall feeling compound itself from that autumn and winter weather. Standing at the roadside at 12:30am on an early Thursday morning, in the dead of night, literally pissing into the wind in say October or November with the cold rain beating down on an area you'd hope would stay cosily tucked away, is never a good feeling. Jumping back into the car Alex would hastily put his seat belt on and snuggle his face into the top part of the belt acting as a makeshift hammock, and by the time the engine was started, and the car would begin to make its way back onto the dual carriageway, Alex would be fast asleep. A companion in physical company only, there would sometimes be the rare occasion where either Alex or myself would stay awake for the entire journey home, talking through anything and everything dance related. But that was a rarity, the only time you'd see one of us wake up, aside from the roadside "pit-stop", would be when the car manoeuvred its way around the cul-de-sac area back home.

During our weekly excursions there would always be some form of element taking place which would render us at the side of the road in some manner of speaking. I distinctly remember traversing to the studio on an early Saturday morning in my black Fiat Punto, its mis-aligned racing stripes plastered over the bonnet and roof of the car, for my morning lessons and training. I say mis-aligned because when I was seventeen and had just bought the car, Bruce (Chris) came over to the house to help me "customise" my new pride and joy.

I've never been a "car guy" I embarrassingly use car analogies during my teaching every now and then with no real idea on the relatedness of the analogy to the actual dance topic I'm talking about. Eventually everyone knows what I'm talking about though, so even though the actual descriptive analogy might be a little rough around the edges, the general point is always made apparent by the time I've finished explaining. After spending the wintertime slowly saving little bits of money to customise the interior of my car. Spray painting all the plastic trim, handles, window winders and various detachable sections of the dashboard with a glittery red spray paint. I then had the fantastic idea to customize-ably alter the actual physical components of the car (you know, those bits that actually make the car work correctly). First it was the gear stick, Bruce had done an awesome job on some of his interior of his car that I also wanted to be able to match him in slick design. I cut away, using a Stanley knife that may or may not (may) have cut my finger as I maniacally cut away the rubber gear stick cover. Next was the gear stick head, off came the top with a pair of pliers, with the remainder being unscrewed, on went a very ice red coloured leather cover for the stick itself and a red and black, leather gear stick head which was nicely screwed into position, the new bag was then super glued to the underside of the gear box frame. Next was the handbrake, again, after hacking, plier-ing and twisting the old original handbreak and its cover away, I then replaced it with a sleek red leather cover and a silver and red cylindrical handle, with red leather adorning the handle. After that had been done, I then decided to change the actual pedals of the car, ideally, I'd have removed the old ones in place of something a little more fancier looking. But I had to save money every month just to do all these custom jobs. Instead, I bought a set of red and silver pedals which were screwed into position using tiny brackets, so they acted more like covers, rather than actually being new pedals. I hooked up a sub-woofer in my boot and routed the wires to the stereo system for that extra bass kick and after evaluating how much I needed to save for changing the actual trim material in the car from its very 90's looking design to a sexy little black velvet (a rather costly endeavour) I decided instead to buy a pack of racing stripes, which would be affixed to the bonnet of the car and run the whole way over the roof of the car and back down thack of the car. I loved the Dodge Viper GTS it looked so cool and having played many hours of Gran Tourismo 3 (where the car featured) I decided that I would aim for something similar in aesthetic. In the summertime of 2007 Bruce came round to mum and dads house to help me affix my new purchase adding more "character" to my "canvas". The issue we had when doing the job, aside from the fact that we'd never done that sort of thing before, was that it was surprisingly windy that day, it was summertime but there was a certain cool breeze blowing as Bruce and I wrestled with the stripes taking around two whole hours to complete. Initially after we'd finished the job, I took a step back and looked at it, it was magnificent...ly shit. After the stripes went on, we went inside to let it dry and set and after another hour had passed, we went back outside to see how it had all turned out. Those stripes were terrible! The stripes had been cut into three sections, one set for the bonnet, one set for the roof and one set for the back of the car. Bruce was in charge of doing the left side and I was in charge of doing the right side, as we left the front door of the house and walked to the front of the car, which was parked facing towards the house on the grassy front lawn. We saw how badly we'd botched it all up, the front two stipes were not running parallel but veered off into a slight V-formation, the roof, that was perfect a nice six-inch space between the two stripes running perfectly parallel with one another, at the back of the car, were two tiny strips of about three or four inches spaced only an inch apart. I was flabbergasted, how could we have gotten it all so wrong? We'd even measured it all, evidentially unsuccessfully, aside from the fact that the stripes didn't align at all with one another, and the interior looked more like a homicidal maniacs' apartment, I loved that little car and I drove the absolute shit out of it. I would drive it all over the town when and where I could, the windows rolled down on sunny days and the sub-woofer doing its best from the band like music and "other" music I would play. I was never one for playing that loud techno crap which has a thumping base as its primary instrument. But that car was a slight extension of myself in some ways and more importantly, it was my chariot which would take me to my lessons on a Saturday morning, as well as the occasional competition. It was during those earlier excursions to the studio in my own car in the early hours of the morning that the stresses of the journey really hit home to me, the mornings were always easiest when either mum (or more often dad) would drive, as that would allow me the chance to have a snooze in the back seats as we journeyed to Wolverhampton in the early hours of Saturday morning. Taking the reins, myself after I'd passed my driving test forced me to step into the shoes of responsibility, no more sleeping in the back of the car whilst someone else was driving, now it was me who was doing the driving. This realization came full circle on a return trip from the studio one Saturday afternoon.

At around 2:00pm, after a long morning of lessons and practicing in the studio, I would make my way to the toilets to change out of my practice gear and into my Tesco uniform, I had a two to two and half hour journey to make to get back home and into work, Where I'd spend the remainder of the evening until 10:00pm, the time when my shift would end and I would return home to crash out until the sound of my alarm would wake me up the very next morning. The drive home on Saturdays always had a very different feel to them, than the drives home on a Wednesday (mainly because Wednesday's drives home would take place in the dead of night). After saying goodbye to everyone in the studio, my dance partner, David, and Helen along with little Dani, their daughter, I'd hop into my Dodge Viper wannabe put the front of my stereo on the CD player, because in those days, you had detachable stereo system fronts, in an effort to deter car thieves looking to make money by selling to your CD player in back ally deals. I cranked up the sound system to Feeder (my favourite band at the time) and I rolled my mean machine onto the road heading out towards the motorway. Every time I was in the car with my favourite music playing, I would always belt out whatever song was playing, in way shape or form am I a singer (although truth be told, I'd like to think I've gotten pretty good). Thankfully, my concealment inside my black Fiat Punto with its partly custom, partly original design and its mismatched racing stripes, acted as a nice barrier of tone-deaf vocalisations, yodelled from inside the car, of which thankfully, the general public were spared from. Those trips home on the Saturday were always tiring, firstly, because I'd personally been awake for close to ten hours and the day was only half done so far. But secondly because in every lesson, in every practice session, I always gave my best version of myself that I could. Trying so hard to push myself further from inspirational viewings of Will and Nicky having their own lessons, to seeing the occasional member of the top six amateurs saunter in for lessons. The studio felt like a hubbub of dancing elites, and I felt a part of it all, all these elements meant that, regardless of how I personally felt, I still had to give 110%. It was always on the drives home that I would feel the effects of my efforts the most, unfortunately. My eyes would struggle to keep themselves open as I barrelled down the A38 or the M1, making up for lost time from whatever accident had resulted in the entire roadway grinding to a halt. As I veered around a corner on the A38, that was used as the last junction to leave the A38 and enter the nearby outskirts of Derby, with the A38 itself ready to follow the roads ascension up towards the main roundabout that would link the A38 to the M1

Motorway. My eyes dipped, my attention blackened and in the literal blink of an eye, I nodded off, my lax hands on the steering wheel pulling the car leftward. As it did so, the raised curb of the roadside junction bounded my car up, jolting me awake, resulting in me sharply pulling the wheel of the car rightward ripping the left-hand side of the car back onto the dual carriageway. The car made all kinds of bangs and clanks as the near-death experience brought me back from the land of nod and into the realm of reality. The car felt off, something wasn't right, and I limped the car past the junction and onto the hard shoulder nearby, the sounds of prominent thudding echoing in my ears and acting as the percussive accompaniment to my mishap. After making it to the hard shoulder and parking up alongside all the random form of grit and debris, commonly seen strewn across any hard shoulder you might happen to find yourself on (regrettably there have been numerous times after this, where this experience has been had). I assessed the damage, two new tyres would be needed on the left side, they were completely flat a really hack job as my desperate attempt to regain control had evidentially caused the possible slight puncture that the tyres would have received to turn into huge ruptures. I was shaking, I'd never experienced this type of thing before, I knew full well that because I'd fallen asleep for a split second, that the car nearly had crashed, and it was all my fault. I nervously picked up the phone and my wallet and whipped out the RAC card I carried for just such emergencies, mum had insisted that we get breakdown cover because of the extensive amount of driving we found ourselves doing every week, it was a no brainer really. As I entered the number of contact from the RAC card onto my phone, I saw my hands still shaking from the experience, I felt sick in my stomach as I put the phone to my ear and followed the instructions from the automatic responses. Eventually, I was put through to an operator where I could explain my plight, 'ok, so where are you exactly?' I was so flustered, where the hell was I? I knew I was on the Derby ring road; I knew I was on the A38; I'd never needed any form of assistance before and so all I knew was the basics. 'Erm, I'm on the A38 heading towards the M1' I nervously replied hoping that the lady on the other end of the phone had some sort of GPS location technology that you see on spy films, where they use some sort of satellite to point your exact location. This, sadly, was not one of those situations, 'where are you near' the operator on the other end of the line replied, 'the A38 is a very long road so it's not easy for me to identify where you are exactly'. I was getting more and more flustered, panicking at the fact that I was going to be late for work, 'erm, I can see the Coors brewery does that help?' I was shooting in the dark now, I had no idea how to reply to this person, why can't they just find me? Reassuringly I heard the voice on the other end respond, 'can you see any small white posts nearby?' White posts? I thought, what the hell do they have to do with my situation? 'Erm, yeah, I can see one up ahead of me. 'Great' the voice of the person on the other end of the phone had now switched from reassurance and Q&A's to progressive and positive. 'Can you read out to me what letter and number you can see on it?', I was so confused at this point, 'erm, yeah, sure' and I made my way along the hard shoulder, walking up to the white post I could see sticking out the ground by the roadside. 'Can I ask why you need me to tell you what's written on the post here?' I asked, I was genuinely intrigued, how is the information on this post going to help with the two flat tyres my car has? 'We can use the information on the post there, to locate your position which can then be relayed to one of our nearby drivers' the voice on the phone responded, after relaying the co-ordinates and few minor follow up questions about the condition of the car, the call ended. I waited for two hours by the roadside in mid-March, watching other drivers and lorries zoom past my now worse for ware Fiat Punto. With every pass of car, lorry, and van both myself and the car feeling the force of the air somewhat sonic boom us. The creaking sound of my car's suspension helping to keep it in place as I shielded my eyes every time a lorry went past and kicked up grit and dirt into my face. Eventually though, I saw the flashing lights of an RAC van join the junction that I had unintentionally renovated and head towards where me and my car had now taken up residency. The guy who greeted me was nice enough and after jacking up my car to evaluate the damage, had told me that we needed to take the two tyres to a local garage to get them fixed. This was because my mean machine, my little black Fiat Punto with its uneven racing stripes also had alloy wheels, and so new tyres had to be fitted around the alloys themselves. Both myself and the RAC guy hopped into his van, my shredded tyres slung into the back of his van where his tools and instruments were kept, and we headed off to a local garage on the outskirts of Derby.

The exchange was easy enough, two new tyres were wrapped around my alloys and for the generous price of £200, which went straight onto the credit card, and we were back on the road, heading back to my car for its replaced tyres to be fitted. After a final exchange and shake of the hand, the RAC guy jumped back in his van and headed off down the road and I made my way around the side of the car, cautiously getting back into the driver's seat of the car. I took a deep breath and started the engine, it was now nearly 4:00pm and I was due to start work in an hour, I knew that the remaining part of the journey home would take at least an hour and a half, 'looks like I'm going to be late for work' I said in exasperation, and I started the engine back up again to drive back homo t Scunthorpe. That's not been the only time that I've had the privilege of being beside the roadside, waiting for some form of rescue because the car either Alex or I would be driving has had some form of issue (created or experienced by us, is a debatable subject). A few years later in 2011 and Alex had to regrettably say goodbye to his beloved red Fiat Punto, in exchange for a brown coloured Vauxhall Astra. It seemed like an upgrade but the passage of time plus the year of the car meant that he'd bought something which was close to the same condition that his former car was like. 2011 was something of a tumultuous time to be honest and we'll get to all that soon enough, but 2011 saw the arrival of a new car for Alex and me to use to traverse to competitions and lessons with and it was also a period where we had found ourselves in brand new partnerships. Alex was dancing with a young blonde girl from Sheffield, whom he would travel and practice with, in a nearby studio run by the draper brothers. I on the other hand, was dancing with a petit blonde girl from Liverpool (or more exactly The Wirral). We'd still be having lessons in Wolverhampton, but now Alex and I were also making concerted efforts to travel to see these girls and have additional practice sessions where they lived. It was clear to us that they wouldn't be able to meet us in Scunthorpe for training sessions and so Alex and I used the car (with Alex occasionally taking a train) to traverse to Sheffield and to Liverpool for extra practice sessions. This inevitably racked up additional milage on the clock of Alex's new car, we'd already driven the absolute shit out of his red Fiat Punto, with Black Fiat Punto following soon after. Now we had a new car which would hopefully last just as long as the previous one, unfortunately, this car had already racked up around 60,000 miles on the clock by the time Alex had bought it and so it was inevitable that something was going to happen to it at some point. One Wednesday evening/ early morning, after having spent an entire day in the dance studio and then traversing over to the local pub for after-hours chit chat, jokes and putting the world to rights, Alex and I saddled into the car, me in the driver's seat and Alex acting as "co-pilot". After making the usual "pit-stop" along the way, where both Alex and I could relieve ourselves, we quickly made our way into the car seats again. It was October in 2011 and the weather was its usual, dreary, wet, cold and windy self. No time to marvel and bask at the sky tonight as the cold rain was beating down hard. After making our way over and under the A38 and the majority of the M1, that's when we felt it, the juddery conk of the engine on the M1 Motorway just outside Doncaster. As the car stuttered and stalled itself, I tried to rev and switch gears, fighting desperately to keep the car alive until we got back home. But it was no use, after I saw the speedometer drop severely, I knew the car was in trouble and I rolled us onto the hard shoulder.

Now, the protocol in such an experience is usually for everyone to get out of the car and to stand by the roadside, safely away from the vehicle, a safety precaution to protect drivers in the event that another vehicle should collide with the car you might be driving. As soon as the hand brake was applied, Alex and I unbuckled our seat belts and made our way out of the car. The rain was beating down hard, and the cold air was made worse from the extremely windy gusts that were intensely blowing. After I'd sauntered down the hard shoulder battling against the elements to find the little white post on the side of the road which would help the RAC find us, I made my way back to Alex who was perched on the guard rail of the hard shoulder. Stood beside the car with the British weather at its finest at 1:30am in the morning, was not a fun experience, that year had already been a hail Mary of punches in the guise of various circumstances and experiences that had really knocked Alex and I around and now we had to contend with this as well. We'd been stood outside for about fifteen minutes and were drenched from the downpour, no raincoats, or umbrellas for us unfortunately, just some thin cotton jackets acting as wind breakers, as we huddled next to one another in an effort to keep a little warmer whilst Alex dug around inside his wallet looking for his RAC breakdown card. 'Fuck this!' Alex exclaimed as he ran back to the car, we were the only ones on the road, no-one else aside from the occasional lorry bellowing past, spraying us with grit, dirt, and spray from the road. 'Absolutely!' I said to myself as I followed Alex back to the car and jumping back into the driver's seat. Alex then typed in the phone number for the RAC into his phone and followed the same procedures that allowed him to speak to an operator. Fortunately, my experience some years earlier had taught me to pay attention to whichever white post is sticking out of the ground, whenever you found yourself in a breakdown situation. As Alex questioningly repeated 'Where am I?' he looked to me, completely oblivious to the answer he was to give and I mouthed to him the details of the white post I'd managed to catch a glimpse of, in the torrential down pour.

The operator calmly explained how it would be about an hour before someone would get to us and after a few minor exchanges, Alex hung up the phone, the sound of the rain and wind blasting the car we were now stationary in, with the occasional ricocheted taking place from whichever lorry bellowed past us. That year had seen us experience quite a lot and that moment sat in the car, first thing in the morning was just another notch on the belt of experiences for us. I'd put out into the universe those earlier years of us travelling together how I'd like to have adventures and escapades with Alex and the universe had clearly heard me and answered. Those experiences were varied of course but it was whilst we sat in that car, the clocking ticking past 2:00am, then 3:00am that Alex and I were able to make the best of the situation. Talk of dancing, of technical details and jokes between us, were what filled the void of occasional silence we'd experience whilst we waited to be rescued. 'Do remember the last holiday we all went on?' I said to Alex, my attempt to break the prolonged silence we'd been experienced for the past fifteen minutes in a hopeful attempt to lift the gloomy feeling looming in. Alex looked at me and nodded 'Do you remember us taking that Pedalo out to where we shouldn't have?' A smirk began to creep along Alex's face as the synapses fired and that memory undoubtedly came into his mind. You see on our last family excursion to Gran Canarias (yes the same one where I was hypnotised) we'd all decided to spend as much time as we could down by the beach, normally the family would keep to the hotel complex, but I eagerly wanted to experience more of the culture on the island and excursions down to the beach seemed to be the only way that could happen. On one particular trip down to the beach, the prospect of riding a Pedalo came up, Alex had pointed them out on the other side of the beach where a pier like structure jettisoned out into the water. After a little bartered back and forth between Alex and me and mum, we were told that we were allowed to go and ride one. Where the bay area of the coast was, there was a netted barrier (probably to keep sharks and other marine nasties out of the bay area). For some reason, Alex and I decided to pedal as fast as we could, rolling our little "boat" over this net and into the deep-sea water, the waves out on that stretch of the sea were really choppy, and looking down you'd see all manner of fish swim by. There must be something deeply wired in the human psyche that gets triggered the moment you experience something you know you shouldn't. We were NOT supposed to be on that side of the net, but Alex and I wanted to see what it was like over on the other side, plus other tourists were swimming in the section of the bay area where the Pedalo's would operate, this way, we'd be able to mess around on the Pedalo and not worry about hitting an unsuspecting tourist. But the waves out on that stretch of sea were rougher than the almost ripple like comparisons experienced in the bay area. Alex and I weren't worried at all though as we'd not long since acquired our dolphin three badge in swimming and were poised to collect a swordfish certificate soon after we got back from holiday (so, y'know, silver linings and all). We were confident that if anything was to happen, that we could just swim back to shore and worry about the consequences of abandoning the Pedalo at a later stage. Panic soon set in though as we'd not really been paying attention to the distance we'd travelled, we'd just kept pedalling after we had cleared the net, which in all honesty, should really have stopped us. But now, because of how far away we were, passing floating buoys as we ventured further and further, we'd found ourselves in a stretch of water used by large ships, with a blare of a ship's horn we glanced to the left, in the distance was a large white cruise liner, heading straight for us! Alex and I had been so preoccupied with just pedalling forwards that we'd been completely unaware of how far we'd actually travelled, as we glanced back to shore, we saw the vague tiny blips of mum and dad standing at the pier where they had watched us embark. With panic and desperation, we hurriedly tried to turn the Pedalo around and pedalled as fast as we could fighting the powerful waves and current. With the cruise liner blaring its horn again whilst Alex and I picked up speed to clear the dividing net once again which put us safely back in the harbour. 'Mum was so pissed at us, when we got back to the harbour wasn't she?' Alex said with a chuckle, 'yeah, she was' I replied, echoing the same chuckle.

It was around 4:00am by the time the RAC van arrived to where our car was stranded on the M1 and because we were unable to discern what the actual issue with the car was, the best that could be done, after the guy looked under the bonnet, was a towed lift back home. As the RAC van hoisted Alex's Vauxhall Astra onto the back of the tow truck, we were instructed to get into the truck. 'What now?' I said, turning to Alex who had just closed the door to the truck, 'What do you mean, what now?' Alex was agitated, he was cold wet and tired and couldn't be bothered to think about anything other than getting back home to his comfy bed so that he could put this whole escapade behind him. In all honesty, I did too, there'd been so many times where Alex and I had found ourselves stranded on the side of the road, both together and individually. That time in October, with the rain beating down and the wind blowing its cold winter gusts, must have been the longest time we'd spent incapacitated. At least it seemingly felt that way, 'do you remember when that police officer stopped us?' I asked Alex trying to help him feel a little more uplifted as the RAC guy winched the car onto the back of his truck. 'You mean the time when we got stopped and the guy thought we had drugs in our bags?' Alex replied, the memory of that escapade coming into full view in his mind.

During our weekly excursions to the studio in Wolverhampton on a Wednesday the small stretch of road that linked the A38 to Cannock was always prone to boy racer drivers hurling down the dual carriageway that linked the two spots. There were speed cameras set up to help prevent that kind of thing, but these were all situated quite far apart so they only worked in particular areas. During one of our excursions in August, the warm sunshine accompanying Alex's broken air conditioning from his red Fiat Punto, we found ourselves on that stretch of road, sitting at a set of traffic lights. Because of the warm weather (and the expected sauna from the car's air-con) Alex and I were sporting tank tops which matched the summer feels you'd get from our sunglasses. As Alex began to drive through the green lights of the traffic lights, there was a police car which drove past quiet slowly, Alex looked across and then back to the road ahead. Suddenly, there was a sound of sirens blaring and the police car which had just past us, was now behind us. Alex moved into the slower lane in case the car needed to get past, but the car mirrored his movement, clearly the police car wanted us to pull over. We rolled the car into a car park of a nearby pub which sat looking over the dual carriageway and the police car slowly pulled up alongside us. The officer who got out of the car was wearing a high viz coat and was evidentially suited and booted, which meant he must also have been baking in the summer sunshine. Alex is sometimes quite funny in serious situations, making something sarcastic or elaborate out of the circumstance which only adds to the hilarity of the predicament he might find himself in. However, on this day, his senses must have sharpened to the circumstance and without trying to seem funny, he obliged and complied with everything the police officer was talking him through. 'Do you know, why I've pulled you over?' asked the officer, 'no I don't' Alex replied, I looked forward to see that the warm engine and the hot sunshine were making the mirage effect on the car bonnet, that type of sizzle look which you often see in movies when a character is walking through the desert. 'We've had reports of some young lads which match your description, racing along this strip here' the irritation of the officer was clear, he was hoping we were the tyrants who had been zipping up and down this little stretch all week and it was made more effectual with the midland twang of his voice. 'No officer, we've just driven down today' Alex responded, I think at this point Alex was genuinely trying to be sincere with the whole situation and after confirming to the officer we'd travelled down from Scunthorpe, things only seemed to escalate. 'So, what brings you down here then?' the officer asked, 'We've come down for dance lessons with our teacher in Wolverhampton' Alex replied. A confident response as that was literally the only the reason, we were there in the first place, the officer wasn't buying it though, he clearly thought we were the hoodlums he was after. 'Is there any way that you can verify that?' the officer asked, a little derogatively, I suspect this was his attempt at an "ah-ha!" moment, 'yeah, we've got our dance gear in the boot of the car' Alex nonchalantly replied. 'Step out of the car boys', this was the moment he must have been waiting for, it seemed as though this officer (let's call him bill from now on, as I can't be bothered formalising the guy as "the officer"). Anyway, it seemed like "Bill" had been playing a back and forth calling your bluff kind of game with Alex, fortunately, Alex knew this, he was savvy enough to pick up on it, (that's probably the reason why he chose not to sarcastically reply or exacerbate the situation further). At this point I'm not sure what Bill was thinking, see, we'd answered his questions as he'd asked them, he'd falsely assumed we were these boy racers he was presumedly assigned to find and now we were about to confidently justify who we were and why we were there. 'Open the boot please' Bill firmly instructed Alex, the very fact that Bill was carrying a weapon probably refrained Alex from doing anything silly, it certainly did for me. As Alex's boot clicked and opened using the key from the engine (thankfully, as the damn thing would occasionally jam) the creek of the old hydraulics revealing some very questionable looking bags.

Normally, dancers will have some sophisticated form of bags at their disposal when they go for their lessons, they'll rock up to practices and lessons with Leather Gucci bags, or Lois Viton bags, all containing their respective dancing gear. Alex and I were a little humbler, Alex had a large red and black Cricket bag (which I believe he still uses) which had all his practice gear, shoes, and drinks in, along with the odd other item and the training weights we used to wear. I was using an old, blue, cool bag which had all my dancing gear folded into it, cans of Red Bull stuffed down the sides and my shoes squashed on top. We were worlds away from looking like any of the more distinguished dancers, but that didn't mean we weren't prepared. As Bill looked into the boot spotting the bags of our gear, it must have dawned on him that we were actually telling the truth, however he must have also been so adamant in his mind that we were up to no good, that he then began to press us further. 'What's in the bags boys?' Bill spoke firmly and more direct, 'just our dancing gear we use for lessons and practicing' I replied, Alex had done all the talking whilst we were in the car, but now we were both being interrogated. 'You mean to tell me that I'm supposed to believe that two young lads, who match the descriptions of some boy racers, have travelled all the way from Scunthorpe to Wolverhampton, to do some dance lessons?' Alex and I looked at one another and then back at Bill, 'yeah, that's exactly right' Alex said. 'I'm going to need you to open those bags please', Bill wasn't backing down, he felt so strongly that he'd managed to catch some nefarious deviants that he couldn't accept the fact that we were dancers from Scunthorpe. Alex opened the large bag and pulled out the black dance shoe bag branded with "Supadance" in red writing, see, these are my dance shoes Alex confidently told Bill, who was now starting to look a little less confident, despite the fact that he had one hand on whatever weapon was on his side holster. 'Open the bag slowly please' Bill was all in, he must have been able to tell that there weren't any weapons in the boot, but maybe, just maybe, Alex was wielding some form of narcotic? His face changed almost in slow motion as Alex unveiled his Latin Cuban practice shoes, poor old Bill, this just wasn't his day, first he thought he'd managed to apprehend the deviant boy racers terrorising the dual carriageway we were on, then he thought he'd caught some other form of criminal which was feeding him bullshit (I mean, who would make up the fact that they were a dancer from Scunthorpe, travelling to Wolverhampton for dance lessons and practice?). Then when Alex unveiled the dance bags, maybe he thought that he'd hit the mother lode with bags of weapons, and then his last-ditch thought being that maybe we were drug dealers transporting stuff from one person to another. He must have experienced at fifty emotions in that one traffic stop, and as soon as Alex had revealed his dance shoes, the whole interaction quickly ended with Bill saying something to the effect of 'well, just make sure you're keeping to the speed limits'.

Alex and I chuckled as we remember the scene that played out and then the swift exit of Bill afterwards. 'Do you lads want to get in the van?' our rescuer mentioned as he began fastening down our immobilised chariot, 'sure thing' Alex replied, and we made our way into the front seat of the truck which had come to help rescue us. Sat up front in the RAC cabin I leaned into Alex 'do you remember that a week later we actually saw the boy racers fly past us?', I began to chuckle as I asked Alex who was wrapping his hands under his armpits in the seat beside me. 'Yeah, and we were keeping an eye out in case that officer was in hot pursuit of them?' the time on the cabin dashboard read 4:25AM, we'd been stuck for quite a while and we were about to make our way home, back to some cosy beds for a little much needed shut eye. Travelling around all the time with Alex in those day was certainly adventurous, there were loads of things that would happen not only when we were together but also when we separate as well, and every time we would espouse takes to one another, there was always a feeling of closeness and comradery. We WANTED to hear each other's stories, what had happened to one another whilst we were separated and reliving the hilarity of some of the shared experiences. These types of excursions never really happened when we travelled with mum and dad, certainly not when driving, every journey was somewhat a straight line (or at least it felt that way to me). Mum and dad had been on every trip with us to the studio and to competitions when we were sixteen and seventeen, and now that we were in our early twenties, it was just Alex and me. It was fine really, we wanted it that way, we wanted to have our own sense of independence and to have "adventures" together whilst we travelled around the country doing our dancing. I certainly felt that way, those days of us figuring out how to manoeuvre in the world, "bounce off the walls" as Steve Jobs would quote, it was fun, it was fluid and it all felt like something we owned, that I owned. The value of those memories are what stick with me the most, because unfortunately, with every high point and upswing, there's always an inevitable down swing and low point. Unfortunately, as the chapter of 2010 with all its experiences and its victories, of wins and accomplishments began to close in December. The dawn of 2011 and the real challenges that this new series of "adventures" began to surface. Unbeknownst to me, was the fact that there was a major shift about to occur and it would nearly bring everything I'd worked so hard to achieve, come crashing down all around me.

Chapter 8 Going Home

It was around 5:00am on a very early, very cold January morning when I received a very important call, a call I can still remember to this day unfortunately, a call that I hadn't expected to receive and that to be completely honest, made me pause and sit down. As I picked up my phone from the table in front of me, it's vibration juddering on the glass table as I drank my morning coffee, I saw the caller ID, it was Alex. Something must have been wrong, there was never any need for Alex to be awake at that time in the morning and the fact that he was calling me, clearly signified something ominous. It was early Saturday morning, and I was in my pyjamas, about to finish drinking my coffee and collect my dance gear to head down to Wolverhampton for a full day of training and lessons as usual. I was living with a friend at the time and so I was trying to make sure that I was awake, organised and out the door before he woke up. 'Hey Ale, what's up?' my voice was concerned, but nothing seemed out of place to me, maybe he was calling to let me know I needed to collect something, maybe mum needed me to swing by after I finished work that night, or maybe there was an update from dad. You see, In December 2010, after a tumultuous rollercoaster ride of dancing, I'd ended the year on a bit of a high note by ranking fourth in the EADA charts, nearly going to the European Championships, making some serious headway at the International Championships in October, and beating some close contenders in the 10-Dance categories along the way. Nat and I had also partaken in an exclusive 10-Dance event that was hosted in the Kings Hall (in Stoke-On-Trent) and showcased the top talent of the 10-Dance Amateurs. It was a black tie, dinner dance affair with the Empress Orchestra playing from the stage and spotlights gleaming from the balconies to help showcase Britain's top contenders. The evening was run as a competition for Amateurs who danced in the 10-Dance category, and we were all the entertainment to be showcased in front of the hundreds of people who had come to partake in some social dancing and watch us all compete. This event was nothing like the types of events that Nat and I had ever done before, not only were we dancing in a specialised event, something about the whole evening almost felt invitational (it wasn't, but it certainly felt that way). But we were also dancing late in the evening to the Empress Orchestra, our respective families and "entourage" watching from the balconies above and it's where I remember my dad watching me dance from. We'd travelled to the event on our own, dad driving the car and me sat in the passenger seat beside him, both Alex and mum were working that evening and so it was just me and dad who would be attending the event. After being ushered in through the rear entrance of the venue we were led through the passageways of the hall to the changing rooms. I gave dad a hug and I made my way into the changing rooms as he disappeared to the balconies to watch the coemption from. The whole evening reminded me a little of growing up and dancing in various medal presentation evenings, where the local dance school would showcase their talents to the parent congregations in attendance. These were always full-on shows, usually taking place on the stage at the back of the hall if the dancing also happened to entail an acting element within it (usually taken from a musical or something) but would more often than not take place on the large dance floor space situated in front of the stage. Each competitor in the event at Stoke was organised in order of their entry numbers in the corridor that ran along the side of the main hall, and we were all briefed that we'd each be called onto the floor individually by the organiser, Duncan, to perform a few bars of a given dance (like I'd always seen by finalists in top international competitions). It felt like I'd made it to the big leagues in a way and before I knew it, Nat and I were soon called to the floor to dance few bars of our Tango. With the Orchestra poised on the stage ready to play the introductory bars of music after Nat and I were called to the floor to present ourselves with the crowds clapping and cheering for us and we soon took up position on the floor for the start of our Tango. We felt the spotlights gleaming over us, showcasing Nat's beautifully gleaming orange and pink dress and its adorning diamantes. Crowds cheered as we twisted and turned and powered down the floor together, performing our choreography to the atmospheric ensemble of the evening's spectators. With the close of the few bars of music, we presented ourselves to the cheering crowds and I gave a look to where my dad was seated, his face blackened by the glow of the spotlights which shone on Nat and me before we made our way off the floor and into the back area where the remaining competitors were all situated. The competition soon took place after the last couple danced their solo segment with everyone making their way onto the floor to dance the corresponding rounds in the events which followed in both the Ballroom section and the Latin sections of the competition and Nat, and I achieved an overall mid-placing in the semi-final in both sections. Not too bad really considering everyone who danced the 10-Dance events was in attendance. The £1000 cash prize was also a big incentive for people to turn up to the event and that aspect resultantly pushed Nat and I down the placings, despite us sitting in an overall 4th place in the EADA charts at the time. Things were feeling like they were at an all-time high, Nat and I were excited for our dancing prospects heading into 2011, if we'd made so much progression and dramatically made strides in our development which had culminated in some very decent results both nationally and internationally, then 2011 was going to be a very, very good year for us both. Unfortunately, around this time, dad had fallen a little ill, it was never anything too serious, but it had resulted in him becoming a lot more of what I would probably call "an old man", he didn't come to the competitions anymore, the last event he attended was the National Championships of 2010, where Nat and I managed to get medium placings in all of the various national titles (when I say medium placings, I mean medium placing In relation to like fifty or sixty other contenders and not medium placing like fourth or fifth, like you'd see in a final, unfortunately). I can still remember hearing his bellowing and sharp voice shouting out my number from the balcony above when I took to the floor over the festival, the memories of seeing and hearing him call out my number come flooding back straight into my mind as I type that out.

In early December, dad had been taken to hospital, it had turned out that he'd contracted pneumonia and was in hospital for a series of checks and overnight stays. Unfortunately, the duration of his stay was extended as doctors and nurses helped organise a series of treatments for him and this had meant that unluckily for dad, for the first time ever, he would have to spend Christmas day in the hospital, with his seat at the dinner table at home remaining empty as the family sat down for Christmas dinner. That was a first, as dad had never missed Christmas, growing up dad was always the first one to go downstairs, the mornings were fun with our dear Papa going downstairs early in the morning on Christmas day, to check if Santa had been. A very young Alex and I, huddled on the top step in our pyjamas, next to one another waiting to hear the good news, with dad every year without fail, walking back from the living room, standing at the bottom of the staircase and looking up at Alex and me with a completely dead pan expression to say 'nope, sorry, he's not been'. Every year he did that and for the first three of four years, we'd believe him, but then afterwards, when we were about eight or nine, whenever he'd come back from the living room, we'd just ignore him and run downstairs giggling.

December of 2010 was the first time that we'd ever had Christmas day without dad, I was living in a house share with a friend from work at the time and so I'd make my way to the house on Christmas day both the year before in 2009 as well as 2010 as well, to wish everyone happy Christmas and to spend the day there. On my visit back to mum and dads house in 2009, I distinctly remember dad sitting in the armchair he'd usually be sat in, with a red tartan blanket wrapped over his legs, the early signs of his pneumonia creeping in no doubt. Although dad wasn't with us for Christmas dinner and for presents in 2010, we did manage to go up to the hospital and see him. We'd bundled a few presents together for him which we then took to the hospital so that he had something to open whilst we were all there. Dad had been moved to a private room which was shared with another older gent who was also in the hospital, I believe dad made friends with this other guy as they'd always have a little back and forth whenever we'd go up to see dad. After unwrapping the few presents, we'd brought dad, we were ushered out, dad needed to rest, every so often we'd all make jokes about dads' predicament, with either Alex or myself picking up his chart at the end of the bed and presuming we could make heads or tails of any of the information listed on it. As we all left, we each hugged and said goodbye to him, leaving him in the hospital room with his gifts and wrapping paper, as we all made our way down the hospital hallway, chatting and making jokes with one another.

Back in the house on that Saturday morning and Alex's voice could be heard from the other end, he was upset, and he'd clearly been crying, WAS still crying in fact, as he spoke, 'Ian?', 'Yes Ale, what's up?' I was so nervous on that call, more nervous than I'd ever been, I was afraid to think that the only reason Alex was on the phone to me, was the reason I'd not slept well the night before. His next words were so heart breaking to hear, 'Dad's dead'. His pain echoed through the phone and into my ear, he was so upset, and I could envision his sadness as his words left his mouth. I was stunned, I'd feared that I'd get a call like this, but dad's last check-up had revealed he was on the up, soon to be discharged in actual fact. When he went into the hospital, he was assured that he wouldn't be there any longer than a couple of weeks, this unfortunately rolled on through to Christmas and then continued into the new year, but there was never any indication that things were getting worse for him, the news was completely unpredictable. There was never any particular reason as to why he'd been required to stay in longer, there was never any serious complication which had arisen. Whatever the reason, the doctors were reassuring to the fact that he would be out in no time, it was only a slight touch of pneumonia which was easily treatable in the hospital. As soon as Alex had finished telling me the situation, he told me he was getting sorted and heading back up to the hospital to meet mum. She was already there and understandably, would need supporting, I told Alex I'd be right over, and I quickly raced up stairs to get changed, trying not to wake my house mate, Steve, in the process. There was no time to be upset, there was no time to cry or work myself up, as I changed out of my pyjamas my upset began to creep in though, I was taken aback by how sudden the situation felt and after changing into a T-shirt and some tracksuit trousers ("sweat pants" for you Americans reading this) with a deep breath I made my way downstairs to put on a jacket and a pair of trainers, ready to head over to the house.

That Saturday morning was a cold one, or maybe it just felt extremely cold to me, it was January, early January to be more exact and the harsh cold air had resultingly settled a little glistening of frost onto the ground. As I raced around to the house, images of my last encounter with dad, leaving him there in that hospital room, flooded into my mind. I knew I couldn't dwell on it though; Alex would need some support and who knows what state mum would be in down at the hospital. After making it to the house, panting a little from the brisk morning run to the house, I slid open the white partition door which separated the cold outside of the world from the front door to the house. Some time ago mum and dad had decided to create a small French door construction on the front of the house. This French door situation would create a more enclosed, undercover area by the front door where parcels or the odd bit of mail could be left. After sliding open the frost covered glass door, I reached for the door handle to the front door, knowing full well the door would be unlocked. But before I was able to grasp the handle, the door flung open, it was Alex, he'd no doubt heard me open the sliding door. Without hesitation he closed the door behind himself and made his way past me to mums' car, his eyes were red and tired. He'd already raced mum up to the hospital not long ago and was just waiting for me to get to the house so that we could both head up together. We jumped into the front of mum's car, a silver-coloured Vauxhall with Alex in the driver's seat. Mums' car was an automatic, contrastingly different to the manual cars Alex and I would have driven before. Alex tore out of the grove where the house was and circled his way around the following streets making his way to the nearby dual carriageway which led to the hospital. As Alex barrelled down the dual carriageway I looked to him, he was holding back some of his tears, his eyes were wide, and his hands were shaking. I glanced at the speedometer to see him doing 60mph in a 40mph zone, he was so stressed, he was so pent up with anguish that I think he was just trying to create some type of focus for himself. Seeing this, I grabbed his shoulder, 'easy mate, we'll get there, you might want to slow down', I tried to sound reassuring, speaking softly to him to ensure that he felt calmer. With a shake of his head, he used his sleeve to quickly wipe his face and eyes and a gradual easing of the accelerator could be heard as the engine hummed to a steady 40mph. One of the car parks to the hospital was situated quite far away, it was the "free one" which didn't require you to pay for the "luxury" of parking close to the hospital. As Alex parked the car up, he immediately unbuckled himself, he wasn't hanging around this morning, he was adamant to get himself up to where mum was. After power walking across the road which separated the two car parks, we made our way to the front of the hospital doors. The green aesthetic framework was the distinguishing feature which segregated what could be termed the "milder" side of the hospital for patients. The red entrance on the opposite side of the complex was used for the more serious affairs which happen in A&E. As soon as we made our way in through the green automatic doors Alex powerwalked his way to the staircase on the opposite side of the elevator and launched himself two or three steps at a time, upward. He knew exactly where to go; he'd dropped mum off not long before and had either already been in the room where dad was moved to or had left mum at the ward to come back and get me. Either way he was like a homing missile, which at times, I struggled to keep up with. As we darted our way up four flights of stairs, to then head down a long stretch corridor which banked left and direct us closer to the ward where dad had been moved to. Alex was getting a little more worked up the closer we got to the ward, and I was too, I wasn't sure what to expect when I got there. So, all I could do at that moment was concentrate on the rabbit warren like maze we were traversing to get to where mum was.

As we entered the ward where dad was being kept, Alex mentioned to the nurse who greeted us, 'Peter Whyatt's room?' his voice was crackled, and I'd be wrong to think that the nursing staff didn't realise why we were there. We were then directed to a small room just by the desk at the wards entrance. As the door creaked open, the sound of weeping could be heard, it was mum, she was sat in the armchair beside the bed which dad was laid in. Stood beside mum was one of the other nursing staff, she was consoling mum as best she could, with a supportive hand placed on her shoulder as mum clenched dads' lifeless right hand and sobbed into the sheets just by where he was laying. That scene was heart-breaking to me, and it evidentially is a scene which has stuck with me. Alex stood by the foot of the bed facing dad as I creaked the room door closed, he was trying to hold back his upset, trying to hold back how sad he was feeling, but it wasn't any use, and it wasn't long before he also burst into tears. I made my way to him, glancing across to mum and then to dads closed eyes as he laid in the bed, and I put my arm around Alex to console him. Unquestionably I was upset, and a few tears rolled down my face as the realisation of the last memory I had with dad was a joke about how death was stood in the corner of the room waiting for him. Suddenly, that joke didn't seem so funny now. When I looked back to Alex, I could see in his face, how incredibly hurt he was, and I realised all too quickly that the last thing anyone needed in that room was for me to also become an inconsolable mess of a person. What was needed, was someone who could provide some type of support, a pillar to lean on if needed, that was something I felt I could do. Mum looked across to me, her face was blood red from the hurt and anguish she was experiencing, with her eyes red and her face all puffy from the extent of her crying, she managed to murmur across to me, 'someone needs to call Lynda and let her know'. Lynda was at that time working down in the south of England a good four- or five-hour car journey away and she'd not long since acquired a working position which revolved around her history degree, of which she undertook when she left her dancing shoes behind to focus on her academic career. 'Don't worry, I'll do it', I wiped away the tears from my face which had emerged from the emotional scene taking place and cleared my throat as I made my way out of the room, with a quick glance back to check on Alex, I saw that he was just staring straight forward, looking on at dads' lifeless body, fully embracing the grieving process with his head in his hands, and I left the room to begin a series of saddening phone calls.

Awkwardly, the hospital had terrible phone reception in the wards (a potential deterrent for people disrupting the patients on the ward and their required rest, I guess) trying to have a phone call push through the walls of the hospital was a nightmare, however after I'd made my way from the ward where everyone was mourning and meandered towards one of the larger open corridors where the phone eventually rang through to Lynda. It was now around 6:30am, the windows in the hallway showing the dark sky outside in that winter period of the year. After a few rings, Lynda picked up, 'Hey Bubba, is everything ok?' Lynda's always had a somewhat calming element in her voice, she has a softness in her tone which allows people to feel very at ease when they're around her. That's probably one of the many reasons why she's become so successful in her pursuits to establish her own hypnotherapy clinic and all the endeavours which have sent her in that direction. It wouldn't have been hard for Lynda to discern what was the matter as my response crackled back to her 'Lyn, we're at the hospital and, well, dads' dead, they've moved him to a separate room on one of the wards here'. I was so nervous of talking about it all and as I elaborated to Lynda the plight of the situation in its entirety, the tears rolled down my face again. Lyn's voice came back with anguish 'what?', her composure was dropped and her upset about the news echoed through the phone. The conversation bounced back and forth a little more after that, as I filled her in on the details of the situation and what had happened. Her upset on hearing the news came through clearly as I held my phone which was pressed against my ear and it was with reluctancy, that I then hung up the phone, with Lynda confirming that she'd be on her way up to Scunthorpe soon. As I leant on the wall of the corridor, I tried to compose myself, the morning situation was a lot to process, and I was already feeling a multitude of emotions. I glanced at the phone, the time reflected back showed that it was nearing 7:00am, there were still more calls I had to make, and the phone reception was terrible in the hospital, my call with Lyn was only just doable and I couldn't bare having to experience a series of following phone calls where I had to repeat the details of the situation. I took a deep breath and shook off the anguish trying to take a hold of me, and I made my way to the entrance of the hospital in an attempt to stop myself from crying, I was also hoping that the reception on the phone was going to be better down there too. The next number on the phone to call was Nat, I figured I'd call her to tell her the news and to let her know that I wasn't going to be at the studio that morning, if I managed to catch her soon enough, then she wouldn't be halfway to the studio, and it would mean that she wouldn't have wasted a journey. As I sauntered around the main entrance to the hospital, the phone began to ring again, after a few rings Nat eventually picked up, 'Hellooo!' Nat was so bubbly and friendly, that her upbeat personality just lifted the weight of the situation a little, I then regrettably began to tell her all the details of the morning and closed the conversation by telling her that I wasn't going to be in the studio that morning. Nat was extremely sympathetic and reassuring as the conversation went back and forth, her understanding to the situation helped to make the explanation of the circumstance a lot easier to talk about. After a little more back and forth with one another we hung up the phone, next on the list of people to call was David, he needed to know what was happening as likewise, if I called him soon enough, he might be able to have an extra hour for himself without feeling the need to get to the studio early by himself. After ringing through to David, I then spent the next few minutes filling him in on the situation, there was a reassurance and understanding from him as I talked through the circumstances of the morning, and I ended the conversation by letting him know I wasn't going to the studio that morning. I'd have to let him know in a couple of days about my Wednesday lessons, as that all depended on what was happening at home. Those conversations were really strange for me, the situation was extremely saddening but I knew that neither David nor Nat needed me to break down as I filled them in about dads' circumstances. I had to keep things together, I still had to go back up to the ward and the room I'd just left mum and Alex in. I felt like I couldn't emotionally breakdown or experience the serious anguish I had welling up inside me, that wasn't going to make anyone feel better. That entranceway downstairs in the hospital was a cold one, I could feel my body shaking from the cold gushes of wind that would sweep through as the automatic doors opened from the combination of my pacing on the phone which would set off the sensors and the new people arriving at the hospital. Or maybe I was shaking because of the severity of the circumstances, maybe my body was shaking as some sort of reactionary aspect to my unwillingness to let anything emotionally out. I knew I had to be tough for Alex and mum, I knew that the last thing they would need is for me to lose all my self-control and to break down into a weeping mess. It would be understandable, no question about that, it's not easy to hear the fact that one of your parents has just died somewhat unexpectedly, but it wouldn't have helped anyone else in the situation. I quickly darted back to the ward both to see how mum and Alex were getting on and, in an effort to warm myself back up. Entering the room where dad was situated for a second time was in all honesty a bizarre experience, I'd already seen the state of dad when I'd gone in the room the first time and so I knew that the initial shock factor wouldn't surprise me. The main element to contend with was the grieving of both mum and Alex, if I could hold my resolve with them both releasing their personal anguish and upset, then I knew I'd make it through the situation and support them both.

I entered the room once again where everyone was mourning, the door creaking eerily as I closed it behind me. Mum was still by the side of the bed holding dads' hand with the nurse from before supporting her and Alex was standing at the foot of the bed, right where I'd left him before my string of phone calls. There was another nurse who had joined them in the room now and she was stood on the opposite side to Alex and was partially consoling him. I leaned across to ask the question I'd initially wanted to ask since I'd first gotten there, the question which I'm sure both Alex and mum could answer but were unfit to do so, 'so what happened?' I tried my best to keep as clear as composure as I could, but I could feel my eyes beginning to water. A prominent feature of dad that had not gone unnoticed when I had entered the room was a partial indentation in his head, rather than seeing the rounded bald head of dads' cranium. What was instead noticeable was a flattened indentation that ran along the top right corner of his head. I'd noticed it when I'd first walked into the room some hour and a half ago, which initially shocked and worried me, but I wasn't able to ask anyone about what had happened. However, with my second arrival, this nurse was able to fill both me and Alex in on what had happened that morning. With Alex and I both stood listening she explained to us that earlier that morning dad had been found in the toilets, a blood clot had travelled through his body and stropped his heart completely. As he collapsed, he had hit his head on the sink unit in the bathroom and that's why his head was concaved slightly. As the nurse explained what had happened to dad, tears began to run down Alex's face again. It had turned out that the blood clot had killed him, the nurse tried mentioning in a reassuring way, how he wouldn't have felt anything after his heart had stopped, referring primarily to the bash on his head as he went down to the floor. The time we spent in that room felt so long to me, time seemingly stood still as the gravitas of the situation was opening up to me, there was a lot to process, a lot to comprehend and there was a lot that would need preparing for, moving forward.

I don't exactly remember what time I actually got back to the house that I was sharing with Steve, all I know is that it was daylight outside after Alex had parked the silver Vauxhall car up at mum and dad's house. We'd hugged tightly and he soon after left me to go inside, I then began the brisk morning walk back to the house I was sharing with Steve. After getting in and closing the front door, I threw my keys to one of the window ledges nearby and made my way into the living room to sit. There were a million things going through my head (as you'd probably expect really) and I was in something of a daze, searching for various forms of rationalisations to the circumstances. Mum had chosen to remain at the hospital with the supportive and consoling nursing staff around her, she was completely devastated, and we'd left her in the capable hands of the nurses as she cried in the embrace of one of them. The next few days were rough for mum, Lynda had come home over the weekend to help console her and to see how Alex and I were doing, she also helped organise a few things in and around the house as well as the funeral arrangements whilst she was with us. But as soon as she had arrived, she had to leave again, Lynda was working down south and she wasn't in a position to be absent from work for too long, which meant that when compared with the rough year ahead, Lynda's visit seemed very brief. In reality it was around two or three weeks that she'd actually been with us, she helped organise the funeral for dad along with a few other arrangements and she had practiced her eulogy like a hundred times in the mirror, trying to make sure she didn't cry when she came to read it aloud a couple of weeks later. To be honest there's a lot of elements that sit in and around this timeline that to be quite honest, I don't have an accurate account of. When I look back to this time and the myriad of events that took place in and around everything that happened, they all seem to form a somewhat cohesive blob which represents that year. Organised in a way where I can work out (roughly) what had happened but there's no specifics as to when. The soup like concoction of emotions, mental states, physical aspects, and circumstances all meshing together like when you clump various colours of Playdough together to form that large brown coloured blob and ball. It's Playdough, but you have no idea what colours are actually in it, that's what 2011 was like for me, a jumble of "mixed up colours" mixed up circumstances and emotions. It probably stems from the likely impactful traumatism of the situation and the multitude of things which transpired over that time frame, well, at least that's what I'm assuming when I look back well over a decade later. Two days after dads passing and Lynda took mum to the Cathedral in Lincoln where she lit a candle for dad and placed in the sand, mum also posted the picture on Facebook, where friends all culminated together to send her well wishes and support. After waking organising a few things upstairs in mums house, my phone began to ring, it was Rach, a long-lasting friend and at that time Bruce's girlfriend (full disclosure they're happily married now with a beautiful young toddler, my godson, Leo). She was calling me after seeing mums Facebook post, I tentatively answered 'Hey, how are you Rach?'. 'Hey, I just saw your mums post on Facebook, I'm so sorry, I had no idea, how are you doing?', 'that's ok, I was gonna call you and let you know, but things have been busy as you'd expect'. As the conversation continued, the back-and-forth sympathies and explanations of what had happened all began to be discussed and Rach concluded by asking if I'd mentioned anything to Chris (Bruce to me). 'I'll let him know, he'll want to talk to you' and soon after she hung up, Bruce was living in Sheffield at the time, he was in his final year of Uni and had a series of exams to conclude. I had every intention of contacting him about everything, but I knew the last thing he needed to hear about was my family bereavement. No sooner had the call from Rach ended and my phone rang, it was Bruce, I'd literally walked four steps on the landing and then gotten a call from him. 'Now then mate' Bruce said, 'How you doing? Why didn't you call or message me mate?'. The conversation I had with Bruce was really reassuring, he's a really great friend, my best friend to be quite honest. He talks straight and calls things as they are, but he's also very understanding as well. As I relayed to him the fact that I didn't want to bother him with my issues, especially whilst he had the most important year in Uni and exams ahead of himself, he told me to stop being an idiot and to not make any plans for the weekend. He was coming back home, and we were going to hang out, I knew there'd be no point in fighting him on it, either way he was coming back to Scunthorpe, if not to see me, then to definitely see Rach. Within two days, there was a knock at the door of mums' house and as I opened it, I saw Bruce and Rach stood there, after a quick hug from them both, we made our way out for the day. Bruce and Rach have always been great friends, the tumultuous tides of the dancing and all its intense requirements can easily throw people out the realm of reality. Bruce and Rach have always been good at helping me stay grounded in the reality of the world, telling me I'm a dickhead when needed is an incredible correction to any ego that I might personally experience. I'm incredibly appreciative of how much they've stuck by me over the years, I think I'd read somewhere that great friends, true friends don't require constant conversations or weekly meet ups. They may only see and talk with one another a handful of times in the year, but you know you can always depend on them. I feel I have that with Bruce and Rach, they're my best friends and really helped me during that turbulent 2011 period.

As best we could, Alex and I trundled the various motorways and A-roads to get to our lessons, but things felt numb for quite a while. The gravitas of dads' absence really sank in over the following weeks after his funeral and those car journeys got a little quieter, there would still be the occasional conversation surrounding the dancing of course. With one of us spurring the other into conversation, but it was clear to see that dads' passing was severely felt. When we were at the studio though, we never let it show too often, I know I certainly didn't, I knew I had to hold a personal resolve to the situation, Alex needed it and as soon as Lynda left, mum needed it too. I vaguely remember arriving at the studio one Saturday morning, Alex and I had decided to forego the following Wednesday lessons and practice after dads' death to console and look after mum and help Lynda in whatever way we could. But we had to do something and so I loaded up the car a week and a half later, on an early Saturday morning and drove us both down to the studio for some dancing, lessons, and practicing. Everyone that knew about the situation was so supportive down in the studio, both David and Helen gave us a supportive hug, Nat was really supportive and reassuring and I think she must have been upset FOR me, more than what I was personally feeling. Alex's partnership with Katherine had finished after the National Championships the year before and so he was once again looking for a new partner, which resultantly meant he was practicing on his own as well as receiving a lesson. I think the reason why Alex and Katherine just couldn't work together strongly, was because there were various clashes in personality and at the time, there was a difference in motivations and drives. As it seemingly looked like the partnership didn't want to work in a way that Alex felt and wanted it to (plus Alex had also referred to Katherine as dancing as slow as a slug in one of their lessons and so I think after that and a few other misdemeanours on his part, that the partnership was destined to come to an end). Personally, I worked even harder in the following few lessons and training sessions, I think that pain is a great motivator in a number of varying cases which would warrant someone to find something deeper about what they are capable of, what they are capable of doing and ultimately who they are as an individual. In my case however, when I look back, I think it was very unhealthy, a couple of weeks after dad had passed and his funeral was arranged, both mum and Alex went to see the family doctor, a lovely man named Dr Ballah. He knew dad and the family very well, he'd treated us all for years and as soon as he heard the passing of dad and that mum and Alex had arranged to see him, he'd prescribed them some anti-depressants and permitted a few weeks advisable bereavement leave from work. I'd chosen to ignore mums advise to see the Dr and chose instead to still go to work though, I needed the money, and I felt like I couldn't just sit around and hope that I'd feel better. My general thinking was that if I just got my head down and "cracked on", that I'd eventually feel ok (a classic case of denialism if there ever was one) and how wrong I was. A couple of weeks after dads' funeral had passed, I reluctantly went to go see Dr Ballah, both mum and Alex had pestered the shit out of me because I'd not been to see him and so, in an effort to make them feel better, I decided to book an appointment and go see him. After arriving at the surgery and waiting to be seen, I was ushered into his office, he greeted me with a hug and asked me to sit. "Your father was a good man" Dr Ballah started, "I was sad to hear he had passed away so suddenly", I tried to remain quite stoic but there must have been something on my face that just signalled that I might not have been doing so great. Dr Ballah, in his infinite Indian wisdom, seemed to have a very good knack for sussing you out, I remember a distinct memory of being very young and after feigning some form of illness or upset stomach, mum rushed me to an appointment to see him. Perplexed at what could be the issue, Dr Ballah began his litany of questioning, and it didn't take him long to figure out what was wrong. After taking his stethoscope and listening to my chest he sat back down, confirmatory noises coming from him as he shuffled a few papers around. "I don't think it's too serious what he has Mrs Whyatt" Dr Ballah began, looking at mum but also with occasional glances back to me. "I recommend a few days rest from school, and he'll be absolutely fine", his eyes moved back and looked directly at me. His words conveyed a few days rest to mum, but his eyes and face conveyed to me "I know your lying, but I'm happy to give you a few days off school, just don't ask me this again". After mum thanked Dr Ballah and we left, I glanced back to him and he gave me a quick wink and a smile, essentially concluding the deal, before his office door closed. This time it was different though, this time he diagnostically knew that something wasn't right, I'd explained the circumstances of dads' passing, how mum and Alex were in bits, how at the beginning of February I'd moved back home to look after mum and to keep an eye on Ale. After a few more conversations back and forth with one another and after a few minor tests using one of those pumps that wrap around your arm to measure blood pressure. He concluded our interaction by prescribing me a recommended dose of anti-depressants (which were immediately thrown in a drawer as I arrogantly didn't feel I was depressed enough to be taking medication and they were subsequently left there) as well as issuing me three weeks off work. I thanked him and soon after, I left, a little dazed by the experience to be honest, I'd purposely tried to keep myself busy, going to work, increasing my practicing at home, continuing to go to my lessons. But now Dr Ballah had thrown a spanner in the works by recommending that I do nothing, I knew I just couldn't do that, I personally felt I wasn't depressed and the last thing I needed to do was sit and do nothing, so I made a plan to use the time away from work to practice more. When I think back to that time, I can see with more clarity how it was all just distraction bullshit (hindsight clearly highlighting that fact to me). But I felt that I couldn't stand still for too long, I needed to be the reliable pillar of support for both mum and Alex and by doing nothing, I was potentially leaving myself open to having a "breakdown" of my own and that was the last thing anyone would need. So, a few days later I sat down in front of the tiny laptop we had at mum's house, and I booked to stay in the Travelodge which Alex and I had used quite often when staying down in Wolverhampton. My plan was to stay down in Wolverhampton for about five or six days (because that's all the money I had available) and get a full day's worth of practice and training in each day I was down there, if I was going to be in the studio space for around 10:00am each morning when David would start his teaching, and I stayed there all day until his last lesson ended at 10:00pm. Then I'd get a solid twelve hours of training done in one day, and if I repeated that for the five or six days I was down there for, well I'd be able to triple my training regime and make incredible strides in my development. After sitting down over the weekend that passed after my consultation with Dr Ballah and by leveraging a little finance around, so that I could afford the £500-£600 stay down at the Travelodge, I packed a case and my dance bag and made my way down the following Tuesday.

When Alex and I used to dance and compete at our dance teacher's competition, down in Wolverhampton, the proposition had arisen from David that if we were able to stay over and help set up the venue on the Saturday evening. Then not only would we be allowed to enter the comp for free on the Sunday, but that also, if we helped stay and clear up the venue afterwards. That on the Sunday evening, when the competition would have ended, we could come with him to the local Indian for something to eat, a pretty good compromise to be fair. Whenever, we'd go with David and the Stagman to the pub on the Wednesday evenings, I'd always try and find one question that I could ask about the dancing industry which could help clear any form of confusion or uncertainty I had. David was never obligated to answer my dancing questions, he was after all "off the clock" and so sometimes the answers David gave were over one exchange or just a general reply and rarely (depending on whether the question had piqued his interest) he would have an answer that evolved into a full discussion that would last the length of the evening. By helping David set-up and close-down his competition over Saturday and Sunday, I knew I had an opportunity to ask more questions about how the running of his events were structured and about all the intricacies that you never fully know about as a dance competitor because you're never allowed to "peek behind the curtain". This was all because primarily, me and Alex had big ideas of running our own dance events at some point in the future and if we could gain some insight from David about how he managed all the logistics of his competition. Then we could both capitalise on the ideas and the "blueprint" way a successful competition should and could be run. This meant that on the Saturdays which coincided with David's competition, both Alex and I would take time off from our jobs and organise to stay down in the nearby Travelodge, just off the motorway junction by Wolverhampton. Now, when it came down to organising our stays there, the most viable option Alex and I had was to (obviously) share a room and due to the already mountain like series of sizeable costs we'd be incurring for doing our dancing anyway (which, on full disclosure was based on a very loose and very malleable form of fiscal planning, which lacked any form of cohesive structure and could very easily have been drummed up by a ten year old on an already used napkin from a restaurant). We figured that the best option would be for us to not only share a room together, but that we should also share a double bed together. It was a far cheaper option for us both, rather than organising a room with two single beds and besides, what's the big deal? We're brothers after all, so sharing a double bed together wouldn't feel awkward or weird (he nervously types as you, dear reader, judgmentally pause after that sentence to give your own verdict on the matter). Anyway, those times we helped David at his competition spanned both the years before and after that 2011 period and because David initially ran two competitions in the year, we'd organise that situation twice a year. A cosy little snuggle situation twice a year, how lucky were we. Fortunately, after experiencing this a few times, we began to see how from an outside perspective, the situation looked and seemed very weird. On one visit, I distinctly remember us making our way into the Travelodge entrance, with me wheeling my little red overnight suitcase behind me, Alex sporting a type of backpack consisting of overnight essentials. That I suddenly realised that the young girl who politely greeted us and began to check us in.

Would see one double-bed room and two young guys doing an overnight stay, the whole thing from the outside, looked a little sus. We never thought about it before hand, we know we're brothers, just doing an overnight stay for the dancing and in our minds, it's all relative and it's all very clear. To the young nineteen- or twenty-year-old girl behind the counter, judgmentally handing us a key fob for our room, that's not the case. I'd occasionally try and justify the situation by exclaiming that we're brothers and just staying for the one night for our dancing, but I think that maybe that hindered the situation more than it helped. So instead, whenever we did our weekend stay there, we'd occasionally lean into the skid of the situation by posing as a homosexual couple. One of us would make our way into the reception first and begin checking us in, by which the time the other one of us would arrive, without prompt, we would then erupt into a domestic dispute exacerbated by hand gestures, poses and a series of over-the-top camp impressions. Appreciably, not every person of a homosexual orientation conducts themselves this way, but we'd experienced the glances and subtleties of the various people behind the counter enough times, to know what was sub textually being thought whenever we checked in together. Our exemplified camp impressions just made the situation a little more amusing to us and a little more awkward for whichever person happened to be sat behind the reception desk. Sometimes we'd be subtle with our impersonations and sometimes on the odd occasion we'd really ham them up. I distinctly remember one occasion where after arriving at the Travelodge and after Alex had parked the car, I grabbed my little red suitcase and made my way into the Travelodge to check us in, as we'd done innumerable times before. Alex had a couple of bags to bring in with him as he was carrying the bag with our tan and hair stuff which we'd be using the following morning to prep for the competition. After making my way to the check-in desk and giving the details of our stay, Alex sauntered into the reception area and immediately we began our "routine". With one arm resting on the counter and a sassy hip sticking out to the side for comedic effect I erupted to Alex, 'Jesus Alex! I thought you were going to take forever!' Alex has always been quick with a comeback in one shape or form and this occasion was no different. With a glint in his eye that conveyed 'oh we're doing this today are we?', he began his retort. 'Well, I'm surprised you're able to make it in here before me, what with the way you minced across that car park!'. You've never seen someone focus their attention so much, as the staff members who greeted us at that Travelodge, I'm sure they've seen all manner of situations but when there's a domestic, nobody wants to be involved. As the guy behind the desk helped organise our room, Alex and I continued our back and forth with each other, until our room key was promptly presented. Alex then grabbed the key and minced his way to the door leading to the hallway and, looking back to me he said, 'get your ass in that room now Mr, I'm going to spank the shit out of you!' I don't know how, but I managed to keep my composure and not laugh as I replied, 'are we using lube this time, or are we going straight in?' After making it to the hallway soon afterwards, continuing our back and forth with one another. We burst out laughing, we could hold our resolve long enough for a few exchanges in our "performance", but soon after making it to the "safety" of the hallway, we just burst out laughing.

This was the same Travelodge I had chosen to stay in for the five or six days I was down in Wolverhampton only this time I was on my own and things weren't as funny. I'd made a rough plan of what I wanted to do in my training, and I'd arranged some extra lessons with David whilst I was there, so I felt confident enough that I'd make immense strides in my progression. In the earlier years of lessons and training with David and Helen, with Will and Nicky and anyone else who I had managed to have a few lessons from. I'd gone to the effort of buying an orange and yellow notebook which I used to diligently write any and every aspect of training, choreography, lesson information and practice exercise in, it was my compendium of dancing knowledge, which sadly is lost to time. By 2011, I didn't need a notebook, I knew what I needed to do in my training and my lessons were the cornerstone blocks to help build a more cohesive structure in my development. If you have a solid training plan which entails clear ideas, the targets you're trying to achieve and satisfactory moments in your development, then in my view, you'll manage to make some decent headway in your understanding and development. The plans I made for my stay down in Wolverhampton, weren't quite so comprehensive. They were more of a loosely guided structure, which from the outset, might have seemed like it had a rationalised structure to it, but in reality, it was largely made up on the spot after arriving in the studio. My training mainly consisted of working on set forms of exercises and drills surrounding basic principles and elements for each of the ten dances, dancing a series of complete routines for full tracks (using the iPods I always brought with me) and then dancing the occasional final (where I would dance five dances of either Ballroom or of Latin consecutively) provided there wasn't too many people in the room. This was all to be done whilst I wore 4kg worth of weights on my arms and legs. The weights were an item I'd been using for years, and they were a regular feature in my training both at home and in the studio. Because I'd been used to wearing them all day in training sessions over the years, having them on my arms and legs this time around was no different to me. But because of the various things swimming through my head, the emotions I was neglecting and the personal drive for greater improvement that I was feeling, I wore them all day, never taking them off. I wore them for the drills and exercises I was doing, for the finals I was dancing through and for the full length of dancing of my choreography too. I was determined to make improvements, I wasn't going to waste any more time, I knew I wanted to be one of the top six dancers in the world, one of the best in the UK. Sheer grit and determination combined with a strategical plan of competitions had powered me through 2010 and I wasn't going to let anything slow the momentum of that progression, not for anything or anyone. If my body aches, that's too bad, other people are hurting too! If my feet blistered then that's tough as well, it's the price you pay for progression. If I'm feeling nauseous because I haven't eaten anything substantial all day aside from a tin of spaghetti and bags of Haribo sweets which would all be washed down with copious amounts of Red Bull, well suck it up Ian, you've got shit to do!

I've always worked hard in my dancing, and I've always wanted the similar output from any partner that I've danced with. Nat was the first person who came along, who embodied that similar ethos of ideas and work ethic, regrettably, she couldn't make it to Wolverhampton and join me for the extra time I was in the studio for. She could only make the Wednesday and Saturday training days, I think she may have tried to come down on Friday as well, but I don't quite remember to be honest. All that toil was enduring was accompanied by the sensation of nausea, blistering and bleeding feet and the agony of my aching body, it was all felt after my first twelve-hour stint in the studio, that was just day one. I knew the week ahead would be a tough one and deterministically, I felt I was ready, I just needed my body to last for as long as I felt it personally could. I was so desperate to make something of myself, visions of dancing in world finals and the dreams of becoming a top-level performer swelled in my mind constantly. There had been so many things that had happened along the pathway to arrive at that singular point, good things, bad things, happy things, as well as sad things, I felt that I didn't want it to be all for nothing, that everything I'd experienced to get to that point had to be worth it somehow. I felt like I was sacrificing so much for doing my dancing, for following my dreams, and living my passion, that everything had to be worth it. Dads' passing was just another nail in the box of experiences for me, now I had even more drive to become something and prove myself (whatever that means). I didn't want to be remembered as someone who never made anything of himself in his dancing career, someone who had potential and was never able to grasp the spotlight for himself. All the toil, physically, mentally, emotionally, spiritually, and financially (really, any "ally" you can think of) all of that had to amount to something, right?

Day two in the studio was more of the same, it was Wednesday and so David was in the studio from 10:00am again, Nat would arrive at the studio at around 1:00pm or so which meant that I had a few hours of intense training on my own before she would arrive. The day passed as most Wednesdays did only this time I was on my own, Alex wasn't with me making jokes during breaks for food or observing my dancing and giving the odd bit of feedback. It was just me and Nat working through everything we needed to, there would be the odd disagreement in the back and forth with Nat and me about things that needed to happen in the dancing, but we both had such a deep respect for one another that our disagreements never got personal or emotional. We'd just park whatever we couldn't agree on to one side, work on something else, maybe a different dance or a series of exercises or something, and then revisit it again to try a resolve the issue we might have had. We were a really great team both in the training and out on the floor and the drive for continual learning and development was definitely a shared sentiment. Day two ended with me sitting in the pub with David and the Stagman talking through dancing stuff, they'd asked how the family was doing back home and we reminisced about experiences we'd all had with dad. All the time I was sat in that pub, I could just feel my entire body burning, my feet had already blistered and bled into my shoes and changing my shoes to do the different practices and lessons of Ballroom and Latin was a task in and of itself. The pair of trainers I was wearing should have added some support, but they really didn't. My entire body ached so much from all the exercises, the drills, the practicing and most of all, from the second twelve-hour day of training I'd pushed myself through, wearing weights on my entire body for entirety of the day and not taking them off until I was finished for the day. After closing time at the pub kicked us all out, I said goodbye to David and Stagman and made my way back to the Travelodge I was staying at. As soon as I made it to the room which I was staying in, after bouncing my way from wall to wall as I made my way down the corridor of the Travelodge, the agony of my body suffering just that little bit more after each collision, that I eventually crashed on the bed in my room. Travelodge beds are like fucking bricks to sleep on, but with the way I was feeling at that moment it was like a warm, snuggly hug. After composing myself and willing myself to sit up on the bed, I began to change out of my clothes, each layer was a task in and of itself to remove. I needed to still grab a shower before hopping into bed and it was 12:30am in the morning, the real damage was felt when I literally peeled my black socks from off my feet, not only had the numerous blisters on the back of my feet and under my feet all burst, but they'd bled as well, drying in a way which resulted in them becoming superglued to my feet. I didn't want to deal with the direct pain of ripping them off my feet, I hurt so much already, and so I left them flapping around on the floor as I made my way to the bathroom to shower. Fortunately, the warm water allowed the socks to fall off easily, however the combination of soapy suds and warm water made the experience of what I'd done to my feet agonising. As I stood in the shower, arms folded, allowing the water to bounce off the back of my neck and shoulders, I asked myself why the fuck was I doing this to myself? It's a valid question, I could have enjoyed the comfort of being at home and doing my usual 10:00pm – 2:00am training as I'd always done, the comfort of having a sofa to crash on after killing myself with weights and exercises and the reassurance that I could grab something (substantial) to eat whenever I wanted, the answer was an easy one though. Mum and Alex were not in a great place and so occupying the living room for a duration of time wasn't possible. Mum was personally coping with a combination of co-codamols and a bottle of red wine every night (a reason for which, is why I personally don't like drinking wine, but more on that later) and I think Alex was having something of an existential crisis of his own with coping with a multitude of things he was unwilling to talk about. Organising to stay down in the Travelodge was my way of escaping, it was a way for me to feel like I could become more connected to the dancing, the thing I'd done since the age of three and actively pursued trying to make a vocational career out of. As day three rolled in, the toll of how brutal I was treating myself started to shine through, I sat for longer breaks, danced for about fifteen to twenty minutes and then stopped for about fifteen minutes to recover. My blisters were bleeding again. Training began at 11:00am and I could feel the aching pulses coming from the back of my feet, I'd stupidly chosen to not let the weight of the situation gravitate on me and decided to wear the weights again for another twelve hours. "Go hard or go home" was probably the mantra in my head at the time, when it came to facing the pain of the circumstances and regrettably by 7:00pm, I was a hobbling, limping mess of a person. I tried to push harder, through gritted teeth and agonising pain, I tried to keep going with exercises and practices, I just didn't want to go home, I didn't want to deal with what was inevitable. By 8:30pm I was collapsed on the floor sitting upright, sweat dripping down my face, my T-shirt having the classic sweat stains of a Rocky movie. I just couldn't carry on, there was nothing in the tank that would allow me to get back up and continue, and that's when David made his way over to me. David had been keeping an eye on me whilst I was staying down in Wolverhampton, he never interfered with what I was doing, maybe adding the occasional insight or something, maybe even the odd joke about how ridiculous I looked, but he never stopped what I was doing either. When he saw the mess, I was in, hobbling and stumbling near a radiator, he came over, telling me that I should call it a day, I didn't listen to him and pushed through the pain, ignoring his advice and viewing it as a weakness. I knew there'd only be a few occasions where David would tolerate my shenanigans and so I'd occasionally leave the studio space and sit in the kitchen/ waiting area next door, for thirty minutes or so, before then re-emerging for more self-inflicting punishment. After my collapse to the floor, he had to step in and he very sternly but reassuringly told me, 'Go home Ian, you're wasting your time doing what you're doing, go home'. He was right, I didn't want to admit it, but he was right, I soon after managed to will myself up from the floor and began de-shedding the weights that I'd been wearing. I then staggered over to the windowsill and collected my towel, Ipods, phone and wallet and gradually made my way into the toilets to get myself changed. That evening of changing to go home was a cold one, in some way I'd felt like I'd failed in my training (a misguided thought) in reality, what I'd really failed at was staying away from my problems and from denying myself any form of grieving process. The car journey back home was torturous, blistered feet and ankles, an aching and tired body worked little in terms of reassurances and justifications from the few days of dance training I'd done. After making my way back to mums' house two and a half hours later. I dumped my bags in the hallway and crawled my way upstairs to the futon sofa-bed in Alex's bedroom which I was using whilst Lynda was staying over, and I slept for a solid fourteen hours.

In all honesty I didn't know what to do the next day when I woke up, my body still hurt from the punishing training sessions I'd pushed myself through, and I wasn't at work for another two and a half weeks. I remember vaguely interacting with everyone in the house and watching crappy TV, no doubt used as a form of mild background noise to everyone's personal upset. Later in the afternoon I rang David to tell him that I was taking two weeks away from the dancing, to rest, recover and be with the family. He understood and we ended the call after a brief form of exchanges. My time off from work would extend from the end of February and into early March which meant I had the remainder of February and early March to get my shit together and plan out the next direction for the dancing. Over this early part of 2011 Nat and I had managed to get ourselves to a few competitions, The Midlands Amateur Dance Champions, the Worcester Dance Festival, and the David Truman Tournament (hosted by our teachers David and Helen) our results had been ok from these events, we'd managed to make the finals of both the Amateur Ballroom and Amateur Latin and we'd even managed to be placed 3rd in the Amateur Latin event. But towards the back end of February, I began to see the severity of the situation at home, Lynda had gone back down south, and I saw just how hard dads' passing had hit mum. Alex wasn't as lively as he had been before, there weren't as many jokes coming from him, and he spent most of his time in the world of Xbox 360 and PlayStation 3 games. Mum was drinking red wine every night, no doubt in an effort to help console her grief of which she would have no doubt felt was too much of an issue to talk about to her sons. In early March though, things took a turn for the worse. It was in or around this time that our Nana, the only grandparent still remaining in the family, had a tumble and suffered a form head injury for herself. We'd grown up with our nana from being young, with school runs, afternoons spent playing games of bingo and dominos and the reminiscent memories of drinking Ribena cordial and eating biscuits as we talked and exchanged various questions on an extensive number of subject matters from countless conversations, we all had with her. She truly was a remarkable lady; she was very worldly despite having not ventured much outside the town she'd lived in. Unfortunately, though, in 2011, there had been some form of incident at her flat and mum and Lynda had to rush in and help sort it out. Nana had fallen and hit her head, it was sometime afterwards that Lynda recounted to me the entirety of the scene she witnessed, of scrubbing blood from the cabinet units and floor after Nana had been rushed to the hospital. But because of this incident, which happened in early February, it had clearly impacted her severely as she would constantly wander up to mums' house asking how everything was and asking how Peter (my dad) was.

Her memory had been impacted from the trauma of falling and regrettably she was on the decline. In early March she was rushed to hospital where the family gathered to say their goodbyes to her, she wasn't going to make it, and everyone was brought in to see her one last time.

I think it was the combination of dads' passing in January and Nanas passing in early March that catapulted mum into a deep spiral that she has later referred to me as her "dark place". She drank at least a full bottle of red wine every night and it wasn't uncommon to see multiple boxes of co-codamols lying around the kitchen counter. The family was given another two-week bereavement from Dr Ballah and it wasn't until Alex shouted down to me one night, that the severity of the situation really fully hit me. After flicking through stations on the TV finding something to pique my interest away from the depressing scenes that had surrounded me of late, I heard Alex's distressed voice bellow down from the landing upstairs. 'IAN! Come Quick!', that was the loudest I'd heard Alex in a couple of months, and I knew something wasn't right. Instantly I flew up the stairs to hear him crying in the bathroom 'I'm in here!'. As I carefully opened the bathroom door, the stench of wine induced vomit smacked me in the face, I almost vomited myself but seeing Alex kneeling in puddles of sick and holding mums head, immediately switched that reaction off. Pink vomit was sprayed all over the walls, the bath, the sink, and the toilet where mum had collapsed, Alex was cradling her head as she groaned and with his face full of tears, he looked up and asked what we should do. There was no time to think, just do, and I jumped into the situation to take charge, I asked Alex fill a nearby jug of cold water, and I began to gently slap mums face to bring her round with Alex frantically filling a jug from the bath. I then propped mum up using my knee and chest, 'mum, drink this, come on mum! Drink this!' I was so scared, so panicked, there was no time to think of what might happen if she wasn't ok, there was no time to worry if this might be a three-for-three scenario all remember at that point was how both mine and Alex's hands were shaking. Mum was groaning so I knew she would be ok, we just had to get her to bed and get her hydrated, after forcing her to sip some of water, I gently poured some over her head, firstly, to clean some of the vomit out of her hair but secondly, to try and cool her down and wake her up a little. Eventually she kicked her feet, knocking Alex back into the washing hamper behind him and her eyes rolled open as she began to realise where she was. Alex and I then promptly helped her to her feet to stand but she was still in a drunken daze, her eyes barely keeping open. Alex and I were both covered in mums' vomit at this point, we were hot, and we were soaking from the jug of water that had been pushed over us both as we helped wrestle mum to her feet. After slinging mums' arm over my shoulder, I instructed Alex to clean down the bathroom as best he could whilst I manoeuvred mum to her bedroom and begin helping her get changed. Eventually, mum was in bed, helping mum into some pyjamas and getting her a fresh glass of water had the unfortunate accompaniment of oral boaks which came from Alex in the bathroom as he cleaned the awful mess left behind in the wake of the situation. That night was a long one for me, I'm sure it was for Alex as well, after we'd gotten mum sorted and cleaned the bathroom up, I called Lynda, I had to tell her what had happened. The phone call was brief as I think Lyn had something she was in the middle of, but she reassured us both that she would be back over the weekend to see how things were. I remember feeling helpless in what should be done but I'd known that something SHOULD have been done in the circumstance. The situation forced me to make a very quick realisation that I didn't know a lot of things, I didn't know how to navigate an intricate situation, mum was hurting but I didn't know how I could help her. Alex needed support, but what could I do? I didn't have any answers and the experience of the evening kept me awake most of that night. The next day was a relatively quiet one, Alex didn't talk much in the morning, and he soon left to go out by himself. I found myself watching a Derren Brown show on the TV where he baffled and bamboozled audience members with mental trickery and his understanding of human nature and the mind. I was massively intrigued; how did he know what people were going to think before they had even thought of it? The simple answer is he didn't, as stated in his TV show, it was all a culmination of various psychological and persuasive elements which resulted in people believing their freewill choice was made on their own accord, rather than from a series of guided suggestions. That evening I sat in my room, alone, mum had remined in bed all day recovering from the previous night, and I remember being sat on my bed, propped up against the bedroom wall thinking. There was some way I could help the family, there was something I could do but I regrettably knew that something was missing and that's when a flash came into my mind of a memory I had. A memory of dad sitting in bed two months before his trip to the hospital reading a book by Bill Bryson called A Brief History On Nearly Everything. I'd never been a huge reader in school, especially as a teenager, but I had read tons as a young kid, encyclopaedias, science books, history books, all sorts really. Reading might not have been the answer, but it was certainly better than nothing, I rummaged through the downstairs bookshelf to find the book I'd recalled dad reading and took it upstairs with me. I then opened my phone and the Amazon app and ordered a string of about twenty to thirty books which were listed on a page of Derren Browns website, there was a solution to my problem here somewhere, I just had to find it.

When the next morning came, I had to make a difficult phone call, it was a nice warm day as I my phone rang through to call Nat, with everything that had happened here at home, with the passing of both dad and Nana and the uncertainty of what might be on the horizon with mum. I called Nat to end our dancing partnership, I've always looked back to that phone call to wonder if it was ever the right decision, was it right or wrong to terminate a partnership that had good potential? I don't think there's a straight-line answer to that really. Ultimately, I knew things weren't going to be right for a while, at least situationally speaking, and I wasn't naïve enough to think that I didn't still have to process my own issues building up from the various circumstances at play. I think I was trying to do Nat a kindness by not involving her, although I know full-well that she would have had no issue in supporting me through whatever I needed to do. With a sorrowful understanding we ended our phone call and our partnership had drawn to a close. Things at home weren't right for a while though and it took me some time to get into the habit of reading, there were always strong incentivises to help nudge me along, what with the emotional and psychological issues facing mum and whatever was eating Alex up that he just didn't want to talk to me about. Things only deepened and got worse when I came downstairs to hear Alex screaming in the living room, mum was face down on the carpet and drooling, she'd been combining her red wine drinking and co-codamol exploits and was now completely passed out. We were prepared for anything by now, Alex had helped mum a number of times whilst I was at work and despite pouring multiple bottles, boxes, and half-filled glasses of red wine down the kitchen sink on a regular basis, there seemed no end to mums' pattern of self-destruction. I placed mum in the recovery position (something both Alex and I had learnt from YouTube as a failsafe precaution from the last time something happened to her) and Alex rang in for an ambulance. The response was quick, and it wasn't long before a team of paramedics were in the house overseeing mum, they concluded their visit by placing mum in the back of an ambulance. The medical team had said that there wasn't a possibility of her being taken to Scunthorpe General Hospital and so instead we had to drive to Grimsby, some twenty to thirty minutes away. Following that ambulance on the M180 Motorway to Grimsby was difficult, Alex was quietly crying and looking out the window next to me whilst I followed the ambulance in tow to the hospital. There was no music, just the sound of the engine and the sniffles come from both Alex and me as we tried to keep our composure, the year just seemed to be going from bad to worse and if the situation worsened with mum, it almost seemed like she wouldn't be around much longer. That drive to the hospital had me seriously contemplating that fact, what would happen to Alex and me if that actually happened? What should I tell Lynda? She had to know at some point what had happened, how would THAT conversation even go? Eventually, we made it to the hospital, my mind still racing with multiple thoughts as we followed the team through the wards to be seated outside a particular ward used for recovery. After the nursing staff had assessed mum and put some tubes in her arms, Alex and I were ushered in to see her. It was almost like déjà vu, Alex and I once again stood at the foot of the bed of one of our parents, in a hospital room that felt cold. Once again, I looked to Alex, he was staring forward as I'd seen him do some months before when dad had passed away, there was a few tears rolling down his face, but what I really saw, was how exhaustingly tired he was. He was completely drained, emotionally and physically, I'd never seen him look so thin in his face before, or at least I'd never noticed it before. Since the beginning of the year, I'd tried my best to be the supportive older brother, I never smothered him with questions or impromptus affection, that wasn't really our style together anyway. We'd joke occasionally, watch crappy TV together or even on the odd occasion, play video games together (or at the very least, watch one another play video games). After seeing mum for about twenty or thirty minutes, the nursing staff came and asked us to leave, mum needed to rest, and so we made our way back to Scunthorpe, the car remaining silent, aside from the hum of the car engine.

There was a lot to process in that early part of 2011, two family members had passed away, mum was in a deep spiral herself, the family was all still in mourning in their own particular ways. A couple of days after mum had been discharged from the hospital, I made another appointment to see Dr Ballah, I relayed to him the escapades that had happened since I'd last seen him and he gave me a Dr's note to take another week off from work. I knew that despite my personal resolve (a façade to mask the reality of my issues really) that Alex needed major support otherwise who knows what'll happen with him and mum needed someone to keep an eye on her other than Alex. After the experience with mum, my Amazon book purchases increased exponentially, huge bundles and boxes of books arrived at the house a few days apart, I needed to know more, become better, I needed to find something to help in any way I could. Suddenly, during a long eight hour reading session in my bedroom, the Anti-depressants which Dr Ballah had issued me with six months prior when dad had passed away, appeared in my drawer, after I'd quickly searched for a note pad to jot some ideas I was reading down onto. I'd realised as the pack of tablets knocked into the front of the drawer from the way that I'd quickly opened it, that maybe Dr Ballah was right, maybe I was suffering from some sort of depression which I was trying to ignore. The pack of tablets was a dosage which would last for two weeks and seeing as though I wasn't distracting myself with work for at least the first week, now might be a good time to do some TLC. I popped two tablets into my mouth and washed them down with a swig of Red Bull and waited to see the affects. I waited for around half an hour to forty-five minutes, but didn't notice anything immediate, so after closing one of the financial books I was reading and wiping my eyes from the tiredness that my eight-hour reading session had resulted in, I made my way downstairs to see Alex. As I opened the living room door, I saw Alex slumped in the sofa his eyes somewhat glazing over as he watched the TV documentary about the 2008 Financial markets crash. Alex has always enjoyed a good documentary although most of them involved serial killers or plane crashes, so in a way the documentary from 2008 was still on theme (in some way) even if the details and intricacies of the topics being discussed were comparatively different. As the interviews with former bankers and Wall Street big wigs continued, the narrative on the TV referred to the CFD trading that had taken place in years leading to 2008. Seconds before any information was mentioned about it, I leaned across to Alex whose eyes were still glaring at the screen and mentioned a bunch of financial details that surrounded CFD trading. Seconds after I had mentioned the information to him, the narrator on the TV repeated what I'd just told Alex. Alex's head whipped around to me, 'How did you know that?!' he asked, the glazed look in his eyes had disappeared and now he was fully engaged with me. I rattled off a bunch more of financial jargon that had clearly stuck in my mind from the books I was reading, and some elements of those details were soon after mentioned on the documentary. Alex was stunned and confused, 'Seriously, how did you know that?' his confusion accompanied by a slight smile that was creeping onto his face. I quickly jumped up from the sofa and headed upstairs to grab the book I'd been recently consuming to show Alex some of what I'd learnt. The memory of seeing dad reading had fuelled a fire of learning inside of me and I was reading all kinds of books at this point, books on History, Science, Finance, Business, Economics, Psychology, Philosophy, Body Language, Persuasion, Sales, Self-Improvement, anything, and everything that was non-fiction I was acquiring and learning from. I emerged back in the living room holding the FT book which outlines the general ideas and understanding of how the Stock Market works and I flipped to the page where the reference of the housing market was mentioned. As Alex read those pages, his eyes widened, 'You learnt about the Stock Market from this book?' Alex asked, 'well, not just THAT book Ale, but yeah I learnt what that guy on TV had said' (that guy being Matt Damen's narrative voice). Alex and I then sat and watched the remainder of the documentary and after it had finished, we sat and talked for another four hours about it all, asking questions to one another and proposing ideas to various topical elements that popped up during our exchanges. I knew I'd found an intrigue for Alex, something that could help guide him through the myriad of turmoil's surrounding us at the time, it was reading, granted, he wouldn't read as much as me, but he did read plenty that culminated in a lively version of discussion in our future travels when driving to competitions and to dance lessons again. A type of revival had happened to his spirit (or so it seemed to me) as our conversations in the car ranged from philosophy, to history, finance, and psychology. We talked about science and a little maths, along with our inevitable conversations about dancing as well, we were back! Not the same as before, in truth we never would be, but we were back in the saddle, the lessons resumed as normal in the studio and after finding ourselves new dance partners, the competitions also resumed. We were back in the car, the stereo playing the alternating CD of choice from one of us and conversations and jokes were flowing once again. Finally, it seemed like there was a little light emerging in the tunnel that represented our darkened experience of 2011, finally, we were rebuilding ourselves.

Chapter 9 A Front Row Seat

'Look, there I am Ale! Can you see me?' I was excitedly standing by the TV in the living room and gloating to Alex, whilst I pointed at the screen of mums' 42-inch flat screen TV on a paused still frame of the new DVD I'd purchased from the British Open Championships in 2012. With a sigh and a huff Alex responded, 'Yes Ian, I see you, Alex's response was exasperated as I'd paused the DVD few times already during the course of our viewing and all he wanted to do was watch the Professional Latin Championship Final from Blackpool. I, on the other hand, was more interested in making him feel bad for making the decision to not to come with me to Blackpool that year and by highlighting him what he'd missed out on. After a rollercoaster of a year in 2011 Alex and I had ended the year without dancing partners once again, My very brief partnership with a girl named Amy from Liverpool had only lasted from around August up until the National Championships in November and Alex had danced with a lovely girl named Emily from Essex for a few months in February to June (of which I believe he established a romantic relationship with) but because Alex wasn't able to travel down south to train with her, the partnership eventually ended. His next partnership was with a girl named Jess from Sheffield, which lasted the same duration as mine did with Amy. Both Amy and Jess were a little bit younger than Alex and me who were now in our earlier twenties, sixteen or seventeen to be exact and they became very good friends with one another during the short stint as dance partners to Alex and me. We'd experience practice sessions together and even though things weren't comparatively the same as when I'd danced with Nat, it did feel like we were establishing those familiar teamwork aspects which were involved over the years prior. Regrettably, both partnerships ended in December of that year at around roughly the same time which meant that as both Alex and I headed into 2012, we would once again be on the lookout for new dance partners.

The British Open Dance Championships has always had special significance to any and all manner of dancer, it's the place where no matter what style of dancing you find yourself experiencing, everything is on the line as you battle to become the champion in the most historic of dancing venues. In my younger years, Blackpool would be home to Disco, Rock'n'Roll, Street Dance, Classical and modern sequence dancing along with UKA medallist competition dancing.

Alex and I never ventured into the world of Open Ballroom and Latin dancing until my early junior years with my first British Open Championship experience taking place when I was twelve and of which was hosted in the Tower Ballroom in Blackpool. It was only the Adults, the Professionals and the Amateurs who were allowed to dance the British Open Championships in the Winter Gardens Ballroom and that's one of the reasons why the venue has so much significance to a lot of people. If you were a dancer from the UK though, you'll find yourself dancing the British National Championships in the Winter Gardens in mid-November and for me, that feeling of familiarity would come rushing back. I'd spent 2011 trying to hold the family together and supporting them whenever and wherever I could and because of this, my dancing had taken a little bit of a back seat. I'd posted adverts and messaged people, looking for a new potential dance partner, but by mid-April, there weren't any possible prospects. As May rolled around, dancers were gearing up for the British Open Championships and I knew I had to get myself there somehow. It was around that time, that I received a Facebook message from a girl named Olga (clearly from Russia). She was a petit girl with a Black bob-haircut, she was the Russian Youth Champion for Latin dancing and she'd seen I was looking for a dance partner and had messaged me to see about organising a dance trial. I'd made friends with a number of Russian and Italian people over the years at competitions and being affiliated with Sergey and Lev (two Russian brothers whom Alex and I had spent time training alongside). Which resultantly meant that there a large amount of people on my social media at the time who were European. Olga's English was passable, and we were able to establish a dialogue with one another, it turned out that she was going to be at the British Open Championships at the end of May and we decided to organise a dance trial together whilst we were at the festival. For me, this was a big deal, I'd never danced with someone of such a high calibre before, I didn't know what to expect. The only relatable experience I had was when I'd trained and danced with Nikki and her stern teaching and disciplined, take no shit attitude. But those days were long gone, after some form of dispute with David (I'm given to understand) they'd left, and we never saw them again. Well… we did see them again at the Nationals in November a few years later in 2009 where they watched the competition and saw us both dancing with our partners. Mum had spotted them in the crowd from the balcony above, where she always sat, and we promptly made our way down to see them. It had been such a long time since we'd last seen them both and we were eager to hear from them again. Making our way down to them, mum went to give them both a big hug. Alex and I hugged Nikki and Will gave us a "cool guy handshake", the type of handshake you see when two characters in a movie who join forces near the climax of the film or something. Nervously I asked them both, 'did you happen to see us dancing?' Alex and I had so much respect for them both, they were initially our first coaches, and we were desperate to know if they approved of how we'd developed since they'd last seen us. 'Will saw you both dancing in the last round actually' Nikki replied, 'but I only saw a little bit of your dancing'. Alex and I paused, waiting to hear Nikki's judgment, like Julius Ceaser she would provide her verdict, thumbs up or thumbs down, would we live, or would we be fed to the lions? 'From what I saw you've both become much stronger, your technique has improved a lot and Will thought you both had developed a lot more power in your dancing'. That was like music to our ears, we didn't care how the rest of the competition went, that praise was something we'd craved for so long and when they had to leave and we didn't hear from them again, we almost felt a little lost. Alex then boldly asked them both, 'what do you think we should focus on in the next round?' a ballsey question really, Will and Nikki weren't our teachers or our coaches anymore, but eagerly I leaned in to hear their answer. 'Try and keep more grounded' Will said as he looked to me and then across to Alex, we both nodded a confirmatory nod and then glanced to Nikki, would she be kind enough to give us a little extra advice? In reality, neither of them really had to give us anything in terms of feedback, it could have all been pleasantries and general conversation, but Alex and I desperately wanted and valued their input, they were hugely inspirational to us both and we had so much respect for them. 'Like Will said, you need to be more grounded, when you're not grounded into the floor with your weight, you look off balance' that was all the advice they had for us, they were kind enough to give us even that, but soon after their praise and advice was given, the band began to re-emerge onto the stage and the fanfare, ubiquitous to the British dance festival (both open and closed) began to play, signifying the re-commencement of the competition. Alex and I quickly said our goodbyes as we had to go find our partners and get ready for the next round and mum left to join dad on the balcony where they could both watch the next round from. As the numbers for the next round were called onto the floor, couples made their way to their starting positions. Alex was in the heat before me and when his number was announced into the next round, he made his way to the centre of the floor to start his Cha-Cha. At the conclusion of Alex's heat, the remaining numbers were announced, and I boldly took to the floor in full awareness that both Will and Nikki would be looking for me. I danced that next round with so much speed, power, and energy, I wanted to do them both proud as I felt them watching from the crowd. Blackpool lighting at those Championships has a type of mystique to it when you're out on the floor. Because of the lighting in the rafters above the floor and the spotlights beaming from the highest corners of the ballroom, you don't tend to see faces in the crowd when you look out to the audience, more like a darkened mass of heads and bodies. As I danced past where Will and Nikki were sat, I heard faint calls for my number being shouted, it was them, they were cheering for me and supporting me as I danced my choreography. At the close of the next round, both Alex and I were knackered, we literally went all out in an effort to do Will and Nikki proud and after we'd managed to recover from the various stitches, we both had received for our efforts, we went to go find them once again to see if we'd done any better. This time though, the seats where they were sat were empty and as the competition progressed and we were resultantly knocked out of the event in the following round. We eagerly surveyed the crowd of people sat watching the competition, from the balcony above to see if Will and Nikki were in the crowd watching to see if we had made it back into the next round. Sadly however, we never saw them and the interaction we had with them at the National Championships that year, was the very last time we ever saw them.

With Alex and I sharing a hotel for the entirety of the British festival in 2011, we regularly made our way to the winter Gardens Ballroom each morning for practice sessions hosted by the organisers. On one of the days that Alex and I were there in Blackpool, I received the message from Olga confirming the location and time of our dance trial. I was so nervous, this was my first international dance trial, all the other girls I'd danced with were from the UK and the sense of familiarity meant that even if the partner was new, there was something common for us to relate to. This time, things were different, I nervously grabbed my towel, shoes and a bottle of water and made my way to one of the upstairs dance space areas found in the Winter Gardens. Making my way into the room, the sounds of clicks and the placing of steps could be heard by Latin dancers rehearsing through their choreography and the sudden and harsh breathing noises used as couples turned and hit poses with one another. You normally don't hear these elements when you watch as an audience member in the competitions, but dancers use their breathing extensively to maximise their movements and to emphasise key highlight moments of their choreography, whether that's by using harsh breaths out, or slow inward breaths to essentially "breathe one another in" and collect energy. These were the sensory elements my ears and eyes depicted after I had entered that room and situated myself by standing along the back row of some of the arranged seating, as I scanned the room looking for Olga. On the right-hand side, sat on the front row, I saw her, Olga was fixing her shoes and was already dressed In her dance wear, I shook off any remaining nerves I had about meeting her for the first time, and I made my way over to her. After a few pleasantries and double kisses on the cheek, that never actually kisses, it's more like kissing the air really, she directly asked me, 'So what dance are we doing?' This was a first for me, I'd never been the one to completely decide what would be done in a dance trial. My previous dance trial experiences were always supervised by a teacher and so I hesitantly thought and responded 'Rumba, let's do Rumba'. We then took to the floor together to dance some basic choreography; I literally had no idea what the hell I as doing. I tried to mimic a general template that David used to use whenever I had danced a dance trial in the studio, but it didn't take long before Olga began to recommend chorographical elements she'd danced with a former partner. To be honest there were a number of contrasting elements at play when I experienced that dance trial. Firstly, I was competently holding my own with a Russian Champion, I didn't feel out matched or incapable in any way you might have thought and any of the suggestions that Olga provided were immediately taken on board and used. Secondly, when it came to inputs that I had, Olga respectfully worked with the ideas to help create a flow for us both, I'd mainly asked and worked with the feeling of the connection, it was too lax for me and there wasn't enough tension for me to use in the connection. As soon as Olga gave me the response in connection, I was able to then place her on her foot more clearly and strongly, which in turn allowed her to maximise her hip movements. There was a flow, a rhythm and I felt so invigorated by the experience, I was dancing with a European girl, and I wasn't shit! Usually, English dancers are terrible when compared to European dancers, but I felt on par with Olga, maybe technically she had better movement, a higher quality in technique when compared with my own ability, but it seemed like it worked. After an hour and a half of working together, she gestured to the side and mentioned she had to go with her coach, I looked to where she was pointing and saw her coach standing behind the row of seating at the back of the room. A tall stoic looking figure in a black turtleneck top, with trimmed facial hair and long, slicked back hair, characteristically adopted by many Latin dancers. He wasn't there when I had first arrived, but he was there by the end of the session between Olga and me. She mentioned that he had asked a friend to make videos of the dancing which were in turn sent to her coach and she concluded the discussion by telling me that they were going to have food together, where he would assess the quality of the dancing to see if it was a good match. Within the space of about five minutes the whole experience was over, and I was left in the hall by myself, absorbing the entirety of what had just happened. I then promptly sat down in the seat that was next to Olga's, where all my stuff was kept and called Alex, I figured we could meet up to go for a coffee and I could then tell him how my experience with one of Russia's finest had gone. Later that evening I received a message from Olga, she stated that after the British Championships were over, that she'd be flying back home to Russia as there was another dance trial she was having and that she'd be in touch with what her coach thought sometime after that. I didn't worry about any of it, I was also still looking for a partner and had another dance trial arranged in a few weeks as well. Less than a week later, she messaged me again to say that they'd decided to move forward with the other partner in Russia (which makes sense when you think about it) and the conversation concluded with her thanking me for the experience at Blackpool.

That experience taught me a lot and it made me realise something very important and somewhat profound which in turn shifted my thinking. Reflecting on the experience with Alex in the Café Nero just down the high street in Blackpool, I became aware of the fact that I wasn't as bad as I thought I was. In fact, my ability had increased so much over the years that not only was I holding my own with a Russian youth finalist, but I was also able to make suggestions to her, which in turn helped make the dancing better and easier for us both. When I look back to that experience, what comes to mind is that scene in the Avengers Infinity war movie, #Spoileralert. During the climax of the movie there's a fight scene between Tony Stark and Thanos, the antagonist of the movie, as they duke it out on a desolated planet far from earth, eventually Tony lands a blow to Thanos which causes him to bleed. This in turn prompts Thanos to disappointingly say, 'All that for a drop of blood'. The scene is compelling because the antagonist, Thanos, is massively powerful with capability of destroying entire worlds. Because Tony sees him bleed, he learns that he can be defeated, or at least he's able to see the fact that he can be defeated. I feel that scene encapsulates my experience when I had that dance trial with Olga wonderfully, the perception I held was that Russian dancers were way up high on a pedal stool with their quality and their overall ability, and that I was much, much farther down the pecking order. That dance trial helped to disprove that idea, all the toil and hard work that I'd put myself through, that BOTH Alex and I had put ourselves through, it had all helped elevate us upward, we just couldn't see to what extent. That experience also helped us realise that the international level of dancing wasn't as high as we originally thought. Nothing is impossible and nothing is improbable either and my experience with Olga helped solidify a confidence and an understanding that, despite the façade that international competitors hold themselves with. They're all beatable, if I can competently hold my own with a Russian finalist, then what's to stop me from beating one in a competition, what's going to really stop me from climbing the ladder of success in my dancing on an international scale? Why can't I become a top six finalist in the world? That's been the goal ever since I entered the arena of Amateur dancing. If I trained hard enough and long enough, I'd eventually be on par with the top-level competitors of the world. My experience with Olga was a confirmatory sign from the universe that I was on the right track with it all, that even though the road was difficult and arduous, it was all slowly coming together.

After the British Open Championships had ended Alex and I sat down together to make a plan for the rest of the season, I still didn't have a partner at the time and Alex's new partner, Emily, was travelling to Scunthorpe from Essex most weekends for extra practice with him, alongside the lessons from David and Helen on a Wednesday. It wasn't long before the partnership reached a breaking point though and it abruptly ended, from what I can gather Emily was emphasising the need for Alex to travel down to London and have lessons down there. She was doing a lot of travelling compared with Alex and despite his inner turmoil of dads passing earlier that year, his part time work in Tesco just wouldn't allow for that to happen. Inevitably after four months of dancing together and dancing three competitions, the partnership ended, and he was once again looking for a new dance partner. The difficulty that we both faced at the time (aside from the grief of losing two family members and the constant worry over mum) was that we soon realised how the aspect of money in the dancing, played a hugely pivotal role in everything. Don't get me wrong, we weren't ever oblivious to the fact that we needed money to do the dancing, but after we excitedly sat down one evening during June/ July in 2011, we excitedly talked about dancing this International Championship and that Russian Open event, of dancing the Italian Open and the New York Open Dance Championships. There were so many events we could go to, so many events where we could showcase our ability and achieve what we were searching for. The only problem was the cost, plane tickets and hotels, entry fees and possible training camps that take place in and around the outlined events. They all had a price tag and after we looked into the surrounding logistics of them all, we soon realised how outmatched we were in that remit, not in actual dancing, that was the easy part (he ironically types, remembering the toil and pain of that evening he collapsed in the studio and was asked to go home). The hard part was actually finding a way to get to these events so that we could compete alongside the very best of the best. We eventually expanded these conversations out to David when we would go to the pub with him and Stagman on a Wednesday evening after training. But what we heard wasn't what we thought we'd hear, after one particular exchange, David responded by outlining how that would be a waste of our time. Alex has always been quite direct when he talks and when he's talking about something he deeply cares about (like his dancing) he generally doesn't care how his words come across, or how you might feel about them. 'Well Jack goes to the Russian and Italian comps, so why can't we?!' Alex's question was direct, and his tone was defiant, he didn't want to hear that he couldn't do something, and he was irritated that David had insinuated that he'd not be permitted to go and do something that he felt would benefit his dancing. The conversation circulated for a little while and eventually the discussion moved on, but the exchange stuck with us both. In the car journey back home, Alex and I began to unpack the discussion to find out what was really being conveyed. WHY was David saying that it would be a waste of time for us? Surely having another English couple competing in an oversees event would be a good thing, right? We'd not be able to participate in the World or European Championships anytime soon, not only because there was a huge inconsistency of partners for us both, but because at a meeting which took place at the National Championships in 2010, the affiliation which EADA had with the European dancing body and an announcement of EADA's dissolving, was the primary topic of discussion.

The outline of the meeting which summoned most of Britain's best dancers (and Alex, me, and Nat) was to surmise the fact that the big wigs at EADA were in a position where they couldn't be affiliated with the IDSF (an international body of dancing, which is mainly centralised in Europe, now known as the

WDSF). It was all politics and the BDF organisation (Ballroom Dance Federation) was banning anyone who would decide to compete in any IDSF events, again it was all politics bullshit. This banning was already being implemented, our friends Jonas and Jasmine had been banned because they had danced at an IDSF event somewhere in Europe and because of the politics (which in reality is just a collection of old men grumbling about who controls the world of dancing). They'd been issued with an official letter from the dancing board of Britain and weren't permitted to compete in any and all of the competitions in the UK for the rest of the year. Voices were raised in that meeting and concerns were put forward and it was outlined that EADA, the official flagship of British dancing and a huge instigator to the development of dancing, was being disbanded. But the dancing body who establish the rules for everything dance related in Britain, decided an overruling which outlined that if anyone is to dance and compete in "non-certified events" abroad, which aren't approved by the British board of dancing. That they will also receive a ban and suspension for the entire year and subsequently won't be permitted to dance any of the major championships. Again, it was all bullshit politics and scare tactics and Alex, Nat and I left the room feeling dejected and uncertain for the following year of dancing. For Nat and I this was a huge deal, if there were no more EADA comps, then what was the point in actually competing and driving all over the country and killing ourselves to acquire points. What was it all for? If the next day the EADA organisation was folded, then there'd be no reason for people to work as hard in their dancing, nationally, and that would mean that the resulting quality of dancing In Britain would decline. It was a real shit-show affair to say the least.

Alex and I had worked so hard in 2010 and all we wanted to do was to join the club of top-level dancers, we wanted to be in that world where discussions on high level dancing, big championship events and hardcore training sessions which could easily be glued together like a montage in a movie, were. The experiences of 2011 severely rocked the boat for us both and the turbulent water, we found ourselves on (keeping with the analogy) deterred us and hindered us, but it never stopped us. Conversations between Alex and David escalated over the ensuing months, and real differences of opinion started to emerge. David also wasn't restrained in calling Alex a twat, which was put forward in a jokey kind of way initially, but over time, became more and more common as Alex talked about differing ideas and potential concepts surrounding the dancing that David contrastingly didn't agree with. In 2012

Alex began to skip the odd Wednesday lesson, we'd always travelled with one another on a Wednesday and understandably 2011 has shaken things up a bit, but Alex still made sure he came to the Wednesday training sessions despite the agony and turmoil he was experiencing from losing two family members and the ordeals of mum's circumstances. In 2012 he'd had enough of the derogative feeling he'd been getting from his interactions with David, constantly being called a twat had moved past the point of being a joke to him and now he took it personally and Alex decided to start skipping the odd Wednesday lesson in 2012. He never stopped training, he just didn't bother to come on a Wednesday as much, maybe once or twice a month he'd skip a Wednesday lesson. Choosing instead to either stay home to train, or to just take the day for himself and relax by playing video games and going out. Whenever Alex didn't go to the studio, the question was always asked, 'so where's the twat?' I'd initially respond jokingly by saying he'd stayed home but after a while I began to see how the term was being used derogatively to him and soon began to voice my displeasure in hearing Alex referred to that name and how he doesn't like being called that. It fell on deaf ears most of the time, as David would occasionally refrain from calling Alex a twat when he did eventually come down to the studio in Wolverhampton. But it wouldn't take long for that reserved attitude to eventually dissipate and for the term to be used more frequently, which in turn would result in Alex skipping the following week or two, depending on how annoyed he'd become at it all.

By the time the 2012 British Open Championships had rolled around Alex was in a flux of not going to lessons and not finding a partner. I'd mentioned how I was looking at going to the Professional Latin night in Blackpool, I fiscally wasn't able to stay all week like I'd done the year before and so I was looking to only go on one night. Unfortunately, this was in and around the time that Alex was putting his foot down with me sharing the use of his car, I'd had to scrap my own car a few years earlier and we'd been sharing his red Fiat Punto interchangeably as we traversed the British countryside attending all manner of competitions. Now he had a new car and was probably beginning to feel forms of resentment from dancing in the studio (no doubt resulting from his exchanges with David and constantly being labelled a twat) and he point blank told me that he was using his car all week and that if I wanted to go to the British Championships so badly, that I should just find my own way there. In that moment I was taken aback by how selfish I thought he was being, and we got into a huge argument over it, which resulted in us not speaking to one another for a few days. I realise looking back on it that I was the one being selfish, I'd decided to buy my own ticket for the night in the Ballroom, and I'd made plans in my own head of how I was going to spend the day there in Blackpool, but I'd not considered the fact that Alex would decide to not let me take his car for the day. I quickly made arrangements to check train times and book tickets for a mapped out journey using Britain's rail network. I don't like using public transport personally, I'm not a big fan of it at all, I rarely use buses and trains and I'll only use taxis IF I really have to. The only acceptable form of public transport I've grown comfortable with is flying and using a ferry, as navigating the sea or the air would be a difficult one for me to do on my lonesome. If I need to get anywhere in the country, I'm much more comfortable and happier when I can hop behind the wheel of the car and drive myself there. I think it's because when I'm driving, I feel like I'm the one whose fully in control, if something happens whilst I'm on the road then that's clearly my fault and I'll deal with it. But if something happens when using public transport, then I'm helplessly stuck waiting for the situation to resolve itself. I much prefer the freedom of travelling independently and autonomously to wherever it is that I need to go to. When the day of the Professional Latin Championships took place, I had to wake up super early, whilst everyone was tucked up in bed, I was grabbing the first train out of Scunthorpe at a brisk and early 7:00am. My journey to Blackpool that day was a bit of a complicated one to say the least, with me taking the initial train from Scunthorpe to Doncaster, changing to get a train from Doncaster to Leeds, which in turn traversed me from Leeds to Preston and concluding my initial trip with a final change of trains once again which would take me from Preston to Blackpool. A total of four train journeys and I'd be in Blackpool. Regrettably, it was the same situation for me coming back home as well and with how late the British dance festival I was prone to run to. I was worried about making it back to the station on time for my pilgrimage home and at 7:00am I was riding the rails on my way to Doncaster, my first stop along the way. I'd chosen to wear a navy-blue suit I'd bought a couple of years ago, a nice clean shirt and a pristine tie, I felt well and truly suited and booted for the day ahead in the Winter Gardens Ballroom and the potential to "rub shoulders" with some of the industry's notoriety.

After reaching Doncaster I waited on the next platform for around half an hour, surprisingly to me, the train for Leeds rolled up exactly on time and after the doors pinged open, I made my way in and found myself another seat. Anytime I've been a passenger in the car my habit since I was very young, has always been to stare out the window at the passing countryside, travelling all across the countryside as a kid, dancing in all kinds of competitions and visiting various places, has meant that I've grown up travelling the British motorways quite a lot. Sundays were always competition days in one form or another and it would be more common for mum, Lynda, Alex, and me, to traverse ourselves around the countryside over the weekend attending any and all manner of dancing event, than it was to sit down all together and have a Sunday dinner (although we did do that occasionally). When I was sat on the train both from Scunthorpe to Doncaster and from Doncaster to Leeds, that feeling of looking out the window at the passing scenery, instantly came back to me. 2011 had been a roller coaster of a year and I'd handled it the best way I could, it wasn't perfect by any means and there were a lot of issues I still needed to sort out, but I'd done my best with it all and 2012 was shaping up to be something entirely different. At the time of me venturing to the British Open Latin Championships, I'd already established a brand-new partnership with a young girl called Leah, from Wales, in the early part of May and unfortunately there just wasn't enough time for the two of us to get our dancing organised to compete in the upcoming British Championships. As I stared out the window of my various train rides from Scunthorpe to Doncaster, from Doncaster to Leeds, and the remaining journey from Leeds to Preston and my final excursion from Preston to Blackpool. I deeply contemplated where I was, both in my dancing and in my life, my newly established partnership had forced me to make the decision to unfortunately give up my Latin dancing and to specialise in the Ballroom section only. I'd gotten pretty good at assessing the various potential partners that came along over the years, having dance trials and conversations about what things would be like training wise etc. Nat had set such a high bar from our partnership that I resultantly measured everyone and anyone that I came into contact with, against her. Simply stated, no one matched her, not her drive or determination, nor her passion and desire for continued improvement. Dancing both styles to a high standard is exceptionally taxing both physically and mentally, dancing the Ballroom requires not just physical tonality and structured training, but a deep understanding of how you move your body and steps in co-ordination with your partner. Dancing the Latin tends to lean more into the physical side than it does its technical side, where the aspect of stamina plays a huge role. People who dance the 10-Dance genre are stereotypically type cast into being seen as doing one side of the genre better than the other and I'd spent my entire dancing career trying to break that stigmatic ideology. The long and short of it all was that I wasn't in a position to have an International/ European partner, there's a huge requirement to essentially support them by providing housing, a means to make a living and few other minor contributory factors. It seemed too much of a trade-off, despite the fact that they would be capable of handling the 10-Dance genre and my ridiculous training structure. So that meant I had to begrudgingly find a British girl to dance with. Most girls don't like the idea of doing finals with weights on their arms and legs, they don't like the idea of getting sweaty and potentially ruining their makeup. Most girls, typically want to "experience" their dancing with swishy Ballroom skirts and the ease of movement, lessons, and practices of Ballroom dancing (which is starkly contrasted with the more intense style of Latin training). That's a huge accusation, I know, but having spent over 30 years in the industry I've rarely seen anything that juxtaposes that statement. My newly established partnership with Leah was where I had to make the decision of dancing back on the floor again or waiting around for another six to twelve months "hoping" for another Nat to come along. Frankly, there wouldn't be another Nat, so I cut my losses and specialised in the Ballroom with Leah. Leah didn't have any objection at doing the Latin dancing, but her background in Modern Sequence and Classical Sequence dancing (a form and variation of Ballroom dancing where everyone on the floor dances the same sixteen bar structure of choreography) meant that specialising in the Ballroom was the easiest option for the couple to pursue, as an incredible amount of training would be required to get her up to scratch with the baseline technique for the Open level Latin dancing. My contemplation as I stared out the window had me wondering if I'd made the right decision, that if I'd held off from dancing with Leah, that maybe someone else would come along. I was also beginning to process my own emotions a little at this stage with the passing of two family members the year before and the turmoil that mum had found herself in, along with supporting Alex. There was a lot to process, and I hadn't handled it in the best way to be completely honest, exhausted of any options of what to do and where to go, feeling lost and isolated I contemplated throwing myself from a random bridge in Scunthorpe. The cold forceful gust of wind knocking me back from the railing had snapped me out the daze like feeling I had experienced and which led me up there, and I gingerly climbed back down nervous of the height which was now triggering my fear of hights (when I say fear of hights, I mean I just don't like them, I'm not scared or anything, but I just don't like hights... well, maybe I am scared of heights, really). There was a lot to unpack and process and I'd neglectfully abandoned any thought or feeling which related to the experiences of 2011 and early 2012. I'd spent so much time "just cracking on" and waking up early and going to be late reading all kinds of books, which covered a vast array of subjects I'd never even considered to be interesting. All that acquisition of knowledge provided me with what I felt was a heightened form of understanding (well, at least when compared to the dumb ass state I was in prior to 2011) the scene from The Count Of Monte Cristo comes to mind as my personal development felt reminiscent of the characters time in jail where he is taught by another prisoner, an old man, the inner working s of the world in a multitude of facets.

As the screech of the train wheels rolled into the station at Blackpool, I began my pilgrimage to the Winter Gardens, it was around 12:00pm by the time I'd made it to Blackpool and so I felt that if I made my way to the Ballroom, I'd still manage to catch some of the earlier rounds of the Professional Latin currently underway. After the security staff scanned my ticket by the entranceway to the Winter Gardens, I began to meander through the various stalls in and around the foyer area of the Winter Gardens, these were the stalls where I'd regularly buy DVDs and CDs from, but not this time, I was somewhat flat broke after needing to purchase the various train tickets to get to Blackpool and forking out money for both a morning ticket and an evening ticket to the ballroom. After perusing some of the nearby stalls I eventually made my way into the ballroom. The winter Gardens has always felt like a home away from home to me, maybe it's the same for every dancer that finds themselves in that venue. There's a history and a form of legacy which surrounds that place when it comes to dancing and in many ways, it feels like I've contributed towards that history whenever I've attended an event there. The smell of the old Ballroom is the first sensation to greet the senses as you enter the foyer to the ballroom and the cushioned carpet springs and squishes under your feet and as you make your way towards the white doors off to the right and you feel the railings on the stairs as you walk down to the Ballroom, there's just something euphoric, something atmospherically ineffable which wraps around you and helps you feel so invited into that ballroom. The whole place comes alive and as I think back to the countless times, I've experienced that feeling walking down into the Ballroom as a kid, dancing rock'n'roll, disco and street dance competitions. Dancing Classical and Modern Sequence events, my medallist Ballroom and Latin, Junior and Youth Ballroom and Latin events and later in life my Amateur and Professional career as well. I have a lot of great memories being there and that feeling of being present in that Ballroom to experience all the sensory elements that it holds, it's something that I feel will stay with me forever. As I felt my hand slide down the central railing of the staircase which leads into the ballroom, memories and experiences of the National Championships came into my mind. Every morning at the National Championships in November, the Blackpool Festival would allow competitors to come into the ballroom for a few hours to do some additional practicing and warming up. This also happened at the Open event too, but at the Nationals, because there's less people, the feeling of being in the ballroom during that practice time in the mornings, feels symbolic, it feels special. There were many times when I'd slide my hand down the smooth golden coloured, central railing, with my fingers rolling over the bumpy connection pieces of the railings, as I made my way into the ballroom to practice. The echoes of voices and footwork being heard across the floor and, depending on what time I'd arrive at, a bit of Blackpool Empress Orchestra Waltz music might also be playing. Those memories, those feelings are what I experienced as I made my way down the steps and into the ballroom for the Professional Latin, the only difference was that the competition was in full flow, the smell of sweat, tan and various perfumes and colognes were in the air, the ballroom was hot, and the crowds of people were bustling. I was in the thick of it, I was where I felt I wanted to be.

When you arrive at the bottom of the steps in the Winter Gardens ballroom you find there's a carpeted walkway which encircles the entire ballroom, allowing people the freedom to move and walk around, without the need to constantly walk across the floor. The red cushioned seating is arranged on a floor space that overlooks the dance floor, of which is arranged with a selection of seating which is placed at the floor level, and a back tier of seating which is elevated onto a slight platform. This form of seating is the standard arrangement for the dance festival events as the idea allows for the audience to have the maximum opportunity to see the dancing. As a I meandered through the bustling crowds of people, the sound of the next heats Samba could be heard playing. As I walked along the long stretch of walkway that extends down behind all the seating which is situated directly in front of the stage. I found myself squeezing past competitors, coaches, the odd renowned dance figure, my plan was to meander down and around the ballroom to where David would be sat as I knew he wouldn't be there at that time of the day and so his seat on the front row, would be available. I didn't want to walk the other way around the floor, as that would take me through what's known as "The Ice Room", a segregated part of the ballroom situated behind the stage and where large fire doors at ither end divided the ballroom from the colder warehouse like backrooms of the ballroom. During National Championship events, that room has a selection of tables and chairs distributed throughout for competitors to place their gear on. At world events like the British Open festival, the number of people back there is tripled maybe even quadrupled which means it's all "argy bargy" to try and get through them all. Walking the other way meant I was less likely to be struck in the face by a rogue hand placement or wildly flung arm line, less likely, but not impossible. Eventually, I made it to the front row seating, I'd been told numerous times over countless years how I looked like William Pino and whenever I competed in international events, that look of similarity really became apparent. When I wasn't in my competition gear, that look wasn't as familiar, but there were still times when dancers would give me a type of look which conveyed the idea that they thought I either was him or looked like him. Anyway, the cluster of Asian people situated on the front row seating, were sat where I wanted to sit. There are two types of tickets you can buy for the British Championships (both the Open and Closed events in May and November, respectfully) seating tickets which as you expect, provide you with a seat and "rover" tickets which allow you to enter the ballroom and hope there's a spare seat somewhere. Tickets with a seat number are stupidly more expensive, as you pay a premium for the guarantee of having an actual seat for the evening. The "rover" tickets are a lot cheaper (by comparison, at the time of writing I think a "rover" ticket for the British Open Championships is in or around £50). I didn't have the luxury of spending the money for a seat at the event and so I'd just bought a "rover" ticket when I arrived at the box office to the Winter Gardens. I knew David wouldn't be making an appearance until a little later in the day, as he was doing the Dance News write up that evening for the Professional Latin, a fact he had told me, the last time I'd seen him in the dance studio. (The Dance News Newspaper is a circulated tabloid within the dancing industry which talks about the latest happenings in the dancing world, in short, it's the Financial Times [FT] of the dancing world). This Asian collective were sitting in those seats and so I knew they didn't have seat tickets, I boldly made my way over and gestured for them to move up, allowing me to sit in David's allocated seat on the front row. As I sat watching the rest of the heats in the Samba section, I studied, who looks strong, who looks like they're going to make it through to the next round and I watched the technique and movements of the couples on the floor. In a way I was at the wrong event, as I'd now specialised in ballroom and so you'd have thought that I should have been watching the Professional Ballroom, not the Professional Latin. But I knew that my Ballroom skill would go from strength to strength with the specialisation, what I really needed to do, was ensure I maintained a solid grip on my Latin technique and understanding.

When Alex and I first began our more independent journeys into the world of Open Ballroom and Latin dancing, traversing the country for lessons and competitions and training every waking moment we could. We knew that we wanted to compete and become professional dancers and eventually, become teachers and coaches. Our friends Sergey and Lev would talk of their coaches back home in Russia and I was confused as to the use of the term, after pressing David about it in the studio one time, he stated that they were one and the same form of expression, but I wasn't too sure, I felt there was a distinct difference. Now, after my competition days and Professional career are behind me, I can honestly say there is a difference. Teachers are just that, teachers, they instruct you using information and guides to assist your learning of whatever technique or specific facet you're working on or need to improve. Good teachers are discerned from bad ones via their competent inner workings of connectivity, the information a "good" dance teacher will provide, versus a "bad" dance teacher, can easily be discerned with how well they can interweave the information they're telling you, with how it relates physically. "Bad dance teachers will tend to relay technique elements or jargon from the technique book and use that to justify their point to you. Coaches, on the other hand, are more involved, they're the ones pushing you, making you do finals, pushing you out of your comfort zone with harsh feedback and disciplined training. Becoming a teacher would require me to gain my qualifications by studying the technique book and pass my exams and essentially turn professional, which in essence was a little way off. The experience of becoming a coach to someone was soon approaching though and it entails an entire saga in and of itself, of which I'm more likely to write about in a future book, as the intricacies and details of the experience and the surrounding elements are quite adventurous and extensive. When I specialised in Ballroom dancing, I knew I had to retain that grip on the Latin dancing and the "spirit of being a 10-Dancer". I wanted to ensure I became a great teacher with comprehensible knowledge in both Ballroom and Latin, I didn't JUST want to be a Ballroom dancer who was also qualified in Latin dancing. I wanted to be a great dancer, period! Attending the British Open Professional Latin Championships would give me chance to see, in the fullest of respects, what I knew and what I didn't and to perhaps learn a cluster of information that I could not only take back to Alex, but that I could use for my own personal benefit. As the day rolled on the following round of the Professional Latin took place, some of the familiar faces from the semi-final stage were now on the floor and the competition was heating up. When dancers in the "big events" compete and make the semi-final and the final, they are permitted to have either one or two passes. This means that they're permitted to skip the first or second rounds of the competition as it's seen as they've "already proven themselves" and so are permitted to join in either the second or third round of the competition. If a top-level competitor ends a partnership and forms a new one, then the rules state that the new partnership must compete from the first round, as they are classed as a new couple. I watched as the semi-final contenders made their way onto the floor, the heats were reducing the number of contenders systematically and that meant that I could get a full glimpse at the dancers who had made it through and proven themselves on the floor. After the end of the ensuing round, there was another break in timetable, I couldn't leave my spot as I knew someone else might come and take my seat. So, I just had to wait and hope that I didn't need to go to the toilet, plus, David would be along shortly to begin his write up for the Professional Latin event and he'd inevitably want his seat. As the recommencement of the third round began, the finalists began to make their way onto the floor to join the remaining competitors. The ballroom was beginning to fill up as more crowd members were arriving and taking their seats and it was halfway through the third round Samba that David made his appearance. I quickly jumped up to give him his seat and after a quick exchange I slid behind onto the second row behind him, all the while the competition was continuing. Now I was in dangerous territory, the seats I was sat in could and probably DID belong to someone and it would only be a matter of time before I was once again shifted to another seat (if I weas lucky). As the last few heats were dancing their Paso Doble in the third round, I inevitably found myself being moved again, some European competitors (identifiable because the guy and girl still had their hair and makeup on and the slight amount of Italian they spoke, of which I could understand) came and shifted me, gesturing their tickets as a sign of ushering as they did so. Now I was on the back row of the seating, my five-foot-four (and a half) stature stretching and struggling to see anything of significance at this point. As the close of the third round ended, multitudes of people rose and left to grab a drink from the bar, the ballroom was beginning to really pack out with thousands of people. I knew I'd have to make a decision at some point and so I chose to stand by a nearby pillar which overlooked the ballroom floor and situated not far away from where David was seated to the right of the stage. The next round was the quarter finals, and I knew that where I was stood had the potential to get a little rough, I was in the crowd, and everyone wanted to get a front view of the competition. I'd have to find a way to keep my ground so that I didn't get pushed around and so that I didn't lose my spot overlooking the floor. During the break, the designated photographer for the Blackpool Dance Festival was sauntering around the floor space area and just happened to see me. There's a very strict understanding at Blackpool, that no-one is allowed to stand in the isles or walkways leading to and from the floor, not only is this because of fire safety regulations (it's somewhat the primary reason actually) but also because competitors need that space to walk onto the floor from. Security personnel patrol the ballroom and its balconies stopping people from congesting the isles and to catch any would be filming which takes place. A big no-no because there is a closed network TV (DSI TV) which films and records the whole competition (as a way of making extra money by selling the copies of the DVDs). The designated photographer (I'll call him Phil for simplicity as I don't remember his name) had a lanyard that allowed him to stand in that floor space and take official photographs of the competition. During the intermission period before and after the quarter finals Phil would chat and joke with me, his wife (for ease of narration I'll call her Sally) was sat in the end seat of the front row by David. It was technically a seat for Phil, but he was up taking photographs and so Sally was currently sat in his seat. David was two seats down from Sally and the seat which separated them was initially a seat reserved for Helen (David's wife), however she wasn't able to make it that night and so David had invited a teacher from Ireland, a lovely lady named Laura O'Brein to sit next to him on the front row. As the competition moved into the semi-final stage I quickly darted to the toilets, I'd not been since my arrival at Blackpool at 12:00pm and now it was close to 10:30pm, I bolted to the toilet, trying to ensure I wasn't gone too long and that the spot I'd been keeping hadn't been sneakily acquired by someone just waiting for a chance to get my front row viewing.

As I briskly made my way back to my selected spot by the pillar, my feet were really starting to burn and hurt (not as much as my stupid training session in the last chapter, but the pain element was certainly high), I'd been stood on them for about two or three hours now, using the occasional lean on the pillar beside me to ease the pain of my shoes. As soon as I re-emerged from the toilets, Phil saw me again and we began to chat again, the semi-final round was to start at around 11:30pm with the final for the Professional Latin not commencing until 12:15am at least. As I talked with Phil, he alluded to the fact that he didn't think his wife would last the night sat on the front row, she was already falling asleep (as both Phil and Sally were easily in their late sixties/ early seventies) and he said to me that, if she felt she needed to go back to the hotel, that I could potentially sit in his seat. As the semi-final round began, my feeling of excitement increased, there was a very real chance that I was going to get a front row seat at the British Championships! Me, humble beginnings Ian had fought through so much and it truly felt the universe was beginning to repay him a little something for all his toil and hardships. The Cha-Cha was the first dance and the best semi-finalists in the world battelled it out on the floor relentlessly against one another. As the competition switched gears for the Samba, the competitors were asked to leave the floor, they would be re-called into the semi-final, one dance at a time. As the same series of couples took to the floor for the Samba and the Empress Orchestra began the first few bars of Samba De La Torre, the crowd erupted, there was so much energy and life in the ballroom and that fed directly into each competitors performance as the Samba music played. The following dance was Rumba and a huge eruption from the crowd signified the fact that a new contender had been re-called into the Rumba, the competition truly was starting to shape up and the crowd went wild for the new arrival onto the floor. As the close of the Rumba ended the crowd extended its applause for the new couple who had fought for their semi-final dance. My feet were hurting so much but as soon as the competitors were called onto the floor for their semi-final Paso Doble, my focus switched to Ricardo and Yulia, an American couple, the number two in the world at that time and a couple I had watched immensely to gain technique and understanding in my own dancing from. As they took position directly in front of where everyone was standing, the crowds began to chant their favourite numbers and the orchestra began to play the renowned Spanish Gypsy music commonly played for Paso Doble. Because Paso Doble is a progressive dance it meant that I was only able to see part of Ricardo and Yulia's dancing before they disappeared behind the obscured view of the stage, fortunately however, the progressive nature of the dance meant that other top contending couples were able pass by, and the crowd roared as the current champions Michael and Joanna from Poland stormed past with their synonymous choreography which pulled elements of contemporary dance into the structure of their Paso Doble. The last dance of the semi-final was the Jive and if you'd thought the crowd couldn't get any louder, you'd have been sternly corrected. As each number was recalled, the crowd couldn't contain itself, eruption after eruption was heard as each of the expected semi-final contenders were announced onto the floor individually and as the music began to play, the crowds continued their support for their favourite couple. Flicks, tricks, spins and impacting movements were abound on the floor and the energy of the crowd was felt and reciprocated by the energy of the dancing on the floor. Dancing a semi-final at Blackpool is exceedingly taxing and harder than you might think. There's a lot happening out on that floor and it's all able to be seen by the best panel of adjudicators the world has to offer. After the close of the semi-final Jive and the extended applause from the crowds, the competitors left the floor, heading for the ice room behind the stage. The crowds which had pushed and shoved trying to squat a view of the competition had started to disperse and my feet were killing me, all I wanted to do was take my shoes off and sit down. But if I did that, I knew I'd lose my spot at the front of the crowds, after David had walked past and we'd exchanged a few statements and quips to one another, he left with Laura and headed to the bar. Phil then soon approached and mentioned that his wife was probably not going to last the night, he'd had to nudge her awake during the semi-final and was organising to send her back to the hotel. As the Empress Orchestra played its fanfare to signify the re-commencement of the competition, front row dignitaries of dance taking their seats for the full show about to be experienced from the world's best Latin dancers in the Professional division, David and Laura squeezed past everyone and made their way onto the front row again. As each consecutive couple for the final was re-called, the crowds erupted and applauded and before the orchestra started to play the first few bars of the Cha-Cha, Phil nodded to me and gestured to his seat on the front row. He was letting me have his seat, a promise he'd mentioned before, but I didn't think he'd actually let me. I quickly made my way onto his seat and prepared myself for the experience of a lifetime, I was about to see the best dancers in world, people I'd only really seen in YouTube videos and lecture

DVDs, I was about to get a front row experience of their dancing and my eyes, ears and thoughts were ready to absorb anything and everything I could comprehend, in an effort to take back and learn from.

The experience of the front row was not squandered in the slightest, everyone was clapping and cheering during the final of the Cha-Cha and it truly felt like I had arrived at a place where I was able to be in and amongst the best in the world. I was sat on the front row along with former world champions and international finalists, I was slowly becoming an integrated form of the dancing fabric that I'd so desperately wanted to be involved with. Everything I'd experienced up until that point, felt like it had all purposely been for a reason, there was a reason why I'd experienced everything I had up to that point, the highs, and lows, the good and the bad. All for a moment to sit amongst the best in the world and be part of something which would catapult me forward to where I ultimately wanted to be. As the end of the Cha-Cha concluded, I absorbed everything I'd just witnessed, there was a huge amount of inspiration I was feeling on that front row and there was an even larger array of ideas and information which I was digesting from everything I'd just seen. As the couples left the floor, I leaned back to see if David had noticed me on the front row, he had, with a look and mouthed wording of 'What the fuck are you doing there?', I responded by giving him a smile and nod before Marcus Hilton (former world champion himself and established MC for any and all Blackpool Dance Festival events) announced the competitors for the Samba back onto the floor. The crowds applauded and cheered as each competitor took their respective positions to begin their choreography. Looking leftward and the music began to play was Michael and Joanna, they powered across the floor into a series of Promenade to Counter Promenade Runs which moved directly toward and then past me. I'd seen the countless times on YouTube videos and even bought their instructional DVDs, watching them a thousand times to learn anything and everything I could from them. After they continued to progress and move around the floor Sergey Serkov and his partner Melia from Russia made their way past me, I was able to see the strength and power ubiquitously seen in Russian dancing and absorbed the impact of his power and digested how his movement affected Melia. Within a whirlwind of rhythm and dynamic movement, one finalist after another made their way past me and I worked tirelessly trying to absorb anything and everything I could from what I saw. Suddenly, my feet and the agony I'd been in from standing on them all day, seemed like a distant memory in the wake of what I was experiencing. The energy, power, rhythm, musicality, performance, technique, I was in awe of it all and I couldn't believe my luck at being in a situation to actually witness it all. The couples soon finished their Samba with the closing bar of the Samba music and presented to the eruption crowd who just wanted to see more and more of them all. Next was the rumba and with the announcement of a new couple into the final the crowd's expectations on what was to unfold on the floor heightened. The Rumba, soon lead into the Paso Doble with the new couple not receiving a re-call into the Paso Doble final and the former six competitors from the earlier dances took to the floor to dance their Paso Doble. Shapes, drama, high energy, power, and fierce performances were given by everyone on the floor, almost as if the previous three dances hadn't happened. As I said dancing a semi-final (and subsequently a final) is very difficult to do in Blackpool, you give your all in the first few dances and you've nothing to give in what remains. Hold something back and you run the risk of being out classed by the ferocious dancing taking place on the floor. At the conclusion of the Paso Doble the dancers were instructed to "stay on the floor" an honour of the highest calibre given to those competitors who manage to climb the ladder of the competition and solidify themselves into each and every dance. Scrutinisingly worked out from the discernible marks of the judges around the floor. The Jive which followed was electric, energy levels were the highest they'd been all evening and it wasn't long before the entire ballroom was on their feet clapping and cheering for each and every dancer on the floor. I truly felt a part of the proceedings, part of the dancing industry that night, as I stood clapping and cheering for my favourite couples and the nearby contenders and by the close of the Jive, the competitors took a much-appreciated series of bows with the crowd still cheering and applauding.

As hundreds of people begin to stir and leave the ballroom for the following break, I once again sat down in the seat from Phil, what followed after the final and the break in between was the prize presentations, not many people stick around for that as they mainly want to see the couples dancing in the final. That means there's a large array of people who leave the ballroom for the prizes portion of the evening (plus the ballroom clock was showing that it was nearing 1:00am. Phil made his way over to me and I began to move and let him sit down, he gestured for me to stay where I was and that he was fine standing as he still had photos to take anyway. With the Empress orchestra once again blasting their synonymous fanfare, the prize presentation was underway. The prize presentation at Blackpool for the professional events (both at the Open and Closed Championship competitions) always had the couples leave the floor after their placing is called. There's significance in this, which dates back to the earlier years of the competition but ultimately, it's because there are sometimes new couples who join the final in selective dances and their placing is not always a 7th position. This means that a type of circular carousel of couples coming to the floor when announced for their placing, present to the audience, collect their envelope of prize money for that dance, and rush round the other side of the stage, through the Ice room at the back to once again come onto the floor for the next dance or for the positionings of the line-up when the champion is crowned and their photo is taken by the official photographer. After each dance was called and everyone received their awards and envelopes of prize money, the competition came to a swift close and I now had to make a B-line for train station, there was only one train leaving at that time in the morning and if I didn't catch it, I'd be stuck in Blackpool. I raced through the Church square and back ally streets of Blackpool recounting the location of the train station and after eventually making it to the platform, the last train was about to depart. I was nervous and unsure as to whether this was actually my train, but as soon as the train tanoy system announced, 'doors closing', I made the split-second decision and bolted to the closing doors of the train now about to leave, narrowly sliding through the closing doors. No turning back now, I was on the train either way, I had three stops to change successfully if I was to make it home and it was around 1:30am in the morning.

As I sat on the rickety ride home early on Thursday morning, I contemplated everything I'd experienced that night, my feet were hurting so badly at this point with my shoes cutting into the back of my heels from the extensive amount of standing I'd been doing. I was hugely inspired by everything I'd just witnessed, the atmospheric feeling in that ballroom lingering with me days after the event had ended and I'd gotten home. I couldn't wait to start working on some of the dancing ideas that I'd seen from the competition and most of all, I couldn't wait to rub Alex's face in it all. I would make sure that when I eventually recounted to him the entirety of the time I'd had at the British Open Championships, that he'd sorely wish he'd accepted my offer and come with me. I didn't care how he personally felt, there were no doubt multiple reasons for why he'd decided to not want to come with me and I wanted to make him really realise how much he should have listened to me and come along. I spared no expense the following morning when I woke up and saw him in the living room the next morning and dove right into it. 'You missed out massively last night Ale!', his gaze was fixed on the TV as he ate his bowl of cereal, trying to act unfazed by presence and the provoking way I was getting him to engage with me. Seeing this, I arrogantly moved myself in front of the TV to continue undeterred at my attempt to make him feel bad for missing out 'not only did I get to see the dancing last night, but I also got a front row seat!'. The statement piqued Alex's interest enough to shoot me a glance but he remained in the same position on the sofa, 'you were sat on the front row?' he replied. He was evidentially not really interested in what I had to say, and his response was more of a challenge to my bold statement. 'Yup!' I quickly replied, eager to keep him engaged in the conversation for the sweet victory taste of his misfortune of missing out on the night. 'I was sat on the front row with all the British Champions to watch the final of the Professional Latin…' my voice trying keep him engaged long enough for me to deliver the "crushing blow" to accompany my enjoyment in his misfortune. 'And you could have been sat there watching along with everyone else if you'd bothered to come with me and not had a stick up your arse about it all'. With a huff and a shrug, he motioned to get up and take his breakfast bowl into the kitchen, dissatisfied with my torment but not actually rising to get annoyed by it either. However, I knew that the entire evening had been filmed and it wouldn't be long before the DVD of the entire competition was available to buy, I'd make sure I got an early copy and I'd make sure to keep playing the DVD so that I could point out me sitting on the front row. My victory would be sweet, and his misery would be brief whilst I gloated about being there and watching the top dancers in the world from the front row. When the DVD came out a couple of months later, I ordered my copy and within a week I had it held in my hands eager to rub Alex's face in my fortuitous experience at the British Open Championships. As we sat and watched the competition from the seats of mums red leathered living room sofa, we talked and compared ideas of what we saw and my experiences of being there that night and seeing it first-hand. As the camera panned right to show the floor on the right-hand side of the stage I'd gesture and point to where I was stood. 'Can you see me, Ale? That's me stood watching the semi-final', I'm sure there was a large amount of disbelief from Alex when I'd initially told of my front experience at Blackpool. But now he was beginning to see the fact that I'd not actually made it up and that in reality, what I'd said was true. With the couples on the TV now on the floor for the final the camera panned over the various dancers in the final and as soon as the camera panned o the right of the stage (well the left as you look at it), I jumped from my seat and paused the TV, 'Look, there I am Ale! Can you see me?', of which I did numerous times during the course of the final and I feel probably made Alex resent the British Open Championships of 2012. But I didn't care, I'd spent all day there and been rewarded with a front row seat to watch the competition and he hadn't and I wasted no time reminding him of it over the following weeks, playing the DVD numerous times to watch and learn from as well as pause and point out to him, the good fortune he'd missed out on if he'd just listened to me and come to the competition. With his eyes rolling at me pausing the TV for the millionth time I exclaimed 'Look, there I am Ale! Can you see me?'

Chapter 10 Trade The Day With Dancing Escapades

Sitting on the bonnet of a warm and old Ford Fiesta, staring at the traffic whizzing by, my mind flooded with all manner of scenarios and uncertainties, I sighed a deep sigh and wiped away the perspiration which had accumulated on my forehead as a result of my unscheduled "work-out". It was March 2012 and the "new" car that Alex had purchased after his last car, a Vauxhall Astra had been sold after conking out on him, his latest "investment" was now sitting in the car park of a Little Chef diner on the A38 waiting to be rescued by the RAC. It was a Wednesday morning and once again Alex had fallen out with David, again, which in turn had meant that he had decided to not attend any of his lessons for that week. This in turn had meant that despite my best efforts, I was once again on my own, travelling to Wolverhampton on my lonesome, just me, my dancing bag, and the stereo system in the car acting as a musical accompaniment to my independent journey. Alex had really started to have enough of the tormenting nature of being called a Twat by David, seemingly on a regular basis by this point and he was now putting his foot down on being involved with anything David was doing by foregoing the occasional series of dance lessons. I'd tried desperately to help Alex through it all and to pacify the situation numerous times before hand, but now Alex wasn't having any of it and he was really sticking his heels in with the whole situation. I'd helped Alex navigate the intricacies of 2011 as best as I could, encouraging a litany of reading materials for him to cast his eyes and mind over, in an effort to stop him spiralling just as mum had done and to help give him focus. I'd felt reading and the vast array of subjects I'd come into contact with for myself had massively helped me, and I figured that they could maybe help him too. The only difference was that Alex didn't read all that much, I think he's become a little bit more of a reader now, but back then he'd slowly make his way through one recommended book after another over the series of a few months. This string of self-study eventually culminated in a variety of conversational subject matter which Alex, and I would have regular discuss and clarify, resulting in the ensuing car journeys to and from the dance studio, the variety of competitions one or both of us would compete in, as well as late night talks in the living room at home which lasted three, four or even five hours at a time, they would all be filled with deep conversations and comparisons of ideas. The discussions were always insightfully intriguing, talking about philosophy, finance, science, history, maths, psychology even politics at one point as well. With Alex laying out a full-scale plan to revamp the health care system using the stated taxpayer money in an effort to "fix things". Our conversations were a buzz of excitement and a vessel where we could help channel any unresolved issues which surrounded our experiences of 2011 and the negative series of events that had transpired throughout that time. With those conversations, came a deep level of understanding and we both became a lot smarter because of the back-and-forth discussions we'd regularly have with one another, which seemed to challenge and develop our ways of thinking. There was so much for us to learn and just like in the years of our dancing beforehand, we were once again "training" with one another, developing our learning and expanding our knowledge, only this time it was more with the mind rather than the physical aspect of the dancing. Halfway through 2011 both Alex and I became deeply aware of the impact of money in our dancing, one Wednesday morning car journey to the studio, we found ourselves traversing the familiar countryside of the midlands area as we headed down the A38 towards Wolverhampton. We were talking numbers and it was essentially a full-on discussion of how we can manoeuvre ourselves into a position of earning around £1500 a month without sacrificing our time in order to do it (meaning we shouldn't have to waste our time working at Tesco in order to make the necessary money we wanted). As the conversation flowed and Alex ran some calculations in the passenger seat next to me, he began to formulate an idea. 'Do you remember that documentary we watched about the Stock Market Ian?'. I was apprehensive as to where he was heading with the conversation and so I tentatively replied, 'yeeees?'. 'Well apparently three trillion dollars flows through the Stock Market every single day', Alex's voice began to fill with excitement as the idea that he'd been sat on during our discussion was coming to the forefront of the conversation. 'Well, what if we were able to trade like those guys in Wall Street and we took a portion of that money?', as Alex proposed his grandiose idea his excitement only increased. 'And how do you suppose we do that Ale?', my pursuit of reading and learning had eventually led me to purchasing a few books surrounding the Stock Market. Learning about how the world of finance worked and some of the big drivers in that remit had resulted in my assortment of books and learning taking a more financial/ sales twist. I remember looking down and around my room one day to find it containing copies of the FT (Financial Times), books on the stock market, on futures trading and a selection of other volumes which revolve around the subject matter. As Alex and I talked the idea grew and grew, I was beginning to amass an immense amount of debt which should really have been paid back. Instead, I fought in a desperate attempt to keep more money for myself, balancing the odd payment of the credit cards which would in turn be used to fuel more of the dancing. This culmination of debt built up significantly from my credit cards at the time and it came after I'd made the brilliant decision (sarcasm implied) of omitting to not pay back any of the debt I owed. Blind to all this (or ignorant) one evening Alex and I sat down with each other and mapped out the actual dancing we WANTED to do (i.e., travelling abroad and competing in places like Italy, Russia, Hong Kong, America and Japan) it became exceedingly apparent that we would most likely not be able to experience that side of the dancing unless something fiscally changed for us both. It was both an exceedingly depressing and incredibly insightful endeavour, we just had to work out a way where we could earn the type of money, the kind of money we knew we needed for our dancing expenditure.

As the year progressed in 2011 Alex and I did our best with everything we could circumstantially and the realisation that we both would need an exceedingly vast amount of money (at least £3000 a month to be exact) which we could then use and spend on lessons, travel, competitions, and outfits. We just needed to come up with a way for us to accumulate it. After convincingly chatting for around three or four hours one evening on the subject and with a small collection of finance books open on the dining table in the living room. Both Alex and I decided that the best and only way we could surely make any substantial amount of money, would be from day trading the stock market. With a string of YouTube videos and internet references as evidence of the fact that the idea was an achievable one, Alex and I set to work with trying to conquer the stock market. We listed out a string of numbers and their composite breakdowns, 'ok, so if we traded an account with this amount in it, and we managed to successfully trade for this amount of time, then we'll make this amount'. 'Why stop at £3000 though?' Alex said, the question of why we should be setting a limit as we talked together intrigued me, 'surely if there's trillions of dollars flowing through the financial markets every day, then we could even accumulate hundreds of thousands, even millions if we did it correctly?'. In principle Alex's idea was sound, mathematically, the numbers all tallied, the only difference was that for us to make that amount of money, we'd either have to trade in huge volumes (not an option given our financial circumstances) or we'd have to day trade for a few years, potentially even a decade. Unfortunately, rational discourse took a back seat as the large numbers we'd tallied were too appealing to us and so the very next morning we excitedly headed into the main high street of the town to visit the local Halifax bank. To ensure we made an impression and that we'd be taken seriously, we decided to dress smart casual, that meant jeans and formal shoes mixed with either a shirt and blazer or t-shirt and blazer, were the chosen forms of style. As we entered the local branch one of the friendly female assistants greeted us 'what can I help you with today?', the young girl was friendly enough in her mannerisms and Alex responded back confidently 'we just wanted to know what the largest amount of money our standard bank accounts will hold?', perplexed at the question the young girl replied, 'erm, I think it's up to a million pounds that the standard account holds'. She was somewhat unprepared for that sort of question early in the morning, clearly that wasn't the type of question she had come across before and she soon made her way to one of the nearby offices to speak to one of her managers with Alex and I being asked to take a seat. As we watched the que of people which snaked its way to the teller windows gradually reduce in front of us, a confident and large gent opened his door to one of the nearby offices and approached us both 'Mr Whyatt?', Alex and I looked and gave a confirmatory nod 'right this way please'. We then made our way into the office of this bank manager (I'll call him Henry for the ease of the narrative), and we promptly entered where were asked to sit down. 'Can I get you boys anything? Coffee or some water?' We must have been the only people who had asked about the limitations of the bank accounts we had, and this must have seriously piqued Henry's interest. 'I'll take a black coffee please' I boastfully requested, and Alex soon chimed in with his own request, 'I'll take a water if that's alright'. It wasn't soon after, that the girl who had greeted us before came in carrying a bottle of water for Alex and a small cup of black coffee for me. 'So, what exactly can I help you both with today?' Henry leaned in on his desk pressing us for more intel. After seeing the viciousness and dog fight like attitudes and mentalities from documentaries and reading about the Stock Market, both Alex and I felt arrogantly assure of ourselves to not be intimidated by this bank manager. Jumping straight into the heart of the matter I asked Henry 'What we really want to know is how much our standard bank accounts can really hold?' Alex soon jumping into the discussion by adding 'would we need to have multiple accounts if we were in a position of having multi millions of pounds at our disposal?'. I glanced across to Alex and smirked, that was pretty good for him especially first thing in the morning, normally he's a lot more direct and I'd have to metaphorically assemble the debris of his poor choice of wording into something less jagged, this time however, he was firing on all cylinders. Henry was clearly taken aback by the questioning, in his mind he may have had the adage of judging a book by its cover scenario, thinking that both Alex and I just wanted to set up some kind of savings account or something. Instead, through a variety of back-and-forth wording, Alex and I had unintentionally convinced him that we were millionaires, and we were looking for a place to store our money. Henry stammered and checked his computer numerous times looking at various possibilities and ultimately the conversation concluded with him recommending some generalised options for what we could do with our money. After a firm handshake to conclude our meeting, he escorted us to the entrance of the bank and Alex and I sauntered down the town high street heading back to the car, a little reassured that we could use our regular banking accounts for storing wedges of cash that we could accumulate in the market. If we needed to make a decision about some of the higher volumes of cash we'd hopefully be expecting, then that could be looked into at a later date. For now, we had to look at how to accumulate the money using the trading platform Alex was looking into.

Waiting for the RAC van to arrive and collect Alex's clap-trap piece of crap, I reminisced about the various adventures Alex, and I had found ourselves on, the ducks in Oxford, Alex's toilet exploits at the Coventry Football Club. There were countless adventures that Alex and I had found ourselves on and yet here I was, alone, sat on the car bonnet of his clearly good for nothing car. That moment of sitting there, watching the world literally race by me and waiting, ultimately helped me realise something. If I wanted to continue to do the dancing and to not have the unsure reliance of Alex who was essentially a loose cannon at this point. I'd need to ensure I had my own car and that I made my own destiny, relying on Alex was too much of a risk as he could decide anything, at any point and that might throw a huge spanner in the works for me. Especially if I'd made arrangements, of one description or another, Blackpool Dance Festival and my collation of train journeys were a testament to that fact. After I talked with David to let him know I once again, wouldn't be down for lessons, I sat and soaked up the sun beaming down through the spaced-out clouds in the sky, reflecting on the money-making strategies Alex, and I had talked about. Coming down the stairs one day after enduring an extensive reading session, I saw Alex excitedly grinning as the pale blue glare of the computer screen monitors now set up in the corner of mums living room beamed onto his face. We'd talked endlessly about how we'd make money in the stock market, but we didn't have any ideas or direction on how we would do it. That's when Alex ushered me into the living room 'Ian, come quick, come quick!' his excitement was uncontained as he gestured to the computer screen set-up in front of him. As I peered round the corner of the monitor closest to me, I saw the ebbs and flows, the ups and downs of the little green and red bars which represented the price fluctuations in the stock market. 'What have you done Ale?' I was shocked but also massively intrigued, he'd set himself up on one of the various trading platforms available to him and had "invested" £125 into an account. 'I've just bought into the S&P 500 Index Market' he boastfully explained, as the peaks and troughs emerged on the screen, the little number representing his position fluctuated wildly. 'Wait you've BOUGHT into it?' I asked perplexingly, 'Why a buy position and not a sell?', the question was a clear one and it became apparent as the expression on Alex's face quickly changed, he'd not considered the option of selling the position he was currently locked in, rather than buying it. I didn't really know much either in truth, but I'd read two or three books on the Stock Market already and was beginning to get at least a clearer idea of how the trading game is played (or at least I thought I did). 'Well, I can't pull out now, I'll lose £70 If I do that!', As we sat and watched the fluctuations in the market wildly swing up and down, Alex's account went from £125 down to £70 up to a nice looking £150 and then at the close of the ten-minute trading candles he was observing, settled on £0. Within ten minutes he had put money in and lost it all, we then began the arduous task of dissecting his trading strategy to understand what had just happened. We were both very green in the territory of day trading and it eventually turned out that we both had two VERY different strategies when it came to creating money in the markets. Alex's plan was to occasionally throw £100, £125, £150 into the trading account he had set up, in an effort to learn by doing with a hopeful attempt that he'd hit upon a winning strategy. He'd chosen his "battle ground", the index markets of the S&P 500, the Dow-Jones 30, the NASDAQ and the FTSE 100, these were his poisons of choice and with the soundbites of CNBC acting as background noise to the constant frustrations of his losses, Alex powered his way through his money in an effort to "beat the market". I on the other hand, had a completely different strategy, I knew that we were up against really smart people (and machines) and in order to do well out of the situation, I felt I had to learn anything and everything I could about the stock market and the instruments we would be using. This idea led me to spend the following year and half studying the market, how it works (roughly) and what option would be the best one for me use, as and when I decided to jump into the trading seat. I'd heard loads about George Soros, Warren Buffet and Ray Dalio, people who all use very different strategies to make money on Wall Street and who are all big hitters in the world of the Stock Market. Which direction was the best one for me? Which option was going to bring me closer to my goal of not only making substantial amounts of money but living a life full of dancing? That's REALLY what it was all about to be honest, it wasn't about becoming a millionaire (although I wouldn't have passed up the opportunity to become one to be quite honest) it was about creating a situation of financial freedom where Alex and I could pursue our passion in dancing without limits. We were constantly shackled to the required "work for money" scenario and "having to make do" with our lot in life, we wanted something more, we wanted something better. The trading seemed like a logical and easier way of achieving that goal and given the timing of how it all came about, it seemed to us that the best direction would be to pursue and understand the world of trading.

It was around this time that Alex decided to cash in on his old Vauxhall Astra, which was suffering some similar pains experienced by his former red Fiat Punto years prior. A combination of engine troubles, resulting in the car overheating, were mixed elements alongside the requirement for a new rear suspension and the costly endeavour of replacing the standard brake pads and brake discs meant that if Alex was to keep his bucket of bolts running on the road, that he'd be out a couple of grand for the experience. This was what had essentially led him to buy a new car, a little Ford Fiesta that was questionably cheap, it didn't really matter to Alex though, by this time he wasn't showing much interest in travelling to David for weekly lessons anymore and so the following Wednesday morning, I asked to borrow his new little car to head to Wolverhampton for my own lessons and training, expecting to hear the agreed upon confirmation that I felt Alex would be happy to accommodate. Alex was extremely reluctant though; I'd been using his cars ever since my own Fiat Punto was scrapped and I think he was getting fed up with the constant request of me using HIS own car at the expense of not being able to use it for himself. We'd find ourselves regularly fighting about "who deserved to use it more" and ultimately Alex would throw in the fact that he was paying for its tax and insurance, which in reality meant that he ultimately, had the final say. I felt like I sometimes had to barter with him in order to use his car and it wasn't until I'd voiced some version of this to David that a suggestion came to the forefront. David suggested that perhaps I should look to getting my own car, the initial problem I had with this idea, was that the mechanic guy who mum and Alex knew back home, sold questionable vehicles that would last for a while, but eventually there'd be some form of issue with them. David suggested I get a car on finance instead, I was working full time anyway so paying back the monthly payments would be easy enough and after the final payment was made, I'd eventually own the car anyway. Sat on that bonnet with a warming sun beaming down on me as I watched the numerous cars zip past on the A38, made that idea seem even more tantalising. I'd managed to get Alex's bucket of bolts past the Derby ring road and as I'd began my drive along the A38 heading towards Litchfield, the car's engine light flashed up on the dashboard. As the car stammered and jerked, the evidential realisation that I wasn't going to make it to the studio hit me and I threw on the hazard lights and bunny hopped into the hard shoulder. Combining a use of the clutch and the changing of gears I managed to just barely make it to the Little Chef diner entrance, but the road leading into it, bent around like a U-turn. This meant that I really had to pray that the car would make it and not die completely, if I could roll it round the corner, I could then just park it up in a nearby parking bay. The car chugged its way into the corner and as the end of the curve neared, the road inclined slightly causing the car to completely give out. I knew I didn't have long to move it before someone else might come along and the last thing I needed to deal with was an accident at a Little Chef. After a few choice words and venting about Alex, as I applied the handbrake, I hopped out the car and readied myself for the seemingly insurmountable task of pushing the thing uphill into the Little Chef car park on my own. I steadily took off the handbrake and used every ounce of strength to keep the car where it was, digging my trainers into the tarmac to stop the car from moving. It was so heavy, and one wrong slip of the foot would lead it to roll down the incline again and crash into the nearby railing that separated the grass verge and the road. One difficult step at a time and I slowly, through gritted teeth and sheer will, pushed the car uphill. My shoulder digging into the frame of the door as I pushed and groaned agonisingly, making inch after inch of progression to get it past the peak point of the incline and onto the level surface of the car park. Eventually, after the wrestling and struggling had brought me to the top of the entranceway, I used the ensuing momentum to roll the car to a parking spot overlooking the A38. With a crunch of the bumper knocking into the barrier which separated the hedgerow by the roadside to the carpark at the diner, the car came to an ultimate stop, and I leaned my back against the now incapacitated mess of a car. Heavy breathing, a sore shoulder and sweat on my forehead were my rewards for avoiding a car accident, which incidentally would have happened had I left the car where it was. This was proven by the arrival of a white transit van, as no sooner than ten minutes after I'd "parked up" did the white transit van roll into the diner car park. I looked at my phone to see the time, 11:15am, I then frustratingly closed the door to Alex's car (I say closed the door, it was more like a frustrated slam of the door that dropped a piece of rust from its undercarriage onto the floor) and I hopped onto the bonnet to catch my breath and regroup, before then dialling in for an RAC rescue.

As I sat and waited on the bonnet of Alex's now incapacitated Ford Fiesta, I began thinking about where my direction in life was heading. Despite my best efforts, I still wasn't where I wanted to be in both my life and my dancing. I'd started a new partnership with a Welsh girl, and I couldn't afford to be situated in a position where I couldn't make my dance lessons and skip training days. I felt a little trapped by circumstance and the unfortunate but evidential facts that had come about from Alex and I's fiscal breakdown for what's needed to at least START competing in the world of international Ballroom & Latin dancing only seemed to act as evidential restrictions that ultimately seemed unclearable as I sat watching the traffic. I also began to think back on and start to process my grief and experiences from the year before, I'd spent so much time taking care of everyone that I'd neglected my own well-being so as to prevent anything worse from happening to mum or Alex. There was still a lot to resolve, and I'd never really come full circle on those issues until a number of years had passed. But sitting on that car bonnet, I wondered if my dad would be supporting or criticising what I was doing at that point. He'd never involved himself with our dancing, more like spectated it and supported it from a distance, I wondered if everything I was doing had any real significance and meaning or was it all just a huge waste of time. Would I even manage to reach and attain the great and lofty goal of top six in the UK? Top six in the world?

Who knows, my outlook was depressing to say the least and I really doubted in my ability to ever make something of myself. After the RAC pick-up truck had arrived, they began to arrange for the car and myself to be taken back to Scunthorpe, Alex's car was hoisted up onto the truck and fastened into position and after a prompt from the driver, I hopped into the front cabin of the RAC van ready for the drive home. Apparently, RAC drivers have certain zones that they operate within, a radius, and if you have a scenario like mine, where I had to travel from the lower end of Derby to Scunthorpe, you are somewhat "passed" to another member of the RAC who operates in that area. This was a new experience for me, after the journey back had led to the service stations at Tibshelf, another driver was sent out to collect me and the car and take us to Scunthorpe. This meant that Alex's car had to be unlatched from one truck and then mounted onto another, as the drivers discussed between themselves how to organise the switch, I made my way inside the service station to head to the toilet. It must have been around 6:00pm by the time the orange flashing lights lit up the little road where mum's house was. I'd been on the road since 10:00am and I just didn't care anymore about anything, I just wanted to get in, get changed into some comfy pyjamas and spend the rest of the evening upstairs, alone. After Alex's car was unbuckled and dropped off, I kicked it in frustration, I'd missed a full day's worth of training because Alex's car had broken and a little more of the rusty under carriage peppered onto the floor. I soon made my way inside though, Alex was in the living room, his face illuminated by the blue hazed glow of the two monitor screens hooked up to mum's old laptop. I threw the keys on the table as I entered the room to him and they slid across the table towards him, knocking into the closest monitor, and falling to the ground. 'Your new car is shit Ale; you can take me off the insurance, I'm not using it ever again!' I was so annoyed, not only had I missed out on a day of training and lessons, but I'd instead spent the day wrestling with Alex's car, experiencing a minor existential crisis and had the accompaniment of two larger than life RAC guys who brought me on a near six-hour journey home with their wonderful body odour smell acting as an accompanying sensory experience. I hated everything about that day, and I left the room to go upstairs and crash out in my bedroom for the rest of the night. I didn't come downstairs until it was time to grab something to eat and even then, I omitted seeing Alex and walked straight into the kitchen to make a sandwich and go back upstairs. Over the next few days, I took the time to calm down and organise getting a new car on a finance deal like David had suggested. At least that way I'd have my own car and could go and do whatever I wanted, without the restriction and worry of whether or not my car would break on me at some point. Two weeks after Alex had acquired his Ford Fiesta and it was sold back to the guy who Alex had initially bought it from, it was a number of months before I'd eventually acquire my own car though as paperwork and other logistics held up the process. This mean that either mum was to drive Alex and me to Wolverhampton (a rare occasion by this point) or we'd be skipping a series of lessons for a while. May Blackpool came and went with my train journey escapade adding additional memories to the time I didn't have a car available to me. My feet would still get a regular workout (aside from still practicing every day at home) by walking every morning to work, a wonderful three mile walk to get to work and another three mile walk to get back home again. It almost felt like I was in one of those adverts on TV, 'poor Ian has to walk three miles just to get to work…'. Eventually, the universe repaid me with the arrival of my brand-new Seat Ibiza which I had to walk all the way across town to collect, another three-mile walk. Needless to say, the time I didn't have a car and had to walk six miles to and from work, along with numerous other excursions, resulted in me becoming very fit, so silver linings, I guess. After I'd acquired my new set of wheels, it was time to get back on the horse with lessons and practices, this time I had my own car, and it didn't matter to me if Alex was going to be joining me for dance lessons and training sessions anymore. I had some independence back, in the shape of a Seat Ibiza and I was excited to get back into the regularity of everything again.

When I first got that car, it had 16,000 miles on the clock and had only one previous owner, it was relatively new (at the time), and it was the first time in a long time that I felt that things were on the up for me. That new car was almost like a representation of my life receiving an upgrade, the stereo was new, the interior had leather interwoven in the seats, it truly felt like my life had been blessed by the universe. This was around the time that I began to travel to Wales for additional practice with my partner Leah who lived in a small village just outside Newport. I'd initially wanted to dance Ballroom with her as that was the most logical direction the couple should go, but it wasn't long before David strong armed me into making the decision of dancing the Classical and Modern Sequence Championships in October with her as well. I'd danced the Classical and Modern Sequence style of dancing years before as a youngster and left it all behind to pursue the Open Ballroom and Latin dancing after an inspirational experience at the junior British Open Festival in

Blackpool. I was reluctant to do it but after some coercion by David I eventually agreed to do it, this meant extra lessons and practice which Leah couldn't do over at Wolverhampton and so, if I was to make things work for the dance couple, I'd have to hop into the car and travel to Wales for extra lessons with Leah's Classical and Modern Sequence teacher. It wasn't long before a routine developed around our commitments and the resulting dynamic was that after I finished work at 10:00pm on a Thursday, I'd hop into the car and drive the whole way to Wales (a four-to-four-and-a-half-hour car journey) which resultantly meant that I'd make it to Leah's mum's house at around 2:00am/2:30am (depending on how held up on the motorway I was). I'd then crash out and sleep and in the late afternoon/ evening, Leah and I would attend lessons with her teacher Anne and practice together at a local hall just down the road from her mum's house. We'd then both wake up on Saturday morning, bright and early at 5:00am and drive to Wolverhampton for our scheduled lessons at 8:00am until 2:00pm/2:30pm, where I'd then hop back in my car and drive back to Scunthorpe and go back to Tesco, working from 5:00pm until 10:00pm. Leah's mum and dad would come collect her from the studio between 1:00pm and 2:00pm depending on what agreement Leah and I had for our practicing in the studio. That was the cycle I did with Leah for the duration of our partnership, for nearly two years I'd hop in the car and leave Scunthorpe on a Thursday night right after finishing work and arrive back on Saturday evening to go straight back into work. The addition of dancing the Classical and Modern Sequence Championships was grating on me though, I did it the first year as a one off, to satisfy the need that Leah had to dance as an Amateur in the competitions she'd grown up doing and we attained a 3rd place position in the British Championships, not a bad result for the couple really. The second year we did it I was extremely reluctant but there was a lot of pressure put on the emphasised fact that "we were next in line to win it", after the inclusion of more Classical and Modern Sequence lessons with additional teachers, we danced the Championships again for a second time and attained another 3rd position, we were now British finalists for two years in a row. As 2014 rolled around, the prospect of dancing the Championships once again came up, statements of how we'd done all the hard work to become the British Champions were all I can really remember people talking about. In January/ February I'd had enough, I didn't care about Classical and Modern Sequence dancing, I felt like the focus for the couple was heading down a direction I never wanted to go down and I point blank refused to do it for a third year, I didn't hold back either when talking to Leah and her parents about it all and I certainly didn't hold back with David either. At one point I remember David saying to me how I'd "become a British Champion" and I think my response was something along the lines of 'becoming a British Champion in something I don't care about doesn't appeal to me'. That vocalisation inevitably terminated the partnership for me and Leah and by early February we both went our separate ways. Leah continuing to dance the classical and Modern Sequence events for another year and me, looking for a new partner and seriously questioning a lot of what I'd been doing again. The whole experience had made me bitter, made me feel like I'd been used, I felt used in the partnership for Leah to achieve something SHE wanted and not what WE wanted, because all I ever wanted was to compete on the highest level against the worlds best. I also felt used by David as well, I was beginning to harbour some resentment as I counted through the amount of dance partners, I'd had over the time I'd spent with him and roughly tried to work out how many lessons I'd had on my own without a partner (some of those lessons being beneficial mind you). In all honesty I was never interested in becoming a champion (well, I mean, that's a stupid statement to say really, of course I'd want to win and become a champion). But what I was most interested in, what I've ALWAYS been interested in, was becoming the best I knew I could be, if I was to become the best of what I can be, then surely my results will reflect that. Trophies and accolades didn't mean anything to me if they were acquired by means of just being the next one in line, like a fucking monarch waiting for their respective parent to die so that they can become king or queen themselves. By this time, I was a lot more clued into how the politics in the world of Ballroom and Latin dancing worked, I wasn't ignorant to the fact that certain lessons with certain teachers, provided better opportunities. But if that was all the reason there was for me to do the dancing, then why bother doing any of it at all? After my split from Leah, I took a couple of weeks to sit and reflect on the experiences with Leah, about how I'd been coerced into dancing a style of dancing I didn't have any interest in. About how my lessons with David were feeling more and more like they didn't matter and that the information and value that David MIGHT have, was being used and developed with other students who "showed more promise". Frankly, I felt like a cog in the machine that was helping to pay for his standard of living and his mortgage, blunt and very dramatic for sure, but I didn't see any evidence that pointed to a contrary idea.

Over the time span of mine and Leah's partnership, Alex and I delved deeper and deeper into the world of the Stock Market. I'd bought tons of books and was experiencing six-to-eight-hour long bouts of learning, note taking and theorising. Alex, once a month, was losing £110, £125 or on the odd occasion £150 in a desperate grab to find some way of "beating the market". My bedroom became a wheel of escalating books, now exceeding the small bookshelf I had in the corner and spilling into random assorted piles which were dotted all around the floor. The white boards I'd nailed to the bedroom wall were strewn with the ideas I was working on for the trading and I had dozens of notes strewn across the walls of my bedroom, along with pages and exerts from the Financial Times (FT) which were all marked and highlighted. On a cork board in the centre of the wall where my white boards were situated was something of significance though, a collation of goals arranged to form what I'd learned to be a "Vision Board". Through such intense bursts of studying and learning my mind craved a release, I was never a serious studier in school, frankly I was the worst, I barely revised for my final exams and coursework was reluctantly done to appease teachers and not really for developing my personal understanding. But this felt different, this felt purposeful and my intense reading sessions would culminate into hours of discussions which I held with Alex. One way I'd release some of this intensity was through the use of Vine, the video platform which I guess was the precursor to TikTok. Making the occasional video on literally whatever came to mind, allowed for my more creative side to feel like it was getting some airtime. Creating a series of characters that I worked on trying to get into the trending page of the app, all in the hopes of "going viral". Characters such as Safety Sam, the character dressed in a yellow fireman's outfit who is so pre-occupied with any and all means of safety that he interferes with everything people do. There was Captain Jack Sparrow looking for his hat, where I'd run around like an idiot (a theme to my life really) looking for Captain Jack's hat. To a character named Posh who was always scheming and plotting to take over the world with his board from the game of Risk acting as a map of the world which he intends to conquer. There were also ad hock dumb videos quite a lot of the time too, like having the screen completely pink which symbolised the idea that the Pink Panther was following me in various different rooms. You might well think that my dancing was acting as the creative vessel to release that intensity of studying, but in all honesty it wasn't. Dancing during that time was becoming more like a fulfilment of criteria rather than an experiential journey. Gone were the adventures of Alex and Ian, the request I'd put out into the world on those earlier teen expeditions to the studio in Wolverhampton. Now the dancing was a fulfilment of obligations, people's expectations and worse, it wasn't becoming anything of my own anymore, I felt like my dancing was the property of someone else, like I should be eternally grateful to someone else for the hard work (and money) I'D put in. After about a year and a half of playing around with various ideas which circulated on the trading, I eventually jumped into the new trading platform Alex had found. My market? The "FX" or currency markets. I'd seen that the fastest way for me to accumulate money was via the currency markets, they traded nearly 24/7, compared with the stocks, commodities, and index markets that Alex was looking into, they all ended their trading at 5:00pm (respective to their time zones). I'd devised a series of strategies and after toying with various "fake trading" ideas (using a demo account to learn and use the system with) I jumped into the market, opening up a trading account and putting about £120 into it, I was all set to make my millions.

On a side note, let me tell you about Alex and I's excursion to Manchester to hear a guy talk to us about day trading. One Wednesday morning Alex and I woke up and organised ourselves early in the morning, it was around 8:00am and we were planning a journey together. This was the first time in a long time that we'd had a buzz of energy about travelling together and we were excited to be heading out into the world together again. We had no car at this point as Alex's last "investment" was sold for scrap and I hadn't quite received my Seat Ibiza just yet. We were planning out our trip using a map to highlight the trains from Scunthorpe to Doncaster and Doncaster to Manchester, our destination? The Hilton Hotel just in front of the train station at Manchester. Weeks prior to our planned excursion, Alex had mentioned to me how he was very interested in going to a "conference" about trading, we'd seen a plethora of YouTube videos which showcased conferences held in the US and we figured we'd be in for quite an experience if we went to one ourselves. We were also hungry to learn more ways we could use the trading platform, maybe there were some additional little indicators or ideas that we hadn't come across yet and this guy (let's call him Michael, because, again, I don't remember his name) could maybe help fill in some of the blanks. After Alex organised for our names to be put down on a FREE seminar being conducted in Manchester, we got ourselves organised and within the two weeks that passed, we looked at getting ourselves organised with notepads and pens, eager to take down any and all notes that we could use. I still had a satchel bag from when I was a college, and I housed a few books and my note pad in it for the journey ahead. After getting off the train at Doncaster and preparing to board our next one, I quickly nipped to a nearby kiosk to grab an FT (Financial Times), not only did I want to see some of the latest happenings in the world, but I also wanted to look smart holding an FT in front of this Trader from London. After boarding our train to Manchester, Alex and I found ourselves a couple of seats with a table and I quickly sprawled out the FT looking at the stats on the back pages and scanning through the other pages to find the LEX column. We were so excited, we didn't know what to expect, we excitedly talked about what we might learn and questions we could maybe ask. It had been such a long time since Alex, and I had talked this excitedly about anything in a while. Alex's absence from coming down to the studio with me on a Wednesday meant that the car was filled with a lot of bad singing and stereo music from just myself. After Alex's Ford Fiesta had kicked the bucket, we'd not really been talking to one another either, this trip changed that, we were once again heading into the unknown (cue Disney track) and it was exciting. There's a lot that could probably be said about Alex and me (and a lot you've no doubt drawn a conclusion about for yourself, by reading this far too) but we've always embraced the aspect of the unknown. I'd confidently say that we've both not been too hesitant on jumping right into a new scenario, a new set of circumstances. We might have doubts, concerns or maybe even a little fear, but none of those elements have stopped us from progressing forward. As the train racketed its way along the rails towards Manchester we conversed and wrote notes about ideas we wanted to ask about as soon as we got to the conference. After the train rolled into Manchester, Alex and I disembarked and our next part on our quest had begun. The information Alex had printed out, regarding the details of the event had a little map and address on it and it indicated that the high-rise building in front of us, was where the conference was being held. Makes sense, right? But the paper never mentioned it was in the Hilton Hotel, we found that out a little later. After circulating the building in front of us a couple of times I whipped out my phone and its Apple Maps GPS App and after typing the post code into the search bar, found that the phone thought we were already at the right place. We eventually navigated ourselves round to the entrance of the Hotel and gingerly made our way through the foyer towards the counter in front of us. Alex and I had decided to dress smart casual for the day, jeans and a T-shirt/ shirt combo with a blazer and either nice shoes or trainers were our choice of attire, as we sauntered through the entranceway of the Hilton Hotel. Alex approached the desk and asked the girl sitting there, where the conference (Conference X let's call it) was being held. After the girl took a look at both of us, she asked if it was the same Conference X that was being run by Michael. After agreeing, she gestured to the right and told us to follow the stairs up into a seating area where Michael would collect us from. Alex and I then made our way towards the marble walled staircase which banked around in a U-shape, leading up to a small foyer/ sitting area. As we entered the area, we suddenly felt a little outclassed, there were at least a hundred people all congregated together, all suited and booted enjoying a host of buffet styled spreads which included, small sandwiches, canapés, coffee, fresh juice, literally everything you can think of. Alex and took a seat in the centre of the room where a type of glass coffee table was situated and looked around at all these "businesspeople". We were the youngest there by about twenty years and were beginning to feel a little intimidated, I leaned across to Alex, do you think we're in the right place? Seems like we've under dressed for this'. Alex just gave a confirmatory grunt as we looked around at the various people deep in conversations and debates with one another. 'I'm going to help myself to some of the spread Ale, you want anything?', I'd figured that when in Rome, do as the Romans do and I would probably feel a bit more at ease relaxing and eventually plucking up the courage to talk to some of these very professional looking individuals. Alex gestured that he wanted a glass of water and a few of the sandwiches, as my little coffee from the machine that was set up by the juices crushed its beans and began to fill up, I poured him a glass of water and grabbed a small glass of orange juice for myself. I then picked up a couple of small plates and grabbed a selection of little nibbles, the canapés, some tiny sandwiches, and some very decadent looking deserts, before collecting the black coffee I had organised from the machine and sitting down with Alex. No sooner had I stuffed one of the canapés into my mouth did I hear a booming voice from behind me, the chat of all the people in the atrium silenced as the voice shouted out, 'Everyone who is here for the Northern Rail shareholders meeting, please come and take your seats! The meeting will soon be commencing!'. Alex and I just looked at each other, our eyes widening as we realised that the buffet, we'd helped ourselves to (or more accurately, that I'd helped myself to) was NOT intended for people attending Conference X. As everyone quickly filed into the corridor where the shareholder meeting was to take place, staff members of the hotel, quickly came by to clear away any and all manner of plates and food. Alex and I quietly sat munching on our sandwiches, watching the staff clear everything away in around two minutes, and the entirety of the atrium was soon empty. Soon it was just me, Alex and the small assortment of nibbles and drinks we had obtained, waiting for Conference X to start. People soon started to emerge though, jeans and T-shirts, jumpers, and trousers, about a dozen people turned up, these were clearly the people for Conference X. The only issue was that both Alex and I, in our smart casual combo, looked like the host, sat eating fine assorted nibbles and drinking coffee and juice like we were one of the elites in the Hilton. When people rocked up, they all looked at me and Alex, giving the type of look that made it seem like WE were running the event. After about ten minutes Michael made his appearance, black trousers with a blue pin striped shirt, opened at the collar, sporting a fancy watch and black shoes, ushering us all down the corridor and into the conference room.

Making our way into the conference room, Alex and I made our way to the front of the seating, overlooking the small table with Michaels Café Nero coffee cup and the white board he was clearly using for his presentation. A lot of other people chose to seat themselves a bit further away, but Alex and I plonked ourselves down right on the front row. We wanted to hear anything and everything this guy had to tell us, a real-life trader from London, who better to talk to about the stock market than him right? We were eager to learn as much as we could. Michael was a boisterous and confident person, typical of the type of middle-class person that would deal in the stock market and his presentation and conference which ran for three hours, was pretty well presented. The issue was, well, the conference turned out to be not quite what Alex and I were expecting. It was essentially an introduction to trading seminar, where Michael would espouse a lot of day trading jargon, that I'd personally spent years reading about and that Alex had exposed himself daily to, in the markets already. Talking about how to spot trends in candles and giving examples for people to try and follow along with. Ultimately the seminar ended with Alex and me asking loads of questions about what certain particular indicators are best used for and what trends are better to use and identify with than others. Michael either didn't know or didn't want to tell us though, his initial reason for setting up the conference was to get people to give him £10,000 which was included in his signup sheet, whereby which he would then "teach" you how to trade the markets. After a discussion with Alex and me, he soon realised we didn't have the £10,000 he wanted, and he very swiftly moved on. What a waste of a journey, we'd taken the time to travel all that way, all for it to be realised that the whole thing was a waste of time. We didn't learn anything that we didn't already know, with Alex and I conferring to one another answers to the questions Michael was shooting out to the room about using trend analysis and EMA's (Estimated Moving Averages), along with a host of other examples. At one point Alex raised his hand to ask about how he could best use Stochastics and Michael immediately moved on to someone else's question, completely ignoring what Alex had asked. (Stochastics by the way is a tool used in trading which uses two lines to show how the current price of something compares to the highest and lowest price levels over a given period of time). As Alex and I sat on the train ride home, we didn't talk much, we'd felt we'd been royally duped and that the whole experience was a waste of time, we did joke about the odd thing that had happened like trying to find the Hilton Hotel when it was right in front of us and the Northern Rail situation, but we ultimately felt dejected to say the least. After getting back home, Alex crashed on the sofa in the living room and I went upstairs, after spending some time reading, I came back downstairs to see Alex. He was still slumped in the same position I'd last seen him in an hour and a half ago. 'Well at least there's one good thing that came from today!' I enthusiastically said, dropping myself down beside Alex. 'What's that?' grumbled Alex, his eyes remained looking at the air crash investigation TV show he was currently watching. 'At least we both know more about the trading than we originally thought', Alex looked up to me confused, 'what do you mean?'. I repositioned myself on the sofa to face Alex as I responded, 'you didn't hear anyone ELSE asking the kinds of questions we asked, did you?', my voice trying to convey an upbeat and positive tone. 'At one point some idiot in the back had to ask what the difference between the red and green colours were, even after Michael had already said what they were!'. Alex's eyes brightened as he began to realise the intricate questions that we'd been trying ask, compared with the dumb questions everyone else had asked. He even recalled how Michael had asked people if they know what a MAC-D is and why it's used, Alex knew full well all the intricacies of using the MAC-D. It was one of the prime indicators he personally used when trading and he gave a near textbook answer that made Michael pause for a second and realise that we were more clued in than everyone else. We'd found our silver lining for the day.

By the time I personally decided to jump into the market, Alex was making more calculated decisions in his own trading. He'd realised (through pain of losses) that his margins were too high, and he began setting safer parameters which only made him a few pence at a time, but at least he wasn't always losing so, y'know? Silver linings, I guess. I'd used Alex's failures as learning opportunities, showing him pages in my technical analysis books on how to use some of the new instruments he was exposed to on the new trading platform he'd found. Through carefully planned structuring, my account grew from the initial £120 I invested in it, to around £250/ £300, I felt like a king and took a couple of days away from the platform to calm myself down. My strategy was simple, I'd use whatever information (FT, CNBC, the news etc) to see how the world was doing and make educated guesses as to what direction the market was heading in the currency exchange markets. I maneouvred my charts with Stochastics, MAC-D's and various EMA's along with the occasional use of Bollinger Bands. I was using the same parameters in my trading throughout, meaning that, if I made say £15 from my £120 trading account, then when the money in the account doubled (say to £240/£250) then my trades would double. I was playing high risk, high reward, but I felt confident in my ability to correctly see the direction of the market and to spot trends. I'd studied the crap out of Technical Analysis reading entire books on the subject, looking at charts and examples, the FT and CNBC charts to work out theories and ideas which helped identify trending patterns. If those trending patterns were successful, I'd find other examples where the data could be repeated and if that led to the same outcome over the course of three times, then that was a good enough confirmation for me that the idea worked and that I could use it. As my strategy persisted, my account grew and before I knew it my trading account sat at around £600 (or there abouts).

2013 had culminated into a large string of varying circumstances, Alex was trying to find a new partner whilst boycotting the occasional string of lessons from David, mum would have her momentary dips and "bad days" but ultimately, she was on the up and doing a lot better. I was doing tons of reading, learning, dancing, travelling and quite coincidentally had begun a long-distance relationship with a Swedish girl named Avera. I had a new car and generally, things in and around itself seemed like they were on the up, nothing ever moved like it was on a straight line of course, but I felt that there had been a culmination and series of fortuitous things which had happened for me, and it now meant that I was in a really good place for myself. During 2013, the first evidential signs that the "The Adventures Of The Whyatt Brothers" were starting to come to an end though, 2012 had been turbulent, but Alex and I still managed to get at least some form of consistency going in our lessons and travelling together. David's jibes to Alex and the subjective ridicule Alex suffered from another dancing partnership coming to an end (in the form of Jess from Sheffield) were all wearing him down. Sitting one Wednesday afternoon in the kitchen after one of David's lessons had finished, the discussion across the table between David and Alex gradually built and escalated. In a former life David used to be a salesman and I guess that's what's made him successful as a teacher, selling people (including Alex and me) on an idea or premise during their lessons. This meant that talks with David weren't straight forward, as Alex and David pulled apart the failed partnership with Jess to discern what really happened (David trying to demean and essentially take the piss out of Alex, and Alex trying to prove the point that British girls are all lazy). The general point that David was making with Alex was that he'd not conducted himself in the right way, Alex (through a less elaborate way of explaining) bluntly stated how David was wrong, he'd done everything he could but the long and short of it all was that the girl just didn't want to do the dancing the way Alex did. The conversation escalated and I sat and listened to it all as unbeknownst to Alex, David was setting the conversation up for a "that's not what you said earlier" moment, a kind of "gotcha", where Alex would once again be ridiculed for being an idiot. Alex wasn't an idiot, he's actually very smart, he just used to lose sight of that logical element when it came to the dancing side of things sometimes, he's gradually gotten better over the years with that though. Eventually David hit him with the sales tactic of "that's not what you said earlier" and through manipulation, tried to twist the wording and narrative to fit the point that he was making. As I sat and listened to the conversation, I realised that's what was happening, sitting and listening in a third person perspective to understand what was REALLY being talked about proved to be beneficial though. Before David could parry with Alex, who was now stammering, trying to recollect what he said before, I chimed in. 'No! That's not what Alex said David, he said…'. To be honest I was becoming a little agitated from the discussion, I'd realised that David was trying to set Alex up in the conversation, to make juxtaposing statements that could be used as ammunition against him and so that David could double down and validate the underlining idea, he was going with himself. David looked at me with a glint in his eye and a with a tilt of his head, realised that not only was I not going to let Alex be made a fool of (as he's quite capable of doing that himself) but that I was also on his side with what had been talked about.

No sooner had I entered the conversation and the culmination of all my various reading on psychology, sales, body language came together and allowed me to not only hold my own within the discussion but also to parry and invalidate some of the things David had been saying about Alex. A few minutes of exchanges ensued with David and me and then Alex and David and he soon realised he wasn't winning this one and promptly left the room soon after. Alex didn't need me to fight his battles for him and most of the time he'd get himself embroiled in a conversation or circumstance that warranted his uneasement and realisation that he'd messed up. But listening in that kitchen, he was trying to tell David that even though he didn't have a partner anymore, he'd done what he felt was the right thing. Time eventually took its toll though and in January 2013 Alex took an unexpected six-month hiatus from dancing, that meant no lessons, no dance trials, no competitions, no nothing. I remember being sat with Alex and talking with him at home for hours after he made the decision, and he made it very clear to me that he wasn't interested in doing his dancing anymore. He voiced how he was massively unhappy with David and the way he'd been treated by him, what with the constant barrage of name calling and being labelled a twat on weekly basis and it left the direction and situation of 2013 up in the air. Now I was travelling to Wales by myself, driving to Wolverhampton by myself, taking excursions to competitions by myself, the only thing that remained with me were the memories and escapades of having Alex by my side in the car as a companion to the series of adventures and escapades we'd found ourselves on, years prior. I genuinely felt a little lost, I felt like this huge element of support and a wedge of companionship had now just been completely removed, like a bad tumour or something and in its place had generated a massive void. Alex had clearly been my crutch through all the ups and downs that had happened from 2011 onward, he'd been someone I could focus my energy and attention on despite the various negative aspects that were being faced, sometimes on a daily basis. His absence had left an empty void in both the car and in me and the thing about a void is, they eventually fill up.

As 2013 progressed my growing frustration in my partnership with Leah increased, differences of opinions became commonplace in the practices and after I'd voiced the fact that October Blackpool would be the last time, I would entertain the Classical and Modern Sequence, things only deteriorated. Alex's absence was difficult to adjust to and there were many times when my dancing felt more systematic, like I was going through the motions of it all. I knew that I needed focus, and I needed direction and that's when I stumbled into the realm of affirmations and an online video called 'The Secret'. In a nutshell, 'The Secret' is a type of documentary styled film created by a woman in Australia who found herself at the end of a string of misfortunate circumstances. Her daughter provided her with a printout version of Wallace. D Wattle's book, 'The Science Of Getting Rich' and she elaborates on how that book was not only life changing for her, but also led her on the path she's on now. The main take away gist that I got from it all (although I did watch it like thirty times) was that if you have what's known as a "Vision Board" with clearly defined 'I Am' statements and goals on it. Including pictures and related things that correlate in your idealised future, that you can eventually manifest the life, car, or person of your dreams. Sounds very pie in the sky and airy fairy, but essentially, it's all about manifesting and seeing it all in your mind and feeling the feelings of having what you want. It took me a while to get into understanding it all and I even bought Wallace D Wattle's book to help clarify the idea to me. But eventually the whole thing started to make sense to me. I knew that if I wasn't careful, that the void of depression, of uncertainty in everything, would fill that void I had and that ultimately, I'd relapse in some major way, I had to find a way to keep moving myself forward. This seemed like a good way of doing it, HOW I went about it, leads to some questionable aspects though. First off though I'd like to say that, in my opinion, the element of manifestation and its entailments I feel CAN work, you just have to realise what it is that you actually want and build from there. Whatever you're imagining, you have to feel and believe it's possible and subjective to how big the goal is and how much you convince yourself, will depend on how achievable the goal actually becomes. I remember stating on my vision board a series of statements of 'I Am..' and one of them was to be a millionaire (a dream everyone has no doubt) but that was too vague, if I'd put, 'I have £5,000,000 in my bank account blah, blah, blah', then that's a more specific goal that can work, but is it believable? Probably not, £100,000 would be MORE believable, but I didn't really understand the concept as completely as I feel I do now. (Just to be clear this isn't the part of the book where I try to convince you to change your trajectory or anything, I'm not going to sell you on the idea of manifestation or anything). So, I made small slips of paper with highlighted sentences to help create emphasis on what my goals were and stuck them to my "vision Board" mounted on the wall. I had the goal of being a top six finalist in the world, of having a dance partner from another country, of travelling and having dance lessons in Italy (a goal I'd wanted for some time, truth be told) I'd even put a statement saying how I would have actual lessons with William Pino on the board. Along with the type of car I'd like to drive, the ideal house I'd want etc. The day trading was a way to help make that happen and so between all the travelling to and from Wales and Wolverhampton, intense and long reading sessions, dance lessons, practices, and training at home. I'd also be trading the stock market in the currency exchanges as well as having a full-time job at Tesco and liaising a long distant relationship via Skype calls to Sweden. There was a lot happening, but I'd read and watched loads of examples which showed meteoric rises to fame or fortune and the intense manner of how that all culminated. This was no different in my view, the only thing that WAS different was how intensely I would pursue the goals and achievements which I was striving for.

Lessons in the studio remained the same with practices with Leah requiring more breaks for the couple to "cool off" (plus Leah wasn't a fan of my intense training style and using weights) this meant that I'd do some of my practicing alone and this was when I decided to buy some of the dance technique books used within the industry. Dance technique books are always treated as floating, golden symbols of knowledge that only qualified teachers can fully grasp. While there is SOME truth in that (the floating aspect tends to happen as the book is launched at your head from a disgruntled partner) the long and short of it all is that, ultimately, it's just a fucking book. I'd read hundreds of them so far, many of which contained vast arrays of complex subject matter far outside the remit of dancing Ballroom and Latin steps. And so, I plunged into my credit card once again and made the heavy expenditure of buying a whole set of Ballroom and Latin Technique books. When the practices with Leah turned stale and I was in the studio by myself, I'd whip out one of the books, read through technically explained elements and then directly apply them to my own dancing to see the effects. Alex's six-month hiatus from dancing and the void it had left me with was in turn filled with reading, learning, manifesting and ideas. It was all growth orientated and it was all directed at moving me forwards and upward, what would be the harm in all that?

The bedroom where I seemed to reside most of the time whilst I was at home, was cluttered with books of every description, notes from trading the currency markets, the occasional Financial Times newspaper and notes I'd made from the twenty odd dance books that I'd bought. I'd then spend time decongesting by making stupid Vine videos and listening to binaural beats or affirmation sounds and because the cork board which represented my own vision board was somewhat directly in front of me, I'd spend hours seeing, sating aloud and exposing myself to the ideas surrounding what I wanted. The money I was making in the trading started to eventually build and by early 2014 my account was sitting at around £750, not bad considering my starting number was £120, I'd done some risky trades and they'd paid off well and I'd also done some dumb ass ones which ended up setting me back as well. One such trade was with the Euro and the Australian Dollar, I'd made a trade to buy the euro and hedged the position by selling the Aussie dollar, risky with an account containing very little in it, but I'd done that type of thing once or twice before and it had almost doubled the account balance. I set the parameters and used the tracking tools to monitor the condition and performance of the market, using things like Bollinger Bands, Moving Averages and the MAC-D, all fancy tools on the trading platform that make looking at the data easier to interpret (and prettier). After placing my trades, I then left to go to work, confident in the direction of the market and the expected "double bubble" my account would receive. I'd moved around Tesco departments numerous times over the near ten years that I ended up working there and by 2013 I was in the Dot-Com department where online orders are collected and arranged ready for delivering to customers who shop using the online service at Tesco. After finishing my shift at Tesco, I made my way back home and confidently opened up my computer, ready to see the takings for the day. From an account that sat at around £600, all I saw was red, I was down massively and because I'd forgotten to set closing parameters which take you out of a trade if the price drops to a certain level. This meant that I was incurring hundreds of pounds of losses, all the hard work of building the account up, day by day, taking the occasional risky trade and the majority of safe ones to accumulate cash, it was all gone! And by the time I'd managed to close the trade my account sat at around £150. I kicked myself pretty hard for a while after that and I got pretty depressed from it all too, so much so that I didn't touch the trading platform for about two weeks. My skype calls with Avera were all that could perk me up, dancing and learning didn't feel as fun when it was happening on what felt like my own, I'd taken DVDs to Leah's which showcased and outlined technique and particular ideas that I was working with from top level teachers, which she did take initial interest in, but it wasn't long before I was sat in the attic space watching them alone. Determined to not let ANY set back deter me, I rebooted myself and got back into the trading again, if I'd worked the account up to doubling and tripling its initial starting capital, then I could do it again and for the following year, I worked the account back up (suffering the occasional £200 loss every now and then) and reaching the height of a very sizable £930 (ish). After I closed the account in 2014 and took my hard-earned money, my bank balance was looking a lot healthier. Early February saw my partnership with Leah terminate itself as differing ideas on direction and more disagreements in practicing led to us ending our dancing together, somewhat right after David's competition. I wasn't going to be used (like I felt I WAS being) so that someone could have their chance of attaining something I had no desire to be a part of. The journeys to Wales on a regular basis were also starting to drain me both financially and through the numerous times I nearly ended my car in a barrier or ditch, or once, very scarily, over the side of a cliff. Things were beginning to grate on me though as during the ensuing lessons which followed with David, he pressed me on another failed partnership and how I was "stupid" for ending things with Nat.

The use of my Vision Board and the updated statements I'd read aloud to myself three or sometimes four times a day were a driving factor of keeping me focussed. I'd also made the brilliant decision (he says sarcastically) of buying a pack of UV pens and a UV light bulb, which I fixed to the ceiling light of my bedroom. The various manifestation influences I was choosing to expose myself to had stated how if you right down what you want, that it can help magnify the gradual attainment of what you are wanting. I personally took this to extreme, after buying my UV bulb and pens I proceeded (like a madman really) writing under UV light, all over the walls, ceiling and floor, the repeated mantras, goals, and ideas that surrounded my vision board. My drive and goals had helped fill the void left by Alex's absence but now it was intense and somewhat unhealthily distracting me, I wouldn't stop in anyway of achieving what I wanted and like a crazed lunatic I wrote on every exposed surface area available to me. I even wrote on the fucking blinds, THE BLINDS! I was having a serious mental crisis of some description, but I'd masked it all with the desire and goals, of "just keeping your head down" and "just cracking on". Now it seemed that those chickens of neglected feelings were coming home to roost, and I couldn't see anything BUT my goals and where I wanted to be in my life. When I dreamed, I dreamed of dancing in Italy, of having various top international teachers and coaches, I spent the time I would be at work rolling down isles picking up shopping items for online orders with a little symbolic note attached to my trolly which helped keep my attention on my goals and Vision Board. In a word, I was obsessed.

After Alex's absence he eventually resurfaced for his lessons with David, he'd put an advert out for a new partner and was resultantly in the discussion with a girl from Leeds called Chelsea. Alex's youth career had ended a few years prior, and he was now only competing in the Amateur segments of competitions and because he'd also chosen to specialise in Latin dancing. That meant that the girl he would dance with, would also only compete in Latin competitions. Alex danced five competitions with Chelsea which stretched from around September 2013 to April 2014, and just like all the other girls prior, Alex's drive and determination for his dancing had forced Chelsea to recalibrate what she wanted. She would do the competitions, dance practices and everything in between, but she didn't want to learn or develop as much as Alex did. Their first outing was at the Warwickshire Championships, which they won (there were only three competitors and that included Alex and Chelsea) the second event was an Amateur Latin competition in Stoke where they were placed fourth in the final. Following that was the Nationals in November in the Blackpool Winter Gardens where they didn't even make it out of the first round, a bit of a disappointing blow for Alex to be honest. But he managed to rally and the next event they attended was David's competition in February where they managed a semi-final placing, the same event which would be the last competition for Leah and me. Alex's final competition with Chelsea was the European Championships which saw them make a re-call into the second round, after that, the partnership was ended and once again Alex joined me on the side lines looking for a new partner. As both Alex and I reminisced over our partnerships the conversations with David began to more notably become derogative, despite Alex and I's best efforts, we were once again without partners. We knew that in order to make serious headway in the competitive dancing world, we needed consistency, but no matter what we tried, consistent partners alluded us. After receiving more jibes from David, Alex made the ultimate decision to part ways with him and sent David a text which outlined how unhappy he was with him and how he wouldn't be coming back for any more lessons. That was quite a bold move from Alex, I can't say it wasn't expected (heck, even you probably figured that this was the direction Alex would eventually take in the end). But Alex was serious, he'd had enough, he wanted nothing to do with David and once again my car journeys during the course of February in 2014 were filled with just me and the car stereo. As

February rolled into March, David had arranged with another teacher in Stoke, to do some guest teaching in his studio. This ended up falling on a Saturday and so David had mentioned to me that if I wanted a lesson, that it would be in Stoke on Saturday morning. I confirmed it with him and soon enough as March rolled on, I was situated in the Quick, Quick, Slow dance studio in Stoke On Trent, having a lesson with David. The standard chat ensued as usual with David in my lesson, and as we worked through content, I found myself repeating the same Foxtrot basic choreography, as I'd always done before when I had a solo lesson. But something felt different this time, something felt off, there was no new information coming from the work, nothing that seemed constructively helpful and pointing me in a direction of improvement and I found myself asking a lot of direct questions to David about what exactly I was doing.

My constant study and acquisition of various technique books and instructional DVDs had culminated into a string of solidified ideas that I'd tried and tested. Bill Irvines principles were a big one for me, to understand better how the feet affected my movement and my body and the overall physiological elements at play. I would practice walking around the dance studio on a Wednesday and Saturday in my socks, my shoes thrown to the side of the room somewhere (with my trousers tucked into my socks) and a book balanced on top of my head. All in the effort to FEEL how the use of rolling my feet underneath myself actually felt like in relation to the controlled and disciplined aspect of the body alignment. I could conceptionally understand anything and everything that was being instructed through the medium of books and videos, but I realised that without a physical application, it was all useless. David would occasionally chime in with a sarcastic comment on my various training methods and in this particular instance he flat out told me that I looked like an idiot (very reassuring from your teacher huh?). Before working through technical aspects gleaned from the books and DVDs, my main source of practice was with weights. I'd wear them all day on Wednesdays and Saturdays and used them for regular finals training at home, physically pushing myself and powering through whatever I was working on. One night during 2013 the full force of life hit me square in the face and no amount of burying my head in the sand, distracting myself could help, and I found myself having something of a complete breakdown. I'd practiced through my Ballroom using the Russian system of dancing all my dances flat out, performing like I was actually at a competition, breaking into a string of exercises including star jumps, sit-ups, push ups and pistons (where you balance on one leg, hold the other one out in front of you off the floor and lower into the ball of the foot you're currently standing on, with the heel raised off the floor). This training was the norm to me, and it was what helped me maintain a tip top element of stamina and strength. But as I did the circuits of training in one of my practices during 2013, something pulled on a thread in my heart and mind with a slew of doubt flooding my head and an emotional bubble surfacing in my throat as danced and turned in my choreography. As I forcefully tried to push myself through the Ballroom part of the training my eyes welled up, my hands felt light, and I began to feel like nothing mattered. I really had to force myself through the Ballroom segment of the training, but just as I was about to begin the Latin section of my training and dance through the new Cha-Cha routine that I had constructed weeks prior, I collapsed onto the floor and bawled my eyes out. All the pent-up emotion and struggle of 2011 and 2012 came flooding through me, I felt like nothing I did really mattered, I felt useless, I felt helpless, I wanted to ask questions but felt no-one had any answers for me. Questions about dancing, questions about me, questions about life, there were so many questions I had and uncertainty which I felt and most of all, most of all.. I missed my dad.

I missed him so much and I just wished in that moment that I could see him again, images of attending his funeral reminded me that as we walked behind his coffin and the bag pipes played an accompanying Scottish melody, symbolising his personal pride of the family's Scottish heritage. That I'd held back tears for not wanting to upset mum, who was tightly clinging to me, arm in arm as we walked behind his casket. I tried to hold everything together as best as I could during the service for him and after he was cremated and everyone was standing outside, I stood next to Alex trying to make a joke as to how it was freezing outside, and that dad had picked a fine day for it all. I remembered experiencing the exact same scenario with nana's funeral only this time I was completely numb inside and the entire day seemed pass me by like a white noise blur. As I sobbed into the carpet in mums house, my feeling of anguish felt compounded by the lack of development I felt I'd undergone since his passing. I realised that I'd never asked dad any of the questions a young man always wishes he could ask his farther. Am I on the right path? What regrets did he have? How did it feel when me and Alex were born? What was life really like when he was my age? And, of course, the classic, Are you proud of me? I cried realising that I'd never have the chance to ask him anything ever again, before his passing I'd never even thought about picking up a book, now, I couldn't get enough of reading. I wished I could go back in time and ask him and talk with him about a million new subjects, a whole host of ideas that reflected my increase in intelligence. I wanted to learn more about him, but I knew that I could never have the opportunity to find that out, unfortunately mum's statements were always vague and genetic and prone to bias. They consisted of things that I'd heard growing up as a kid, things dad had sporadically relayed highlighting the odd sliver of detail on how he grew up. But I wanted to know more about HIM, who was he as a person? What did he think of ME as a person? I'd never have the opportunity to actually find out and that, along with a whole host of other sentiments, led me to unbuckle the weights shackled to me, to turn off the sound system and my iPod and to just sit on the sofa for the next three hours, sniffling and wiping away tears, the chickens were beginning to come home to roost.

Shooting into my mind, as if like lightning, the full extent of my lesson with David was reaching its peak. As our conversations went back and forth with one another, I pressed him on elements of technique that I'd derived from the Bill Irvine book (compiled by a man named Oliver Wessel Therhorne in commemoration of Bill and his wife Bobby) the ideas seemingly contrasted what David was asking me to do and had questions on it all. Things came full circle to me when David then began to press me on turning professional, a topic he'd brought up numerous times last year and in the early months of 2014. I'd told him at every junction of the subject, how I wanted to maximise my Amateur career like Simone Segatorri had done (he was in his early thirties before he eventually turned professional, and I'd seen his progression as a good template on which to mirror my own dancing direction with). David had other ideas though, he tantalisingly dropped the idea of making money from teaching, of potentially becoming involved with the Dance News Newspaper that circulated the dancing scene. My answer was always the same, no, it's not what I wanted to do. I knew I had more to give in my Amateur career, there was more that I wanted to experience, and I wasn't going to be swayed by the idealised prospect of "just making money" by teaching dancing. I held myself to a different standard and if I followed the lead of what David was trying to get me to do, then I'd be contradicting that personal standard for the sake of making money. I'd already tried setting up a dance school in Scunthorpe, creating the brand, a YouTube channel, business cards, along with a slew of flyers that I personally distributed on cold and rainy days in an effort to drum up business. I even tried to organise Alex into running some fitness classes to help us generate extra revenue whilst we worked and traded as well. Right idea and correct concepts, wrong timing though as the family as a whole was still in the slump of depression and grieving processes from 2011. Despite having read the rule book for dance competitions cover to cover (that's right, there's a rule book for competition dancing, which I imagine nobody reads) I'd found a loophole that I could exploit. You see, Amateurs aren't permitted to teach dancing, primarily because it pulls revenue from qualified and established teachers, but also its related to an insurance thing. Technically speaking these parameters can be liaised around, but if the governing body for dancing finds out, you could be banned and as a result, not be permitted to partake in any of the major events taking place over year. It's ultimately a way of policing the industry so that qualified professionals have a justifiable pillar and significance to stand on, compared with the Amateur level dancers. The whole thing opens a tin of worms which isn't warranted for discussion here, but the long and short of it is that Amateurs aren't allowed to teach dancing. Unless… (cue sly cutaway to the camera to break of the fourth wall).

Unless of course you teach under the "supervision" of a professional (i.e., use another professional's name/ school to teach under). I found that loophole nestled in the fabricated wording of the rule book and decided to exploit it to the max using mum as a namesake or "scapegoat" for the dance school (even though she wouldn't be qualified) and with Alex and me doing the ACTUAL teaching. The plan was easy enough, the timing of it all wasn't though and I soon found myself delivering business cards and leaflets all by myself trying desperately to move myself away from Tesco's, trading and any other "work for money" scenario and to move myself more into the world of dancing, a place I so desperately wanted to belong. The conversation with David was initially proposing that to me (ask and ye shall receive, I guess) but it came at the cost of losing my chance to dance and compete, the sole reason why loved to do the dancing in the first place. I just couldn't do that and the discussion with David escalated with David spending the remaining fifteen minutes of the lesson being the most "hands-off" he'd ever been with me. Suddenly everything became clear to me, the shroud of mystery surrounding my lessons with David becoming removed. I was being primed to move into the professional arena, not as a dancer, but as a teacher. I saw it as a cop out, a "failed Amateur" (failed in terms of not reaching my own ambitious goals) turns pro and spends the rest of his life teaching. I was only twenty-five and I was being coerced into turning professional, that's not what I wanted, and it juxtaposed my Vision Board. It didn't take long for the lesson to end and I promptly paid David, after changing and grabbing my bag, I went to the entrance door to the studio and said goodbye to David, he pretended not to hear me, choosing instead to be more involved with the couple he was teaching and as I walked away, I heard the 'oh, bye Ian', a statement of which I'd heard David use numerous times and said in a particular way conveyed his effort to be sarcastic or pessimistic with someone who had agitated him. That was the deciding element for me, there were a number of other factors too, the lack of development I felt I'd NOT received over the previous six months. The mild ridicule I'd receive personally but witnessed in spades with Alex regarding "failed" dance partnerships, and the string of inconsistent partners that Alex and I had both had since we'd first been with him, that served more like insurances of making money than actual development lessons. I skipped my following week of regular lessons, and it was with sadness that I messaged him the following week to tell him I was no longer going to be attending my lessons with him. He'd made me feel like a number, like I didn't matter, like I was an idiot (of which I knew I wasn't). All the ridicule and backhanded comments amounted into a form of resentment, and I spent the remainder of that day driving home and contemplating the next direction of my life and in what shape my dancing would take. Avera would provide great company whilst I talked through my issues in the dancing over our Skype calls and when Alex found himself free of his lessons from David, he also found a sense of personal liberation.

A strange word to use really, "Liberation", the initial lessons which Alex and I had with David all those years ago had moved us so enthusiastically and deep into the world of Ballroom and Latin dancing, something we'd both wanted so badly. Now we were both at the end of that road, we thought that involving ourselves as intensely as we did with the level of commitment we'd had as well, would all yield huge results. When it all came down to it though, we were just another product, another number which helped tally someone's bank sheet, we were made to run around in circles as the clock on the wall ticked time away. I don't mean to insinuate that we got NOTHING from the experience of being with David and Helen for eight years, we did, we'd progressed so much in ourselves and our dancing since the early days of lessons with them both. But I began to wonder if that was because of the sheer will and drive, the passion to progress and improve and to climb the national leader board in the FADA (Fee-aah-daah) table. Or was it because of the quality of teaching that we'd received? For me to honestly answer that, is a difficult one, there are a number of things I feel I've been able to learn from my lessons down in Wolverhampton. But I also know that the extent of disciplining that technique and skill was 100% down to me. I learnt and applied many elements that came from DVDs, lectures and workshop videos on YouTube, the inspirational drive to become a similar type of dancer that I would see of others in major championship events, that was all a huge element of contribution in my developing skills and something that WASN'T taught to me. You can't teach DESIRE you either have it or you don't, those that do have it, will ALWAYS go further than those that don't in my opinion and maybe that's what's been encapsulated from the experiences of Alex and me. David and Helen were my teachers, but I guess what I was hoping for was someone to genuinely give a shit about my dancing as much I as I did, I wanted a coach, I wanted someone who was on the side lines coming over and giving me advice and direction in my competitions and pushing me further during my lessons and training and it was unfortunately clear that I wasn't going to get that in Wolverhampton. The lessons were more like scapegoats to the discussion of trying to convince me to become a professional and I had to find a way of keeping myself going in the Amateur field a little longer, so that I could learn more of what I felt I needed to know. After deciding to no longer have lessons down in Wolverhampton, there was almost a weight lifted from me, an ease of breathing to be experienced, finally, I felt like I was back in the driving seat of my own dancing.

My relationship with Avera was difficult in many ways as we had decided to have a long-distance relationship that was primarily substantiated with Skype calls to one another. We'd come into contact with one another after Alex had initially gotten in touch with her about a possible dance trial, but with no means to actually get to Sweden, it soon fell flat on its face. In the wake of it all, Avera and I became friends on Facebook, and it wasn't long before we got talking with one another. We'd talk about dancing, pop culture and other personal interests with one another, she was never a big lover of reading books like I was, but that didn't matter to me. After a while we decided to start a relationship together and things seemed to be getting better, she soon told me in 2014 that she was moving to Italy to join Team Diablo (an Italian dance studio that housed some of the top European talent currently on the WDSF circuit). After talking with Avera about the intricacies of how it all worked, where she'd be staying etc. My lessons with David were coming to a close. Avera had moved over there in February in loom of finding herself a new dance partner. At this stage you'd probably be wondering why Avera and I didn't dance with one another (how very astute of you to ask) and the reason was simple and twofold. Firstly, Avera was a Latin dancer, and I was a Ballroom dancer, so that meant that one of us would have to switch styles in order to dance with the other. Avera hated Ballroom and so it would have meant that I would have been the one who would have needed to switch, not difficult to do, but the reason for me switching styles had to be legitimate and not just because "my girlfriend doesn't dance Ballroom". The second and most crucial reason was simply that I NEVER got involved personally with a dance partner, I knew it would make the training and structure too complicated. Avera and I were a couple and there was no real reason to contradict that element by dancing with one another as well. The last thing that I wanted to have happen, was to have a domestic dispute and for that to then effect the next three or four hours of practice and training. So, I clearly stated how that wouldn't be an option for us both and that we could just enjoy our relationship together, without the added pressure of dancing with one another thrown into the mix. After my lessons with David ended in March, I then spent the following April and May periods messaging all manner of top-level teachers and currently competing professionals. I knew I had the desire and the necessary mindset to push myself to the pinnacle of my dancing, all I needed was the right teacher, the right coach to help guide and train me. After egotistically bragging to Alex the brief element of conversations I was having with top level teachers and professionals, eventually I contacted Marco (the same Marco from Chapter 4) he was living and teaching in Italy and coincidentally was involved with Team Diablo. After confirming some details, I made a plan, the next step on my dancing journey was going to take me internationally abroad. Lots of things were now different, I wasn't the same person I was before, I'd changed so much since the last time I felt like I was catapulted into a new dancing environment, into another level that required me to "learn the ropes" of. By June I'd booked my first ticket for a week's visit to Molinella, the small manufacturing town just a forty-minute train ride from Bologna. I was excited for the future, I was excited to finally see Avera, who I'd arranged to stay with once I landed out there, and most of all I was excited to see what direction my dancing was going to take after I'd gotten out there. It was all very exciting, I packed my little red suitcase with a series of clothes and practice gear and with mum in the passenger seat next to me, I drove myself all the way down south to Stanstead airport (the cheapest flight I could find and a four-hour car journey from Scunthorpe). Mum would drive my car back once we'd arrived at the airport and then once again drive back down to pick me up after I returned home. I said my goodbyes to mum and gave her a huge hug and as I walked towards the entranceway of the airport, I felt for the first time, in a long time, the thrill of adventure calling me into action. My vision board was giving me back my desire to train in Italy and to train with the world's best dancers, I felt ready to embrace that new challenge ahead of me. With the sound of the clattering wheels from my suitcase rolling along the paving slabs of the airport entrance and the turbine engines of planes landing and taking off in the background, I nervously looked up to the board above me to see where I should head to. This was a brand-new adventure in the dancing for me, the sad thing was that Alex wasn't by my side to experience any of it as well. But that's the thing I guess, you have to let go of some things in order to experience newer things, there's always a trade involved, an ironic life comparison derived from an intense couple of years of Wall Street and Stock Market activity. I was both nervous and extremely excited as I made my way towards the security check-in, my head was held high, ready to fully embrace the new adventures that awaited me. I'd asked the universe for a new life, a new direction, of which was now beginning to come to fruition, that same feeling of adventurous purpose I'd had with Alex in the car in our late teens as we headed to Wolverhampton for the first time on our own, all those years ago. Was once again being felt as I made my way through that airport by myself, my little red suitcase resultantly being the only companion I'd have on my new journey and with that, I both nervously and excitedly made my way forward, my ticket in hand ready to embrace the uncertainty of the future that awaited me on the other side of the runway.

More By The Author

Just search **Mr Ian Whyatt** on Amazon to find more collections made by the Author.

Complete The Latino Rhythms Collection!

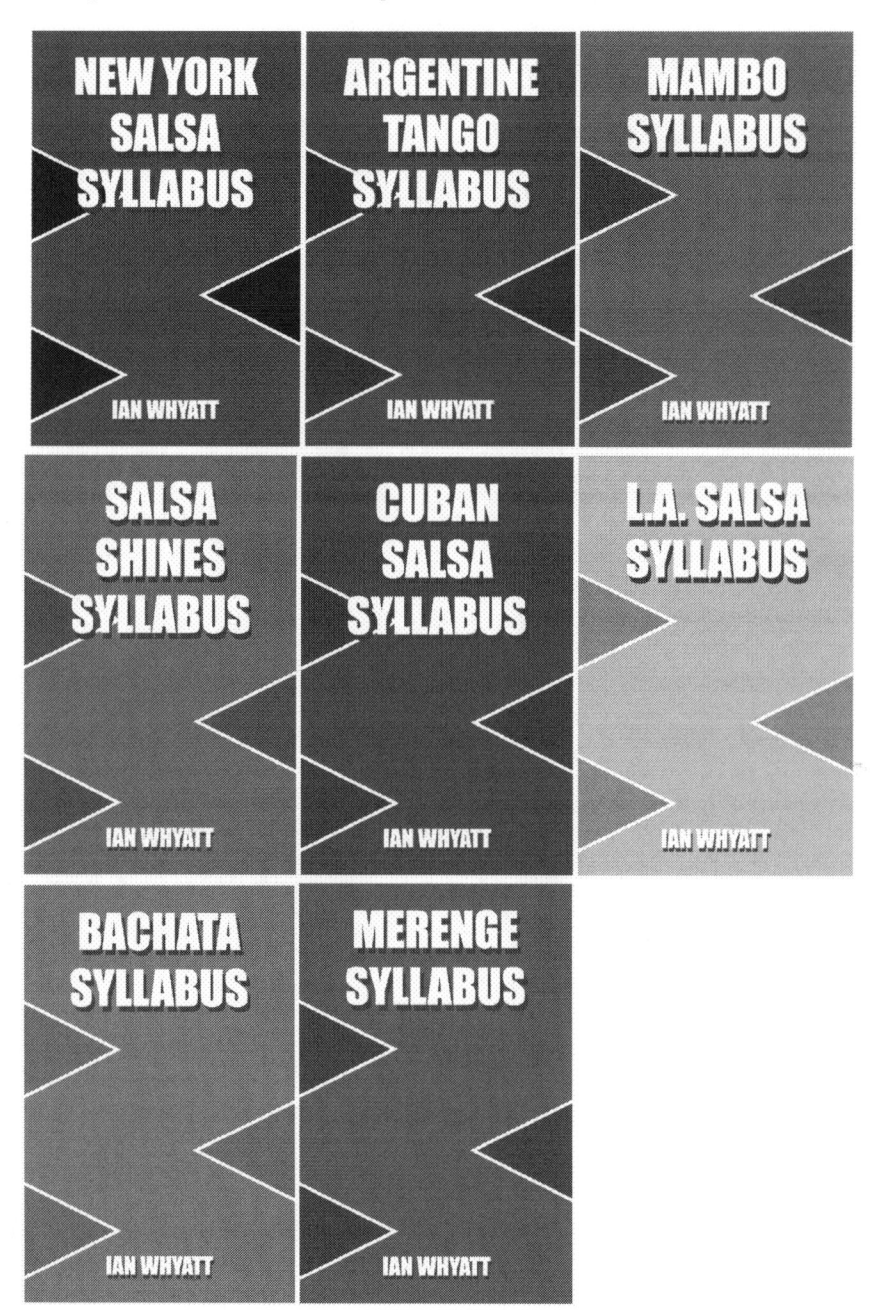

- NEW YORK SALSA SYLLABUS — IAN WHYATT
- ARGENTINE TANGO SYLLABUS — IAN WHYATT
- MAMBO SYLLABUS — IAN WHYATT
- SALSA SHINES SYLLABUS — IAN WHYATT
- CUBAN SALSA SYLLABUS — IAN WHYATT
- L.A. SALSA SYLLABUS — IAN WHYATT
- BACHATA SYLLABUS — IAN WHYATT
- MERENGE SYLLABUS — IAN WHYATT

Additionally...

Printed in Great Britain
by Amazon

0341cfc4-dd95-4c85-8bc6-a0c1aea1cf56R01